The Geography of Words

Languages around the world organize their lexicons, or vocabularies, in myriad different ways. This book is a celebration of global linguistic diversity that brings together fascinating cases from a wide range of languages to explore how and why this lexical variation occurs. Each of the thirty-six short chapters shows how different culturally specific words, relating to a range of phenomena such as kinship, color, space, time, objects, smells, and animals, vary across languages and geographical locations. The book also explains the mechanisms of development in vocabularies, showing why this variation occurs, and how languages and cultures interact, to deepen the reader's understanding of one of the most important aspects of linguistics. Assuming little to no prior knowledge of linguistics, and introducing concepts in an accessible way, this book is an entertaining, informative read for anyone who wants to learn more about the incredible variation and diversity of the human lexicon.

DANKO ŠIPKA is Professor of Slavic Languages and Applied Linguistics at Arizona State University. His research interests include lexicography, lexicology, morphology, and computational linguistics. His publications encompass over 150 papers and reviews as well as 30 books.

The Geography of Words

Vocabulary and Meaning in the World's Languages

DANKO ŠIPKA
Arizona State University

CAMBRIDGE
UNIVERSITY PRESS

University Printing House, Cambridge CB2 8BS, United Kingdom

One Liberty Plaza, 20th Floor, New York, NY 10006, USA

477 Williamstown Road, Port Melbourne, VIC 3207, Australia

314–321, 3rd Floor, Plot 3, Splendor Forum, Jasola District Centre,
New Delhi – 110025, India

103 Penang Road, #05-06/07, Visioncrest Commercial, Singapore 238467

Cambridge University Press is part of the University of Cambridge.

It furthers the University's mission by disseminating knowledge in the pursuit of education, learning, and research at the highest international levels of excellence.

www.cambridge.org
Information on this title: www.cambridge.org/9781108841658
DOI: 10.1017/9781108894548

© Danko Šipka 2022

This publication is in copyright. Subject to statutory exception
and to the provisions of relevant collective licensing agreements,
no reproduction of any part may take place without the written
permission of Cambridge University Press.

First published 2022

Printed in the United Kingdom by TJ Books Limited, Padstow Cornwall

A catalogue record for this publication is available from the British Library.

ISBN 978-1-108-84165-8 Hardback
ISBN 978-1-108-79501-2 Paperback

Cambridge University Press has no responsibility for the persistence or accuracy of URLs for external or third-party internet websites referred to in this publication and does not guarantee that any content on such websites is, or will remain, accurate or appropriate.

Contents

List of Figures	*page* viii
Acknowledgments	xiv
Introduction	1

Part I How Words Are Studied

A What Is a Word?	7
B The Internal Affairs of Words	10
C The External Affairs of Words	13

Part II How Words Are Carved Out

1	1 = 2, 5, 6, or 7	19
2	Beer Eyes and Wine-Dark Sea	25
3	Second Cousins Twice Removed	31
4	I Have Three Sons and a Child	37
5	Concepts on the Chopping Block	43
6	Unripe Bananas and Ripe Tomatoes	49
7	Mums and Clocks Mean Death	54
8	The Past Is in Front of Us and the Future Is behind Our Back	62
9	Far and Wide, Here and There	68
10	Bottles with Throats	74
11	Setting the TV on Fire and Extinguishing It	79

v

Part III How Things Are Done with Words

12	Traduttore, Traditore!	87
13	May You Suffer and Remember	92
14	I Screw Your 300 Gods	98
15	Either He Is Crazy or His Feet Stink	103
16	Shoo and Scat	108
17	A Dog and Pony Show	112
18	Blah-Blah-Blah, Yada-Yada-Yada	117
19	Acts of Darkness	122
20	This for That	128
21	Me Tarzan, You Jane	133
22	How Many Languages Do You Speak?	138
23	Harmful and Shitty People	143

Part IV How Words Are Born

24	Cars with Tails and Leadfooted Drivers	151
25	Monkey, Dog, Worm, Snail, i.e., "Crazy A"	156
26	Rovers and Ski-Rolls	161
27	Extra Crispy Soccer Players	165
28	Chinglish and Eurenglish	170
29	Comrade, Sir	175
30	Beer and Whiskey Mighty Risky	180
31	SOFs and SOWs	186

Part V Where Words Live

| 32 | Old-Lady Torturers, Horse Killers, and Bad Mornings | 193 |
| 33 | A Fleeing Bus | 199 |

34	I Wish That You Enjoy in What You Have Deserved!	204
35	Happy Hunting Ground	209
36	A Language Is a Dialect with an Army and Navy	214

Part VI A Word After

Part VII Words about Words

Selected Chapter Readings	221
Pronunciation Respelling	229
Language-Specific Latin Characters	231

References	235
Index of Languages	245
Person and Subject Index	253

Figures

1.1 East German muscle (or to be precise, mussel) car: Trabant (hrstklnkr/Getty Images)	page 20
1.2 The author jumping with the Maasai in Kenya right before the sunset at 6 p.m. (photo by Ljiljana Šipka)	22
1.3 US and Slavic handwritten numbers (photo by the author)	24
2.1 A bottle of Grüner Veltliner (photo by the author)	27
2.2 Children in Rajasthan, India, playing with paint during Holi, an ancient Hindu festival (Bartosz Hadyniak/Getty Images)	28
2.3 Red and blue eggplant, red onion, and other colorful produce (David Malan/Getty Images)	29
3.1 A family tree (johnwoodcock/Getty Images)	32
3.2 A Putin T-shirt that reads "everything is going according to the plan" (photo by the author)	35
3.3 Family resemblance (Jasmin Merdan/Getty Images)	36
4.1 A non–Serbo-Croatian marriage (Peter Dazeley/Getty Images)	38
4.2 An expert at *onna kotoba* (electravk/Getty Images)	41
4.3 Loonie, a currency of choice for Canadiens and Canadiennes alike (Bloomberg Creative Photos/Getty Images)	42
5.1 Chopped-up anatomy (appleuzr/Getty Images)	44
5.2 Planes, trains, and automobiles (MHJ/Getty Images)	45
5.3 Past, future, and present (porcorex/Getty Images)	47
6.1 Test tube tastes (Shana Novak/Getty Images)	50

List of Figures ix

6.2	The spice map of the world (Cavan Images/Getty Images)	51
6.3	Variety is the life of spices (fcafotodigital/Getty Images)	53
7.1	Taiwanese building with no fourth floor (photo by Mladen Šašić)	55
7.2	Dangerous Japanese crows (photo by the author)	56
7.3	Ćevapčići (photo by the author)	59
7.4	Raw-fish sushi: all smiles in Japan, all frowns in the Balkans (photo by the author)	60
8.1	A winding clock (DigiPub/Getty Images)	63
8.2	An astrological clock in Prague, Czech Republic (Craig Hastings/Getty Images)	66
8.3	"No future here: Stop! This is the Empire of Death" – written above the entrance to the Catacombs of Paris (photo by the author)	67
9.1	The meeting of waters in Manaus, Brazil (photo by Mladen Šašić)	69
9.2	Ljubljanica River (photo by the author)	69
9.3	An address in Sapporo, Japan (photo by the author)	72
9.4	Baldwin Street in Dunedin, New Zealand, known as the world's steepest street (photo by the author)	73
10.1	Assorted spirits sticking out their necks (Chay Chay Chiy Ceriy/EyeEm/Getty Images)	75
10.2	A floating island (thelinke/Getty Images)	76
10.3	A snake shepherd (photo by the author)	77
11.1	A hang-up phone (PKM2/Getty Images)	80
11.2	The starboard side of a Saxon ship (duncan1980/Getty Images)	82
11.3	A fiery speech (akindo/Getty Images)	83
12.1	A somewhat rusty reset button (Jupiter Images/Getty Images)	88
12.2	A less than ideal choice of words in a Chinese-English translation (photo by Mladen Šašić)	89
12.3	A turkey from Turkey (PeopleImages/Getty Images)	90

x   List of Figures

13.1 Interpunction cursing (IntergalacticDesignStudio/
     Getty Images)   93
13.2 A *nazar* (photo by the author)   95
13.3 A *hamsa* (photo by the author)   96
14.1 Dropping the F-bomb (JakeOlimb/Getty
     Images)   99
14.2 The lightning curse would not have worked on him:
     Nikola Tesla (Stefano Bianchetti/Getty Images)   100
14.3 One of 300 Slovene devils (chud/Getty Images)   101
15.1 Going flamingo (RyanLane/Getty Images)   104
15.2 Exploding with anger (John M. Lund Photography
     Inc./Getty Images)   105
15.3 Hitting the jackpot (AdShooter/Getty Images)   107
16.1 Shooing pigeons (aka flying rats) (Qiang Dongliang/
     EyeEm/Getty Images)   109
16.2 Japanese beckoning cats talismans: Bringing good
     luck without meowing (Yagi Studio/Getty
     Images)   110
16.3 Tweeting (pixelfit/Getty Images)   111
17.1 A silent dog command (westend61/Getty
     Images)   113
17.2 The author with faithful dog Hachiko in Shibuya,
     Tokyo, Japan (photo by Ljiljana Šipka)   115
17.3 Where bulls and bears live (Mateo Colombo/Getty
     Images)   116
18.1 An empty talk (Lisa-Blue/Getty Images)   118
18.2 A crying baby – annoying, whatever the
     onomatopoeia may be (yuoak/Getty Images)   119
18.3 Kaboom: As American as apple pie (zak00/Getty
     Images)   120
19.1 Fear the fork: The Sun Devil's hand gesture (photo by
     the author)   123
19.2 Taboo: Some roads are best not travelled (Adél
     Békefi/Getty Images)   125
19.3 A cocky rooster (GeoStock/Getty Images)   126
20.1 A missing piece (JoKMedia/Getty Images)   129
20.2 Dictionary, a fathomless well of unknown words
     (Angela May/Getty Images)   130

List of Figures xi

20.3	Doing (im)possible things with words (Isabel Pavia/ Getty Images)	132
21.1	Me Tarzan (Zulapi/Getty Images)	134
21.2	A monument to Dr. Esperanto in Odessa, Ukraine (Martin Ebner/Getty Images)	136
21.3	Raw materials for the words of constructed languages (Catherine Falls Commercial/Getty Images)	136
22.1	A promo T-shirt of the author's School of International Letters and Cultures (photo by the author)	139
22.2	Hard at language learning (Ian Nolan/Getty Images)	140
22.3	No language knowledge can be found in this hat (Sean Gladwell/Getty Images)	142
23.1	A monument to Joseph Stalin, the leader of the Soviet Union at that time – collateral damage to false friends (Craig Pershouse/Getty Images)	144
23.2	Stop so that I can shoot you (by_nicholas/Getty Images)	145
23.3	Back of an envelope waiting for a calculation (kyoshino/Getty Images)	147
24.1	Lights are lit, but the head and the tail are in the dark (Michael Duva/Getty Images)	152
24.2	Electric hands (Yagi Studio/Getty Images)	153
24.3	A T-bone steak (Diane Labombarbe/Getty Images)	154
25.1	The @ seal (Laurent Hammels/Getty Images)	157
25.2	All hat and no cowboy (photo by the author)	158
25.3	A computer at the time when its name became relevant (Weerayut Renmai/EyeEm/Getty Images)	159
26.1	A modern "woodcycle" (photo by Mladen Šašić)	162
26.2	Waiting to scoot away (Brian Bumby/Getty Images)	163
26.3	Roller skaters rocking and rolling (Flashpop/Getty Images)	164
27.1	Capital punishment with no life lost (Image Source/ Getty Images)	166

27.2	The Conquistador side of a Brazilian chess set (photo by the author)	167
27.3	The Indigenous side of a Brazilian chess set (photo by the author)	168
28.1	Chinglish gone wild (photo by Mladen Šašić)	171
28.2	The Motherland Calls – a monument in Volgograd, formerly Stalingrad, Russia (Victoria Sedykh/Getty Images)	173
28.3	Cohen's crack (Slavi Korchev/EyeEm/Getty Images)	174
29.1	A comrade quartet (Dina Alfasi/EyeAm/Getty Images)	176
29.2	This sir is present but nowhere to be seen (Sean Gladwell/Getty Images)	177
29.3	A dean (or perhaps an associate dean) hard at work (andresr/Getty Images)	179
30.1	Are they going to heed the Russian voice of reason? (Izabela Habur/Getty Images)	181
30.2	An orange-tail cocktail (Jordan Lye/Getty Images)	182
30.3	A meeting of the Maases (Westend61/Getty Images)	183
31.1	A R.A.D.A.R. (Vyacheslav Arenberg/Getty Images)	188
31.2	FYI, this is an acronym (Melinda Podor/Getty Images)	189
31.3	Information-age acronyms (Vladimir Godnik/Getty Images)	189
32.1	A bad morning (sturti/Getty Images)	194
32.2	A memorial plaque in Saint Petersburg, Russia, on a house where Dostoevsky lived (photo by the author)	195
32.3	Sixteenth-century Janissaries (duncan1890/Getty Images)	197
33.1	A fleeing bus (ljubaphoto/Getty Images)	200
33.2	Privacy requested (Image Source/Getty Images)	202
33.3	A piece of cake: No problem (ArxOnt/Getty Images)	203

34.1 Congratulations are in order (Luis Alvarez/Getty Images)	205
34.2 A nonverbal approval (Kiyoshi Hijiki/Getty Images)	206
34.3 Onto your health! (Teeramet Thanomkiat/EyeEm/Getty Images)	208
35.1 The Old West straight from a Karl May novel (Matthias Clamer/Getty Images)	210
35.2 They have all said goodbye (nokee/Getty Images)	211
35.3 Cat condolences (Benjamin Torode/Getty Images)	213
36.1 Boomerang (photo by the author)	215
36.2 The author at the Australian National Dictionary Centre (photo by Ljiljana Šipka)	216
36.3 A T-shirt with Aussie expressions (photo by the author)	218

Acknowledgments

My gratitude goes to Wayles Browne, who supplied spot-on comments on earlier versions of this text. I am equally grateful to Motoki Nomachi for providing most valuable comments on an earlier version of the manuscript; I am obliged no less to Elly van Gelderen, who also gave very useful comments, and Vedran Dronjić for his astute comments on an earlier draft. Gina Scarpete Walters also provided superb comments.

I am grateful to three anonymous reviewers for their excellent comments. I would like to thank Helen Barton for her strong support throughout the process of writing and publication, and I am grateful to Isabel Collins for her assistance with the project. In addition, I would like to thank Kevin Hughes for editing the manuscript and providing interesting examples, and I am furthermore grateful to F. Franklin Mathews Jebaraj for his coordination of the production process.

I am indebted to Nina Berman for meticulous comments and support, and I am grateful for the encouragement that I received from David Foster: his comments on a draft of the manuscript were very useful. I would also like to thank Lee B. Croft for his encouragement.

My debt of gratitude goes to my wife, Ljiljana Šipka, for providing useful comments and photos that were used in the book, and for tolerating me over the decades. I am also indebted to Mladen Šašić for various most valuable comments throughout the text and for making his photos available. I would like to thank Kim Smith-Stout and Michael Traubert for numerous, very useful comments, and for their encouragement. Thank you also to Vera Zalar for valuable comments in several places in the text. I am grateful to Xia Zhang, Khatuna Metreveli, and Motoki Nomachi for checking some examples.

I would also like to thank Olja Šipka for proofreading a draft of this manuscript and McKenna Kellar for her assistance with identifying some of the artwork in this book.

Thanks are also owed to the Melikian Center of Arizona State University for their research assistance and travel support, and I would also like to thank the School of International Letters and Cultures at Arizona State University for travel support. Many examples from Japanese and several Slavic languages have been enabled by my research professorship at the Slavic-Eurasian Research Center of Hokkaido University in 2017, for which I am most grateful on many levels. Similarly, examples from Aboriginal languages and Australian English are a consequence of a visiting professorship at the Australian National University in 2014. Many examples from German stem from my short research stay at Ludwig-Maximillian's University in Munich, Germany, in 2011, which was enabled by the Alexander von Humboldt Foundation. Some Slovene examples were collected during a 2019 research stay in Slovenia funded by the National Council for Eurasian and East European Research, by Arizona State University, and by the government of Slovenia.

Introduction

This is a beach book, a long-flight book, a public-transportation book, a before-I-go-to-bed book. It has been written to entertain first and educate second. What is meant by a geography of words here are language-specific and culture-specific configurations of words. Fascinating cases of differences in the way that languages organize their vocabularies are portrayed here. As famous Russian-American linguist Roman Jakobson once noted, languages differ in what they must convey, not in what they may convey. The examples discussed in this book concern situations where various languages express ideas in their word stocks in a way that may be curious to English speakers and those where English may be strange to speakers of other languages. The choice of English is determined not only by the fact that this book is written in English and intended for English speakers but also that for many years now the English language has held a special place in international communication.

An anecdote involving the aforementioned brilliant linguist and philologist Roman Jakobson is illustrative in this regard. The saying has been circulating among linguists for many years that Jakobson fluently spoke five languages – all in Russian. It is only recently that I learned, thanks to Anatoly Liberman, another brilliant scholar, that the statement is incomplete – the full version, which actually celebrates multilingualism, reads, Jakobson fluently spoke five languages, all in Russian, and Jespersen was fluently silent in ten languages (Jespersen was another prominent mid–twentieth-century linguist). More importantly, I learned that this statement is fake news altogether. Jakobson did have a strong Russian accent in English, but, per Liberman, he spoke French, German, and Czech almost without an accent. This story shows the special place of English. The prominence of English dwarfs other languages, so anything impressive relating to other languages was trumped by Jakobson's nonnative Russian-colored English. This is akin to the inaccurately narrow usage of "bilingual" in the United States, where it actually means 'speaking English and Spanish' and nothing else, or in Canada, where it means 'speaking English and French', whereas bilingualism can include any given pair of languages.

Since this text is meant to be short and entertaining to read, no references have been inserted in the body of the text; however, in Part VII, there is a section on recommended readings for each chapter and a list of references. Languages that use the Latin script are given in their original spelling. Those that use other scripts are given in the original and also transcribed using the closest English approximates and in the so-called pronunciation respelling. This kind of transcription does not always reflect all the nuances of the sounds in the original language, but rather gives a general idea of how the word is pronounced using English sounds. Transcription tables for non-Latin scripts and the specific characters of Latin-based scripts are provided in Part VII in the sections titled *Pronunciation Respelling* and *Language-Specific Latin Characters*.

Given that this book is intended for a general audience and is not a scholarly monograph, some common-parlance shortcuts are made in it. When stating that a language has or does something, I am using a shorter way of saying that its speakers, or most of them, commonly have those features or engage in such practice. Needless to say, languages do not do or have anything; they are aggregations of their speakers' linguistic knowledge, habits, and practices.

The cases of cross-linguistic differences presented here are a testimony to the diversity of the human condition, thought, and its linguistic expression. This richness should be cherished – a world in which one language prevailed would be as boring as a natural world with only one kind of tree and animal. This book is thus meant as a small contribution toward preserving the richness of human linguistic diversity.

The architecture of books can assume various forms. Slovenians, speakers of the Slovene (aka Slovenian) language in south Central Europe, have a useful distinction when talking about series (as in series of stories in a book or TV series/shows). The term *nanizanka*, literally, 'beaded series', refers to a series where the plot is separate in each story or episode. By contrast, the term *nadaljevanka*, literally, 'continuing series', refers to those where the plot stretches over the whole series. This book is a *nanizanka*, so one can hop from one chapter to another, without the need to follow their order.

As already noted, Jakobson once observed that languages differ not in what they may express but rather in what they have to express. In numerous cases discussed in this book, a peculiar feature of one language can also be rendered in another, but it does not have to be. It is often so that one language has a so-called culture-bound word, which is not rendered in one word in many other languages, although they may have something similar. Thus, the Portuguese language has the word *saudade*, which can be rendered in English as a feeling of longing, melancholy, or nostalgia. The Internet is awash with examples of these culture-bound words from various languages, from Bantu *bilita mpash* 'an amazing dream, opposite of nightmare' to Finnish *myötähäpeä* 'vicarious embarrassment'.

To further illustrate these differences, Russian speakers need to differentiate two nuances of blue and use separate adjectives for them: sky-blue голубой (*galooboy*) and deep blue синий (*siniy*). This is possible to do in English, but it is not obligatory; one can simply say *blue*. Similarly, Mandarin Chinese has to differentiate between one's older 哥哥 (*gēgē*) and younger brother 弟弟 (*dìdì*). In English, this is not a compulsory distinction, so the word *brother* can simply be used in both cases.

Part I, *How Words Are Studied*, addresses the issues in the scholarly studies of words. It outlines some key concepts in the study of words for those who would like to look at the cases of global lexical diversity presented in Parts II–V with a more focused lens. The first chapter of this part is titled *What Is a Word?* It tackles questions such as how to differentiate a word from a nonword and what features should be ascribed to a word. The second chapter, *The Internal Affairs of Words*, looks at the inner structure of words, the intricate networks of their senses. Finally, the chapter *The External Affairs of Words* looks into the issues of the links between words in the lexicon and how words cross from one language to another.

Starting from Part II, the chapters present fascinating cases of cross-linguistic variety, each in its subject-matter area. Chapter 1 in *How Words Are Carved Out*, the second part of the book, is titled *1 = 2, 5, 6, or 7*. It focuses on the differences in how languages construe their numbers. Chapter 2, *Beer Eyes and Wine-Dark Sea*, looks into peculiarities in the perception of colors. Kinship terms are discussed in Chapter 3, *Second Cousins Twice Removed*. Chapter 4, *I Have Three Sons and a Child*, looks into the construal of gender in various languages. Chapter 5, *Concepts on the Chopping Block*, explores cases where languages exhibit differences in carving out their concepts. Chapter 6, *Unripe Bananas and Ripe Tomatoes*, uncovers differences in how tastes are perceived, while Chapter 7, *Mums and Clocks Mean Death*, addresses the connotations around certain objects and then common prototypes. Chapter 8, *The Past Is in Front of Us and the Future Is behind Our Back*, is about the conceptualization of time, while Chapter 9, *Far and Wide, Here and There*, looks into the conceptualization of space. Various metaphors are explored in Chapter 10, *Bottles with Throats*. Chapter 11, *Setting the TV on Fire and Extinguishing It*, looks into the encapsulation of previous periods in the society in some terminologies.

Part III, *How Things Are Done with Words*, is opened by Chapter 12, *Traduttore, Traditore!*, which looks into the glitches in translation and interpretation. Chapter 13, *May You Suffer and Remember*, explores maledictions, while Chapter 14, *I Screw Your 300 Gods*, discusses expletives. Unusual idioms and sayings are explored in Chapter 15, *Either He Is Crazy or His Feet Stink*. The next two chapters explore onomatopoeia – those used in talking to animals are covered in Chapter 16, *Shoo and Scat*. Words used in reference to animals are addressed in Chapter 17, *A Dog and Pony Show*. Words used to imitate surrounding sounds are discussed in Chapter 18. *Blah-Blah-Blah, Yada-Yada-Yada*. This is followed by the discussion of obscenities in Chapter 19, *Acts of Darkness*. Chapter 20, *This for That*, discusses the strategies of referring to concepts for which we do not have words. The next two chapters are about words in planned languages and pidgins, *Me Tarzan, You Jane* (Chapter 21), and the words one is expected to acquire to speak a language, *How Many Languages Do You Speak?* (Chapter 22). The so-called false cognates are addressed in Chapter 23, *Harmful and Shitty People*.

Part IV is titled *How Words Are Born*. Chapter 24, *Cars with Tails and Leadfooted Drivers*, gives a general introduction to this part, discussing the ways in which new words and their meanings emerge. Naming new concepts is explored in Chapter 25, *Monkey, Dog, Worm, Snail, i.e. "Crazy A"*. Chapter 26, *Rovers and Ski-Rolls*, addresses the names for new nonmotorized vehicles. Chapter 27, *Extra Crispy Soccer Players*, looks into the peculiarities of athletic terminology. Chapter 28, *Chinglish and Eurenglish*, discusses words in hybrid varieties of English. Forms of address are discussed in Chapter 29, *Comrade, Sir*. The story goes on with Chapter 30, *Beer and Whiskey Mighty Risky*, which talks about terms for alcoholic beverages. Chapter 31, *SOFs and SOWs*, discusses acronyms and abbreviations.

Part V, *Where Words Live*, looks more closely into the relationship between language and culture. Chapter 32, *Old-Lady Torturers, Horse Killers, and Bad Mornings*, discusses unusual personal and place names. Chapter 33, *A Fleeing Bus*, talks about different encapsulations of the locus of control. Chapter 34, *I Wish That You Enjoy in What You Have Deserved!*, is about congratulations and responses to them. Chapter 35, *Happy Hunting Ground*, is about the words used to talk about death. Chapter 36, *A Language Is a Dialect with an Army and Navy*, is about the degree of lexical differences and their role in determining if something is a variant of the same language or a separate language.

Part VI, *A Word After*, is a brief reflection on some broader consequences of the global language diversity presented in Parts II–V.

Part VII, *Words about Words*, contains the apparatus of the book, that is, a collection of notes, references, tables, and indexes to accompany the main text. *Selected Chapter Readings* for each chapter are provided first for those who seek more detailed information about the topics discussed in the chapters. A list of *References* is provided next, followed by *Pronunciation Respelling and Language-specific Latin Characters*, which should enable those who seek to pronounce the words used as examples throughout the book. Finally, an *Index of Languages* is provided with references to the pages where they are used and the information where they are spoken and how many native speakers they have, followed by a *Person and Subject Index*.

PART I

How Words Are Studied

An unsolicited piece of advice to the reader (I am a Slav, after all, and that is our national pastime)

If you are not interested in the technical aspects of the study of words, please skip this part and go straight to Part II

A What Is a Word?

This book is primarily about global linguistic diversity in the LEXICON (a collection of words in a language) and LEXICAL SEMANTICS (meanings of these words), seen through the eyes of the linguistic field of LEXICOLOGY (the scholarly study of words). It then makes perfect sense to preface the discussion of concrete cases of lexical and semantic diversity with an introduction of key concepts in the field that are of relevance in the main chapters. Those who are just looking for interesting cases of cross-linguistic differences should skip this chapter, and the next two chapters, and proceed straight to Part II of the book. Only those concepts immediately relevant for the discussion in the main chapters are discussed here. Consequently, Sections A, B, and C, are not an ABC of the linguistic study of words, but rather an ABC of navigation (hopefully, cruising) through this book.

As noted, the field of linguistics that studies words is called LEXICOLOGY, not to be confused with LEXICOGRAPHY, which is the art and craft of dictionary making. The vocabulary items that dictionaries define are often one word long but can also be multi-word items. The technical term that covers both is LEXEME or LEXICAL UNIT (not out of sheer whim, but because there are one-word lexemes, such as *break* and *spring*, and also multi-word lexemes, such as *spring break*). The level of the language system that is formed by lexemes is called the LEXICON, a level distinct from that formed by the sounds, called PHONOLOGY or that formed by combination of words, called SYNTAX.

Lexemes and lexicons do not hang in the air; they belong to their respective languages and cultures. One of myriad definitions of culture was proposed by Hofstede and Hofstede, "[Culture] is the collective programming of the mind which distinguishes the members of one group or category of people from another." (see Part VII for this and all further references). Cultures around the world are very different, and scholars of cultural anthropology have identified the parameters of cross-cultural variation. Two of these researchers are of relevance here, Hall and Hofstede.

Edward T. Hall proposed the so-called classic patterns. The first is the opposition between MONOCHRONIC and POLYCHRONIC cultures. The former cultures perceive time as one line with past, present, and future separated. In the latter cultures, past, present, and future mix with each other on multiple timelines. As a consequence, members of monochronic cultures are more punctual, they separate private from work time, etc. Those in polychronic cultures are less punctual, and personal relations dominate the schedule. The mainstream cultures of the English language are much closer to the monochronic end of the scale. The second of Hall's classic patterns differentiates LOW-CONTEXT CULTURES, where one tells things directly, and HIGH-CONTEXT CULTURES, where much needs to be inferred from the context. Slavic cultures are low-context. If a Russian dislikes something, he/she will tell you about it. Japanese culture is high-context. When a Japanese dislikes something, he/she will convey the idea via subtle contextual clues rather than directly.

Hofstede and Hofstede established the following dimensions: POWER DISTANCE (the level of tolerance for unequal distribution of power in the society), INDIVIDUALISM (feeling independent) versus COLLECTIVISM (feeling interdependent), MASCULINITY (the use of force is endorsed), and UNCERTAINTY AVOIDANCE (society's tolerance to ambiguity and uncertainty). Later, Geert Hofstede added two additional dimensions: LONG-TERM ORIENTATION (the idea that one should prepare for the future) and INDULGENCE (the idea that it is a good thing to enjoy life). If we take a look at the mainstream culture in the United States, it is strongly individualistic, very tolerant to power distance, somewhere in the middle of the masculinity scale, tolerant to uncertainty, that is, low on the uncertainty avoidance scale, in the middle of the long-term orientation scale, and indulgent.

Hall's classic pattern and Hofstede's dimensions alike are underlying factors of some lexical phenomena. For example, high-context cultures develop fine-grained linguistic means of expressing things indirectly. Similarly, languages of collectivist cultures are likely to maintain more elaborate systems of kinship terms for a longer period of time in their development. To add another example, indulgent cultures are likely to have more elaborate networks of adjectives describing fun and enjoyment, etc. For those of you who were wondering about my unsolicited advice at the beginning of this chapter (that you did not follow, given that you are reading this), that too has to do with my coming from a collectivist culture, where giving unsolicited advice is the national pastime.

The notion of the lexeme (which is, as mentioned, a technical term for what is known as a "word" in common parlance) is most elusive. Various criteria have been proposed to define a lexeme. First, there is independent use. For example, the word *word* can be an independent utterance, and the sound *d* cannot. Another criterion is whether it is separated from other words in a text through pauses, or blanks in writing systems that have blanks. So, to provide an example, *this word*, not **thisword* (* means 'impossible'). Then, there is pronunciation unity, the fact that the sounds belonging to one word are pronounced or written together, without a break or something inserted (e.g., *word*, not **wo rd* or **woexrd*). Another criterion is the ability to change the meaning of other words (for example, *word count*, changes the meaning of *count*, and it does so differently than *number count*). Next, there is the ability to convey meaning. For example, the word *word* has a certain meaning; among other things it means a unit of the lexical system of a language, different from, say, the word *number*, which is a unit of the numerical system. Finally, its parts cannot be reshuffled, so, it has to be *word*, not **rdwo* or something like that. Various authors have ascribed varied degrees of importance to all those criteria. While they are all useful in differentiating lexemes from other linguistic elements, there is no single criterion or cluster that can unequivocally define a lexeme. This concept remains a prototype with a core of typical lexemes and a periphery where lexemes and non-lexemes (e.g., prefixes such as *bio-* and suffixes such as *-logy* in *biology*) overlap. One can assume various strategies in this field, but, for all practical purposes, I will consider lexemes to be those items one would normally look up in a dictionary: words, idioms, and lexical affixes, such as the aforementioned *bio-* and *-logy* (but not grammatical affixes, such as *-s* in *he works*; syntactic frames, such as Subject Verb Object; collocations, such as *drink beer*, etc.).

As noted, vocabularies belong to their respective languages and cultures, and the need to talk about separate languages comes from the fact that there is a practical need to translate one language into the other and to learn languages different from one's mother tongue. Establishing links between any two out of some 7,000 world languages is a highly intricate task. Words are involved in the process primarily in establishing LEXICAL EQUIVALENCE. The essence of the process is to find the most appropriate lexeme in the TARGET LANGUAGE for the one in the SOURCE LANGUAGE. For example, when translating from Estonian into English, Estonian is the source language and English is the target language. In the process of establishing lexical equivalence, the situations where one would encounter one-to-one equivalence are extremely rare. Normally, something is always off (a word exists in one language and it is absent from another, a word in one language has more equivalents in another language, etc.), which makes translation and study of languages a difficult process.

These differences are a consequence of a complex organization of words. On the one hand, they feature complex internal semantic structure. Most of them are POLYSEMOUS, that is, they feature multiple senses. On the other hand, words are included in various external networks: they show affinity to combine with some words more than others, they share some components with other words, they are likely to be found in certain types of texts more often than in others, etc. The internal workings of words will be discussed in part B, and their relations with other words and contexts will be addressed in part C. Needless to say, the internal affairs of words are connected to their external affairs. For example, very often one sense of the word may show combinatory affinity of its own, as in *cool* being neutral when meaning 'cold' and informal when meaning 'good'.

B The Internal Affairs of Words

Special monographs and introductory textbooks about LEXICAL SEMANTICS (meanings of words), and those about SEMANTICS in general (meaning of all language elements, words included), have been advancing various models to account for the internal affairs of words, their meanings. The same is true about monographs looking into cross-cultural aspects of semantics.

Many of these intricate models are certainly important in solving various theoretical linguistic problems. However, for the purposes of this book, a simple model proposed by Zgusta for practical work in lexicography will suffice. In this model, meanings of words have three primary components, DENOTATION, that is, what they signify, CONNOTATION, that is, what kind of attitudes they invoke, and APPLICATION DOMAIN, that is, to what they can pertain. For example, *food*, *chow*, and *feed* all have the same denotation. They signify the solid matter used to sustain living organisms. However, the connotation of the word *chow* is quite different, given that it is informal, so the attitude toward using it in formal situations is negative. Similarly, the application domain of the third word is much narrower, given that it is used in conjunction with food for domestic animals only. The cross-linguistic differences in the lexicon, as will become clear in Parts II through V, are most commonly caused by differences among denotation, connotation, or the application domain.

One important contribution to linguistic diversity of our world comes from different developments of new senses. New senses of words are developed from existing ones. This is known as SEMANTIC TRANSFER. For example, human and animal leg were first, and leg of a table was a new sense developed from the existing ones via semantic transfer. The most common mechanism of semantic transfer is METAPHOR, in which the link between the existing and the new meaning based on similarities of some kind is established. There are various approaches to metaphorical transfer. The simplest of them all, the two-domain approach, will suffice in navigating this book. The model encompasses the SOURCE DOMAIN (e.g., the human and animal leg in the aforementioned example), the TARGET DOMAIN (the leg of the table), and the LINK between them (the leg of the table looks like and performs a similar function of supporting something, just like the human and animal leg). Needless to say, these links can be different in different cultures.

Senses of each word can be organized in different ways. In some, there will be a central initial sense from which various other senses develop. For example, the word *bed*, riverbed, bed of flowers, bed of a roadway, bed as a layer of rock, etc. all developed from the initial sense of the piece of furniture. This is known as the RADIAL MODEL, where new senses sprout like rays of a source of light. Then, there are words like *grave*, where there is successive development of one sense from another. Literal 'excavation where somebody is buried' comes first, 'the place of interment' developed from it, and this sense sprouted a new one – 'the place where something dead, lost, or past' (e.g., the grave of one's hopes). So, there is a line of semantic extensions: physical grave -> place of interment -> symbolic place of loss. This is then the LINEAR MODEL.

Not all words are so nice and neat that one can trace clear lines of development. Among other important observations about words and language in general, Wittgenstein points out the so-called FAMILY RESEMBLANCE. He uses the word *games* to demonstrate the phenomenon. There is no one single feature that stretches across the board. It is rather that some of them have some things in common with some games, some other features will be shared with other games, etc. Similar to games, some family members have similar noses, some similar eyes, etc. He also notes that the meaning of a word is its usage in the language, comparing the words to chess pieces, and that words are used to achieve something (comparing them to tools in a toolbox). Elaenor Rosch who, interestingly enough, wrote her undergraduate thesis on Wittgenstein, adds the concept of PROTOTYPES. The word *bird* exemplifies this concept. There is an idea of a prototypical bird, which flies, sings, has a certain size, etc. Many birds fit this profile, and they are in the core of the concept; they are prototypical birds, "birdy" birds. However, there are birds that do not fly, those that do not sing, those that are very big, etc. Birds such as the ostrich or penguin are far from the prototypical core but still within the concept.

One important distinction about the meaning of words was made very early on by Gottlob Frege. He differentiated between SENSE and REFERENCE. The two words for Venus in German, namely, *Morgenstern* 'morning star' and *Abendstern* 'evening star', have the same reference. They refer to the planet Venus. However, each of them has its own meaning; it builds its own mental picture. It should be noted that not all words follow this simple schema. Some of them do not have a referent (for example, *freedom*) and with some, making references is the only sense they have (e.g., with *here* or *there*, which are only pointing to a place close to or distant from the speaker).

All these theoretical distinctions are prominent in the main parts of this book. Things are done differently with words and the context of their usage is different. Prototypes vary from culture to culture – in some, the prototypical fruit is the apple, in others it is the banana. In many cases, languages will share the reference of their words but not their sense.

C The External Affairs of Words

Words interact with other words and with texts of their own language. They also interact with words from other languages. Words share part of their meaning with other words. Lexicology has identified a number of LEXICAL RELATIONS, such as SYNONYMY (words that are very similar in their meaning). Words also have a propensity to be used more frequently or exclusively in certain types of texts. These are their USAGE CHARACTERISTICS. Finally, words may be borrowed from other languages, and this is known as LEXICAL BORROWING.

Lexical relations encompass the aforementioned SYNONYMS (e.g., *desk* and *writing table*), ANTONYMS (i.e., words with opposite meanings, as in *good* and *bad*). Then, there are HYPERNYMS (higher-order concepts, as in *furniture* being a hypernym of *desk*) and HYPONYMS (lower-order concepts, as in *desk* being a hyponym of *furniture*). Finally, there are MERONYMS (part-of relationships, as in *leg* being a meronym of *desk*). Through these lexical relations, words form LEXICAL NETWORKS. TAXONOMIES, classifications of the segments of reality, are also based on relations such as hyponymy or meronomy. As can be seen, the network of the word *desk* contains *leg*, *furniture*, *writing table*, etc. Words also form LEXICAL FIELDS if they share a subject matter. For example, the word *desk* belongs to two such lexical fields, home and office. Words furthermore form WORD-FORMATION NETWORKS if they share LEXICAL STEMS but not AFFIXES, or their stem forms a new word with a stem of another word. For example, the verb *to pay* forms a word-formation network with prepay (where *pre-* is a PREFIX, i.e., an affix that comes before the stem) and *payer* (where *-er* is a SUFFIX, i.e., an affix that comes after the stem). These networks with affixes show the process of DERIVATION. The link between to pay and roll in payroll shows the process of COMPOSITION, uniting more stems into a new word. In the English-language traditions, word-formation is usually studied in the field of LEXICAL MORPHOLOGY, morphology being the study of the forms of words.

All these relations with other words are so-called PARADIGMATIC RELATIONS, that is, relations that exist in the lexicon rather than in the text of the language in question. There are also SYNTAGMATIC RELATIONSHIPS, the affinity of words to combine with certain words more than others. For example, the verb *to drink* will typically be combined with the words for liquids, such as *water*, *milk*, *beer*, and so on. This is the COMBINATORIAL POTENTIAL of this verb, which then enforces SELECTION RESTRICTIONS (what is not likely to be used together with it). Combinations of words that usually go together are called COLOCATIONS. However, syntagmatic relationships go beyond just being next to each other. For example, the word *aforementioned* can be connected to a word that was used much earlier in the same text.

Words also change; they stem from other words in the earlier stages of the same language or other languages. The origin of words is studied by ETYMOLOGY, which mainly looks into the ROOTS of words. It is not to be confused with entomology, the study of insects. Thus, for example, the root for the word *book* is probably *bokiz*, the Proto-Germanic word for *beech*, as Germanic runes were carved on the beech bark. More about lexical relations can be found in various books on lexicology mentioned in Part VII. One can also use Wordnet to see lexical networks of English words.

As said, words have usage characteristics, that is, a higher or lower affinity toward certain types of discourse (where discourse should be understood as any situation where language is used, written, or spoken). Oversimplifying, one can imagine a CORE of the vocabulary (another word for the lexicon), words that are likely to be found very frequently in various written and spoken texts, and its PERIPHERY, words that are not so frequent, primarily because they are restricted to certain types of discourse, or CONTEXTS, as they are technically known. This affects the so-called LEXICAL FREQUENCY. It is higher in core vocabulary and lower in the other fields of the lexicon.

Words that do not belong to core vocabulary are typically marked by one or more usage characteristics. First, there is the REGISTER. It is neutral for core vocabulary, and for other words it can be FORMAL (as in *superfluous*, which is likely to be found only in very formal texts), COLLOQUIAL (when a word is found in general informal, mostly spoken, texts, e.g., *cop* for police officer), SLANG (used in the texts of limited social groups, for example *pig* for police officer), LINGO (found in informal use of members of certain professions, as in *perp* for perpetrator in law enforcement lingo), etc. In many cases, it is the ATTITUDE (vulgar, obscene, offensive, etc. and even facetious, ironic, etc.) that disqualifies the word from general and even more often formal use. Words can also be marked by their SUBJECT MATTER. For example, they can be TECHNICAL, as in *cardiac infarction* for *heart attack*. They can also be bound to a certain REGION, as in *lorry* being British English for North American and Australian *truck*. Words can also be bound to a certain period of time. DATED WORDS or ARCHAISMS were used in earlier periods but less so today, as in *Nipponese* for *Japanese*. NEW WORDS, as in *vlog* for 'video blog', have only recently entered the lexicon. For those who wish to find out more, the previously mentioned books on lexicology offer extended discussion of the contextual parameters of words.

One of the things that words do is transfer between languages. This is known as LEXICAL BORROWING or LEXICAL TRANSFER. The whole word can be borrowed, as in English *computer* being borrowed in many languages. It can happen that only one or two senses are borrowed and not others, for example, English *corner* is borrowed into many languages but only in the sense that it has in soccer, and not in mathematics or when describing physical objects, such as houses. In the process of borrowing, languages can develop senses that cannot be found in the lending language. These are known as PSEUDO-BORROWINGS, as in German *Handy* for cellphone or *Beemer* for projector, words that are based on English elements but are not actual English words. In addition to borrowing words and their senses, languages also create CALQUES, that is, more or less literal translations of words and phrases in other languages. In many languages, rather than borrowing the word for computer, they have calqued it, as in Czech *počítač* or German *Rechner*, which are direct translations of the English word *computer*, as they are also derived from the word for 'to compute' in their respective languages.

All these external and foreign affairs of words influence cross-linguistic differences. Some fields feature more synonyms in one language than in another. Some languages rely more on borrowing in creating new words, others resort more frequently or exclusively to semantic extensions. Taxonomies are sometimes different in different languages, as are usage characteristics of their words.

PART II

How Words Are Carved Out

1 $1 = 2, 5, 6,$ or 7

In the 1970s there were thousands upon thousands of Serbo-Croatian speaking guest workers (or *Gastarbeiter*, which is one of many German borrowings in English) from the former Yugoslavia in Germany, whose numbers were surpassed only by Turks. A curious thing happened during Yugoslav guest workers' annual vacation "down there" (as they refer to their country of origin in southern Europe, lower on its map, as opposed to "up there," which is Germany, in the north, and thus higher on the map). The proud *Gastarbeiter* parents would brag that their offspring had nothing but 1 grades, while the compatriots who stayed in their home country would be wondering why the guest workers would even mention such a disgrace. The cause of miscommunication is that the grade scale in Germany is inverted compared to that of the former Yugoslavia – 1 is the best grade in Germany, but it is the failing grade in southeastern Europe. So, to those listening, the *Gastarbeiters* were bragging about the failing grades of their children. This is one of many situations where languages differ in the scales they use and the meaning of numbers. This linguistic difference just reflects a cultural difference. In this particular case, the ranking underpins the German scale (much like grades A, B, C, etc. in some other countries), while quantity determines the southeastern European scale (the number representing the highest quantity is the best). Some of those differences are well-known. I still remember the horrified face of my Thai tour guide when he heard from my fellow passengers from Florida that winter temperatures over there are around 80 degrees – they were using degrees Fahrenheit and he was thinking in degrees Centigrade. All those who have confused Fahrenheit and Centigrade in cooking recipes have had similar looks on their faces when they saw their burnt food. In a related example, the American expression "from 0 to 60" (measured in miles) reads from "0 to 100" in many other languages that measure distances in kilometers. The running joke in East Germany about their low-cost

Figure 1.1 East German muscle (or to be precise, mussel) car: Trabant (hrstklnkr/Getty Images)

and low-performance Trabant car was *0–100 am selben Tag* 'from 0 to 100 in the same day' (Figure 1.1).

Many differences in how numbers are used are much subtler than in the aforementioned cases. To return to the grades in Eastern Europe, further to the north of the continent, Poles and Russians have a similar scale, but both 1 and 2 are failing grades. This then causes a difference in meaning between the Serbo-Croatian versus Russian meaning for the "2 student." In Serbo-Croatian, *dvojkaš* means 'a D student, one who hardly passes'. In comparison, the Russian word двоечник (*dvoeshnik*) means 'failing student'. Both terms are derived from the word for "two," двойка (*dvoyka*) and *dvojka*, yet what is the lowest passing grade in one language is the first level of failing in the other.

Similarly slight, yet equally confusing, differences can be found in the field of real estate. The American ground floor of any building is numbered the first floor, the floor above it the second floor, and so on. In many other languages, the first floor is reserved for the floor above the ground floor, so one would need to add or subtract numbers depending on the direction. For example, the German third floor will be the American fourth floor. In the same field, an interesting case is offered by the numbers used to refer to the size of apartments and houses. Americans measure their homes by counting bedrooms (and there are rather clear criteria for what makes a room a bedroom – a regular door and a closet are a must), while Germans and other Europeans include living rooms, dens, recreation rooms, TV rooms, and so on in their count of rooms. So, an American two-bedroom apartment would typically be the equivalent of a "three-room apartment" (*Dreizimmerwohnung*), given that the living room would be counted, but it can also be a "four- or five-room apartment" if it has an additional room or rooms, such as a den, TV room, or recreation room.

All of these aforementioned differences in the use of numbers have been arbitrary; however, in some cases the differences are in the natural environment. For example, in Swahili, which is spoken around the equator in Kenya and several other countries, where the sun invariably rises at 6 a.m. and sets at 6 p.m., the hours of the day are measured against observable phenomena of the transition from darkness to light and from light to darkness, as opposed to the variable and not always observable point when the sun is in its zenith. So *saa moja asubuhi* in Swahili, 'one in the morning', is one hour after the sun has risen, or 7 a.m. Consequently, six hours need to be added or subtracted when time is translated, depending on its direction (Figure 1.2).

Scales and cycles in various languages can exhibit differences and be possible generators of miscommunication, even without numbers attached to them. Months of the year are an example of this. In several Slavic languages (Belarussian, Ukrainian, Polish, Czech, and Croatian), the names of the months are based on the natural and agricultural cycle. Their names denote either what happens in nature at any given moment in time or a certain type of field work that takes place at that time. Poles and Croats have similar names for months: *lipiec* in Polish and *lipanj* in Croatian both mean 'linden tree month', and *listopad* (spelled the same in both languages) means 'leaf falling month'. However, they refer to different months: *lipanj* is June in Croatian and *lipiec* is July in Polish, and *listopad* is October in Croatian but November in Polish. The natural calendar cycle in Poland (in northern Europe) is delayed compared to that in Croatia (in southern Europe).

These underlying differences create so-called false cognates. A similar type of confusion can be caused in English, which has the traditional week starting with Sunday and the business week starting

Figure 1.2 The author jumping with the Maasai in Kenya right before the sunset at 6 p.m. (photo by Ljiljana Šipka)

with Monday. In most other languages, Monday is the first day of the week. In Mandarin Chinese, days of the week are even named based on their place in the order of the days: Monday is thus literally 'first of the week' (星期一, xīngqīyī), Tuesday is 'second of the week' (星期二, xīngqīèr), and so on. So, to return to English, when the week starts depends on which of the two English conventions one uses, which may be rather confusing to speakers of Mandarin Chinese. Greek is a bit different from Chinese: Sunday is Κυριακή (kiriake) 'Lord's day', but then Monday is Δευτέρα (deutera) 'second day', Tuesday is Τρίτη (trite) 'third day', and so on.

The start of the year offers similar differences. While the Gregorian calendar, in which the new year starts on January 1, is definitely most widespread, in other calendars the year starts on many other dates. Eastern Orthodox Christians still observe the Julian calendar, in which New Year starts on January 14. In Russian, that New Year's Day is known as 'old new year' старый новый год (stariy noviy god). The Chinese New Year is usually in February, and Persian people observe the نوروز, *Nowruz*, the new year that usually falls around the vernal equinox. The Assyrian New Year is on April 1, the Sinhalese New Year is in mid-April, the Yoruba New Year starts in mid-June, and the Jewish New Year, רֹאשׁ הַשָּׁנָה, Rosh Hashana, is in September or October. So, every now and then, a new year starts around the globe. In cases such as the Muslim calendar, which is eleven to twelve days shorter than the Gregorian calendar given that it follows lunar cycles, the Muslim New Year starts with the first day of the Muharram month, with a vast variation as to its date (historically, it was observed during any of the twelve Gregorian months – from January to December).

Languages are fascinating in the way that they combine single-digit numbers to create two-digit numbers. For example, ninety-three in French is literally 'four-twenties-thirteen' (*quatre-vingt-treize*). French, along with several other languages such as Basque, Celtic, Georgian, and so on, uses a partial *vigesimal system*, where the number 20 is the base for counting up to 100. Around the world, we can find languages that have 4, 5, 6, 7, 8, 9, 12, 24, 32, 60, and 80 as the base for counting, of course along with the most widespread *decimal system*, as found in English. The German and Slovene languages use simple units before tens, so fifty-seven is literally 'seven and fifty' (*siebenundfünfzig* in German and *sedem in pedeset* in Slovene), and Czech can go both ways: either 'fifty-seven' or 'seven and fifty' (*padesát sedm* or *sedmapadesát*). Contact between German on the one hand and Slovene and Czech on the other is responsible for this similarity.

Confusing situations can arise from differences in how numbers are written. For example, in the US manner of handwriting, one vertical line is simply used to write the number one, seven is never crossed with a sideline, and the top line does not have to be perfectly horizontal. In Slavic languages, the number one is written with a slanted top line, and seven is typically crossed while the top line is perfectly horizontal. In consequence, the number one, written by a Slav, can be mistaken for a seven by Americans. Similar problems are created by the English decimal point, which is the decimal comma in many other languages that use the point to separate parts of big numbers; therefore, 10,000.00 in English would be written as 10.000,00 in numerous European languages (Figure 1.3).

Practicalities can also create peculiar situations in terms of how numbers are spelled. For example, in Mandarin Chinese, regular

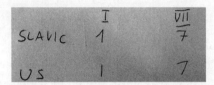

Figure 1.3 US and Slavic handwritten numbers (photo by the author)

numbers are very simple to write (e.g., the number one is just a horizontal line), which makes numbers vulnerable to falsification as new strokes can be added to make a different number. For that reason, there are special number signs with many more strokes that are used in official documents and on checks. For instance, the number one (yī) is 一 in regular use and 壹 in official use. In Japanese, there are two ways of writing numbers: the regular Chinese way and the English way. So, the number one can be written as 一 or as 1. Japanese texts can be written vertically (top-down) or horizontally (left-to-right, just like in English). Traditional Chinese numbers are more common in vertical usage, and the numbers that English uses are more common in horizontal writing. Japanese also has two ways of pronouncing numbers. For example, when counting, "one" would be pronounced *ichi*. When ordering something, "one" would be *hito(tsu)*. If that is not complicated enough, in Japanese, just like in Mandarin Chinese, one has to insert a counter word (also known as the classifier) after the number. This counter is different for words of different shapes and sizes. For example, two birds is 二羽の鳥 *ni wa no tori* (literally, 'two', 'counter word for birds and rabbits', 'of', 'birds'), but two dogs is 二匹の犬 *ni biki no inu* (literally, 'two', 'counter word for small animals', 'of', 'dogs').

As could be seen, the number one can be two, three, or any other number when we go from one language to another, when we confuse it with something else, or when shady characters modify its simple one-stroke character. The underlying existence of different scales and the lack of their correspondence are testimony to the diversity of our linguistic world, in which one size does not fit all. Some of these differences are purely linguistic, and others exist outside of the language but are reflected in it. We are looking at the world through a language spyglass, but the spyglass is at least partially defined by that same world.

2 | *Beer Eyes and Wine-Dark Sea*

In a short story titled "A Marshmallow-Colored Garden," Serbian author Branko Ćopić explains that his grandfather recognized only the following four colors: the bean color, the pigeon color, the rotten sour cherry color, and the white metal color. While the author's grandfather definitely remains quite peculiar in the domain of his mother tongue (which describes the same basic colors as English), his outlook is not particularly unusual globally.

In their groundbreaking 1960s study of basic color terms, Berlin and Kay found that some languages recognize only two colors. They established seven degrees of precision used by different cultures when dividing the color spectrum. They are as follows: one (black and white), two (black, white, and red), third A (black, white, red, green, and a possible extension to blue), third B (black, white, red, and yellow), fourth (black, white, red, green, and yellow), five (black, white, red, green, yellow, and blue), sixth (black, white, red, green, yellow, blue, and brown), and seventh (black, white, yellow, blue, brown, violet, pink, orange, and gray). So, different cultures examine the same segment of physical reality and identify its values with varying degrees of precision. Obviously, these are only basic colors, and their shades form an incomparably more diversified system. This field of study has evolved since Berlin and Kay's work, and their study has been criticized, but it has initiated an intriguing debate at the nexus of language and culture.

Differences can also be found in isolated areas of the spectrum. For example, Russian speakers need to differentiate between two shades of blue and use separate adjectives for them: light blue голубой (*galoobóy*) and deep blue синий (*síniy*). Some research suggests that these linguistic differences cause Russian speakers to be better at color identification than speakers of languages that do not contain such a lexical distinction. Russian is not alone in this regard, as Hungarian features two words for red (*piros* и *vörös*), and Turkish historically had three (*kırmızı, al,* и *kızıl*). In Proto-Slavic (the language ancestor of

25

Russian, Polish, and other Slavic languages), there were two colors for black: *črn* and *vorn'*, with the second of these being used for the color of animal fur or feathers. Animal fur, most notably horse's hair, is widely found in names of finely nuanced shades. So, horses are described as *bay, sorrel, palomino, buckskin, grullo, appaloosa*, and many other colors in English. Human hair is no different: The hair coloring industry uses dye names such as *cognac, tropical strawberry blonde, dark ash brown, violet light brown*, and many others. However, compared to the shades used by painters, this is as nothing. *Blue* is not precise enough, so it becomes *azure, cerulean, cobalt blue, periwinkle, turquoise, ultramarine, zaffer*, or one of many other shades. Painters are known to be prolific wine drinkers, and wine offers interesting cross-linguistic differences. White wine is not really white, yet the term is widely used, as in French *vin blanc*, Spanish *vino blanco*, Italian *vino bianco*, German *Weißwein*, and so on. Red wine is a shade of red and again we find it in many languages. Compare French *vin rouge*, Italian *vino rosso*, and German *Rotwein* (all meaning simply 'red wine'), but there are languages that describe red wine as black, as in Sicilian *Nero d'Avola* ('black from Avola'. The grape variety used for this wine is rather dark) or Serbo-Croatian, where any red wine is named *crno* 'black' much more often than *crveno* 'red'. The best known Portuguese white is named *vinho verde*, literally 'green wine', but the etymology of the name refers to the fact that the wine is young, that is, it is consumed shortly after being bottled, which was historically the case. *Grüner Veltliner* 'the green one from Veltlin', a white wine named after the city of Veltlin in the German-speaking Italian province of South Tyrolia and popular in Vienna, is not really green, but its grapes are bright green (Figure 2.1).

Scholars of Homer have crossed swords regarding the meaning of the phrase "wine-dark seas," which can repeatedly be found in the *Iliad* and *Odyssey*. Similar confusion is caused by the phrase *синее вино* (*sinyeye vino*), which today literally means 'light blue wine', and is mentioned in the classic Old Russian manuscript *The Tale of Igor's Campaign*. Scholars eventually agreed that this was not wine at all but rather a hay-colored vodka. Even now, there is a vodka named *siwucha* in Poland, meaning 'ash-gray vodka'. The root adjective of that noun (*siwy*) is used for gray hair.

Furthermore, Serbian and Croatian scholars of folk epics were puzzled by the phrase *rujno vino*. The question was whether it was

Figure 2.1 A bottle of Grüner Veltliner (photo by the author)

red or white. The month of September in the Croatian system is named *rujan*, using the same adjective, and both yellow and red leaves are seen in that month.

Cross-linguistic color-based differences are not restricted to wine and spirits. In Mandarin Chinese, black tea is known as (红茶, *hóng chá*)

Figure 2.2 Children in Rajasthan, India, playing with paint during Holi, an ancient Hindu festival (Bartosz Hadyniak/Getty Images)

'red tea', while Russians may describe it as black, чёрный чай (*chorniy chay*), or red, красный чай (*krasniy chay*). Also, a peculiar thing happens with in Polish, in which language 'beer' is an eye color. So, *piwne oczy* 'beer eyes' is a lighter shade of brown. English has a similar term involving beer and eyes: *beer goggles* (the effect of alcohol on perceptions of attractiveness), but this is very much a different type of meaning. In Serbo-Croatian, blond hair is literally blue: *plava kosa* 'blond, literally blue, hair' (the meaning of this adjective shifted to blue much later than it began to be used for hair, at which point it actually meant 'blond') (Figure 2.2).

Food offers further interesting examples. Historically, Serbian (influenced by Turkish) had the following terms (which are still used but increasingly less widely): *plavi patlidžan* 'eggplant', literally: 'blue eggplant', and *crveni patlidžan* 'tomato', literally: 'red eggplant'; *crni luk* 'onion', literally: 'black garlic/onion', and *beli luk* 'garlic', literally: 'white garlic/onion'; *beli bubrezi* 'testicles,' literally: 'white kidneys', and *crni bubrezi* 'kidneys', literally: 'black kidneys'; and finally *crna džigerica* 'liver', literally: 'black liver', and *bela džigerica* 'lungs', literally: 'white liver'. And yes, all of these are not-for-the-faint-of-heart

Figure 2.3 Red and blue eggplant, red onion, and other colorful produce (David Malan/Getty Images)

food items served in traditional restaurants in the Balkans. As in Serbian, garlic and onion are differentiated by color in the Indonesian variety of Malay. A popular fairy tale is named *Bawang merah dan bawang putih* ('Red and white garlic/onion': *bawang* 'garlic/onion', *merah* 'red', and *putih* 'white') and it is the Indonesian version of Cinderella (Figure 2.3).

Profound cross-cultural differences are found in the associations attached to colors. For example, what are known as *blue movies*, that is, pornographic movies, in English are known as 'yellow movies' in Mandarin Chinese (黄色电影, *huáng sè diàn yǐng*). In Japanese, they are known as 'pink movies' (ピンク映画, *pinku eiga*). Colors are also used to symbolize political allegiances, so much so that some parties are simply known by color, as in the *Green Party*. When describing coalitions, Germans use political colors profusely. There is a traffic light coalition (*Ampelkoalition*) composed of leftists (red), libertarians (yellow), and environmentalists (green). Then there is a Jamaica coalition, named after the colors of the Jamaican flag (*Jamaica-Koalition*): conservatives (black), libertarians (yellow), and environmentalists (green). The Kenyan flag is also included. There is a *Kenia-Koalition*: environmentalists (green), socialists (red), and conservatives (black). Not surprisingly, there is also a German flag coalition (*Deutschland-Koalition*, abbreviated *D-Koalition*): conservatives (black), socialists (red), and libertarians (yellow). Dutch has a *paars kabinet* 'purple coalition', which includes liberals and social democrats (and excludes Christian democrats).

Interestingly enough, two neighboring countries, Canada and the United States, assign opposite political meanings to red and blue. In the United States, Republicans (somewhat more conservative) are red and Democrats (somewhat less conservative) are blue. In Canada, Liberals (somewhat less conservative) are red and Conservatives (somewhat more conservative) are blue.

Needless to say, colors can have different meanings in different contexts within the same culture. For those who drive, red means stop and green means go, and for those who navigate the seas and the skies, red means port (i.e., the left side of the vessel) and green signifies starboard (i.e., the right side of the vessel). The global linguistic variety in perceiving colors and attaching meaning to them clearly shows how shared physical realities represent only a departure point for a wide range of cultural contextualization. Languages define perceptions of color, as well as connotations and additional meanings attached to these. All of this makes our cultural and linguistic world abundantly colorful.

3 | *Second Cousins Twice Removed*

Kinship is a well-known field of cross-cultural variation, which is then mirrored in cross-linguistic differences. Kinship terms do not only vary cross-linguistically; they also change from one historical stage of the same language to another. The trend in many languages is toward simplification (Figure 3.1). English is a case in point. Old English had separate words for paternal uncle (*fædera*) and aunt (*faþu*), and their maternal counterparts (*ēam* – uncle, maternal, *mōdriġe* – aunt, maternal). It also featured a number of other precise kinship terms expressed in one word, such as *tācor* 'husband's brother'. All of these have been lost. The breadth of today's English kinship terms can be seen by examining the word *cousin*. Defined in the Oxford English Dictionary (OED) as "any collateral relative more distant than a brother or sister," it covers vast areas of kinship. For that reason, it needs to be pre-modified, as in *first*, *second*, and so on, "expressing the degree of relationship between one and a collateral relative who is descended from a common ancestor by the same number of generations as oneself." It can also be post-modified with *removed* "in phrases expressing one's relationship with a cousin who is descended from a common ancestor by a different number of degrees of descent from oneself."

Similar very broad kinship terms are found in Pirahã, an Amazonian language, in which terms such as *ahaigí* 'a person of my generation', *tiobáhai* 'a person from the generation younger than mine', *baí'i* 'a person from the generation older than mine who has some power over me', and so on can be found.

More precise one-word kinship terms can be found in many other languages. Even closely related languages differ in this respect. To return to aunts and uncles, among Slavic languages (all of which have inherited a rich Proto-Slavic system of kinship terms), Russian is exactly the same as English, because дядя (*dyadya*) covers whatever *uncle* covers (i.e., both paternal and maternal uncle), and тётя

Figure 3.1 A family tree (johnwoodcock/Getty Images)

(*tyotya*) has the same scope as *aunt* (paternal and maternal). Polish is on the way to becoming like Russian in this regard, because *wujek* is used for 'uncle' and *ciocia* for 'aunt'. However, it still has a (somewhat archaic) term for paternal uncle: *stryjek*. The Old Slavic system of kinship terms is still relatively well preserved in standard varieties of Serbo-Croatian. The word for maternal uncle is *ujak* and for his wife it is *ujna*; for paternal uncle it is *stric* and his wife is *strina*; and for one's mother's or father's sister it is *tetka* and her husband is *tetak*. The level of precision in this language includes one-word terms for one's husband's sister (*zaova*) and brother (*djever*), one's wife's sister (*svastika*) and brother (*šurjak*), and even one's husband's brother's wife (*jetrva*), one's wife's sister's husband (*pašenog*), and one's husband's sister's husband (*svak*). Some of these are in the process of being lost, but they continue to be used by older people and in more traditional rural areas. Similarly, Serbian ethnographic records show the existence of terms for sixteen generations of ancestors, starting with one's mother and father, and ending with what is literally named "white eagle" and "white bee." However, only distinct names for four previous generations are actually used.

Mandarin Chinese is known for its lexical precision in expressing kinship terms. For example, it uses separate words for older brother (哥哥, *gēgē*) and younger brother (弟弟, *dìdì*), and terms for one's sister follow suit. To say 'brother', speakers need to say 哥哥弟弟, *gēgē dìdì*, literally 'older brother younger brother', as the more powerful person comes first, as in the rule of primogeniture and the many stories about three sons of kings found in European languages.

There are languages, such as the Amazonian rainforest language Shipibo, in which the speaker's gender determines the word used. Thus, a male will use the word *epa* for his uncle, and a female will call her uncle *koka*; aunt is *nači* when a male speaks, and *huata* when the speaker is a female.

Kinship terms are commonly "stretched." Thus, in Yandruwandha, an indigenous Australian language, *ngandri* primarily means 'mother' but it is also used for maternal aunt, her daughter (one's mother's sister's daughter), and other female (plural) kin. Similarly, *ngapiri*, which is primarily 'father', is used for paternal uncle and other male (plural) kin. In various languages, kinship terms are extended to non-kin, as in the common use of 'brother' as a form of address to males in some dialects of English (*bro*), Spanish (*hermano*), or Arabic (my brother: اخي, *akhi*). The use of *auntie* in Indian English as a term of respect for any older female is a similar case. Macedonian does the same with тетка (*tetka*) 'aunt' and чичко (*chichko*) 'uncle', which are both used to respectfully address any elderly female or male, respectively. German offers a further example, in which *Schwester* 'sister' also means 'nurse' and 'nun'. This is paralleled in many Slavic languages and possibly in English, albeit not that often.

One treads carefully around mothers-in-law in many cultures, but that is nothing compared to Uw Oykangand, an Australian indigenous language, in which there is a special register when one speaks in the presence of someone related to one's potential mother-in-law. For example, 'foot' is *embal* as used in the regular register. However, when the groom-to-be speaks with someone related to his potential mother-in-law, he uses the word *arrmubun* to show his respect.

Addressing family members is yet another story. Bart, of the Simpsons, habitually uses *Homer*, the first name of his father, when addressing him. In doing so, he is being disrespectful because the expected form is *dad* or (in the deep South of the United States and military families) *sir*. Many languages, such as German and various Slavic languages, formerly followed the custom of using the formal form of address (equivalent to using *sir* or *ma'am* in English) when addressing one's parents. This system has now become defunct. Polish is an interesting case. Many speakers use sentences such as *Jak się mama czuje?* literally 'How is mom feeling?' (as opposed to: How do you feel?), which is structurally the same as formally addressing a non-peer: *Jak się Pani czuje?*, literally 'How is ma'am feeling?'. However, an increasing number of younger people are abandoning this practice and using *Jak się czujesz?* 'How do you feel?' when speaking to their mothers (and fathers, but with *tato* 'dad' replacing *mama* 'mom' in the phrase). The development of Romanian *nene* (roughly: 'sir'), a respectful form of address for one's older brothers, which was once widely used, but it is now restricted to rural areas of southeastern Romania, is similar.

Kinship relations are expressed in names and surnames in some languages. Thus, Russians have a PATRONYMIC in addition to their name. For example, the middle name of Владимир Владимирович Путин, *Vladimir Vladimirovich Putin* (*V.V. Putin* for short, and even shorter, given the prominence of the person, *VVP*), is a patronymic that means 'the son of Vladimir', as the Russian leader's father bore the same name as him (Figure 3.2).

Arabs also have patronymics. For example, the Arabic name of Avicenna, a famous medieval Islamic polymath, in its short version, is *ibn Sīnā* (ابن سينا), 'the son of Sina'. However, in the complicated structure of Arabic names there are also PAEDONYMICS (also known as TEKNONYMS), adult names derived from their first-born child. So, if a man and woman have a first-born son named Ali, the father would be called *Abū Ali* (أبو علي) and the mother would be *Umm Ali* (أمّ علي).

Icelandic surnames are, in fact, patronymics. Differences between English and Icelandic last names offer an interesting example of lexical and semantic differences. The last name *Johnson* in English links all members of the same nuclear and extended family and, additionally,

Second Cousins Twice Removed 35

Figure 3.2 A Putin T-shirt that reads "everything is going according to the plan" (photo by the author)

there are coincidental links with all other bearers of the same last name, but there is no significant link with people named *John*. In contrast, the Icelandic last name *Jónssson* links one's father and siblings substantially, and then all people whose first name is *Jón* and their direct descendants, but there is no link with one's grandparents, cousins, and so on. The Icelandic system uses the father's (and occasionally the mother's) first name as the basis for a child's last name, as can be seen from the following example. The son of Jón <u>Einar</u>sson is called Ólafur <u>Jón</u>sson, and his daughter Sigriður is called <u>Jón</u>sdóttir. Son is 'son' and dóttir is 'daughter'. There are some minor exceptions to this, for example, Geir Haarde, the hero of the Icelandic financial crisis of 2008. There was a similar tradition in southern Serbia in the past, except it was based on one's paternal grandfather's name. So, if your paternal grandfather's name was *Jovan*, your last name would be *Jovanović*. This practice was abandoned in the mid-20th century, so that the existing last names were used from then onward rather than the patronymic.

Figure 3.3 Family resemblance (Jasmin Merdan/Getty Images)

On the other hand, one's middle name does not have to relate to one's father. It can be a baptismal name, which is common in Poland, where it is known as the *drugie imie* 'second name'. In addition to baptismal name, in English it can also be part of a two-word given name, as is common in the American South (e.g., *Billy Bob* or *Mary Anne*), or mother's maiden name, as in *John Fitzgerald Kennedy*.

People around the world and across centuries have the same biological relations with their ancestors and successors, but each culture views the world from its own perspective, which reveals some parts of the picture and hides others. It seems that collectivist societies have a greater need to precisely define these terms than their individualist counterparts. This chapter has examined the gradual loss of elaborate systems of kinship terms. This may be a sign of collectivist societies shifting toward the individualist end of the scale as a result of globalization (Figure 3.3).

4 | *I Have Three Sons and a Child**

The sentence in the title of this chapter is likely to be heard in rural areas of Montenegro, a small southeastern European country known for its pockets of patriarchal conservatism. "Child" is, of course, daughter, that is, a child that does not continue the family and clan line (yes, they have clans, just like Scots, but without kilts and their identifying tartans). Other areas in southeastern Europe may not feature extreme examples of this kind, but linguistic expressions of gender inequalities are abundant and widespread.

Foreigners are confused by the practice in Serbo-Croatian, the language of the region, of using the form *sine* '(my) son' to affectionately address any young people of any gender. So, a father may say to his daughter: *Marija, sine, da ti nešto kažem* . . . 'Maria, my son, let me tell you something'. The language also features sexist proverbs that literally read: "long hair, short mind" (in reference to female reasoning), "first (child) and already a male" (originally used when a couple produced a boy at the first attempt, but now referring to anything that works first time).

Another expression of sexism is that the word *žena* is used for 'woman' and 'wife' (while there are two separate words for male: *muškarac* for man and *muž* for husband). In this regard, Serbo-Croatian looks curious even in comparison to other Slavic languages, such as Russian (where женщина, *zhenshchina* is 'woman' and жена, *zhena* 'wife') and Polish (where *kobieta* is 'woman' and *żona* 'wife'), but similar to languages that are not particularly known for sexism today (which does not mean they were not so in the past). The two meanings are merged in German *Frau* and Dutch *vrouw*.

A similar configuration can be found in Serbo-Croatian kinship terms, where there are two words for uncles: paternal (*stric*) and maternal (*ujak*), whereas *tetka* is either paternal or maternal aunt.

---

* A chapter with this number is officially not in this book.

Figure 4.1 A non–Serbo-Croatian marriage (Peter Dazeley/Getty Images)

Some features of this kind are more widespread and shared by other Slavic languages. In addition to the word *vjenčati se s nekim* 'to marry somebody, lit. with somebody', which can be used in reference to males and females alike (straight and gay), Serbo-Croatian has two additional verbs referring to the act of marriage. The first is used in reference to males and reads: *oženiti se nekim* 'to marry (of a male)', lit. 'to bewife oneself with somebody'. The second is used in reference to females and reads: *udati se za nekoga* 'to marry (of a female)', lit. 'to give oneself in for somebody'. The female verb for marriage (*udati se*) is used disparagingly for males perceived to be dominated by their wives (Figure 4.1). A similar gender imbalance can be seen in the most common verb for copulation. Unlike in English, where he can screw her and she can screw him, in Serbo-Croatian, he can screw her, but she cannot screw him, but only: 'screw oneself with him' (literally).

All this is not to say that English is free from linguistic expressions of sexism. They range from using *men* to mean all people to all those proverbs with the pattern *he who* (e.g., *He who laughs last, laughs best*) to writing invitations for Mr. and Mrs. Jack Jones. All these colorful examples are but a fraction of the cross-linguistic variation around gender and sex.

Gender awareness is one prominent area of differences. While English sometimes marks gender (as in *waiter* and *actor* versus *waitress* and *actress*, with *server* and *actor* being increasingly used for both sexes), most of the time, unisex words are used, which is not the case with many other languages. The English word *friend* is rendered as *amigo* (male friend) and *amiga* (female friend) in Spanish, *ami* (male) and *amie* (female) in French, and so on. Similarly, if one says *I feel lucky* in English, we do not know if that person is male or female. In Spanish, a male would say *me siento afortunado*, and a female *me siento afortunada*.

Global diversity is even more prominent in grammatical gender. In English, the masculine gender is reserved for males, and feminine gender for females. If we disregard pets and other animals (who are just like people to their owners), areas where a nonperson is not "it" are extremely rare: ships, engines, and countries get to be a "she." Grammatical gender is social gender and social gender is largely sex in English. In contrast, grammatical gender in Slavic languages spreads far beyond sex. While males are, as a rule, still masculine and females are feminine in their grammatical gender, everything else is a "he," "she," or "it," depending on its final sound. Thus, in Czech, *hlava* 'head' is feminine (she) because it ends in an -*a*, *oko* 'eye' is neuter (it) because it ends in an -*o*, and *nos* 'nose' is masculine (he) because it ends in a consonant. There are minor exceptions, but all Slavic languages (Russian, Polish, Bulgarian, etc.) have this feature and that feature also determines how these nouns form plurals and what form their adjectives and some verb forms assume. In Macedonian and Bulgarian, gender additionally shapes the form of the definite article. It is not unusual to hear a Slavic language speaker say in English: *She is not good*, referring to his/her children's school. The noun for 'school', pronounced *shkola* (spelled differently in individual Slavic languages), is a "she," given that it ends in an -*a*. Nouns have different plurals, and their modifiers (such as my, big, etc.) and verb forms (as in: I worked) will differ depending on their gender. Plurals are particularly interesting. Some Slavic languages are very stubborn in maintaining separate genders in the plural form. Take, for example, the following verbs. In Slovene, 'worked' (as in: we, you, they worked, when talking about three or more people) is *delali* (if the group contains at least one male), *delale* (if they are all females), and *delala* (if they are all children). Russians do not distinguish these differences; 'worked' is делали (*delali*) in the plural form, whoever performs the action. Poles, on the other hand, have developed something known as the masculine-personal gender. This gives *pracowali* if the group contains at least one male, and *pracowały* in all other cases.

However, there are non-Slavic languages, such as Hungarian or Finnish, where gender does not play a role in the grammatical system, that is, where there is no distinction between masculine, feminine, and neuter. There are also languages that classify their reality using completely different categories. A well-known case are classes in Bantu languages, such as Swahili, where classification in the first eight classes is as follows: Class 1 and 2 (in this and all other cases, the odd number stands for the singular form and the subsequent even number for the plural form) persons, 3 and 4 plants, 5 and 6 fruits, and 7 and 8 things. For example, 'person' will belong to class 1 and the word for it is *mtu*, whereby *m-* is the marker of class 1 (marking the singular form). In plural, when saying 'persons' *m-* is changed into *wa-* and the form is *watu*. In the word for 'plant', class 3 (singular) is *mmea*, and class 4 is *mimea*, so the initial *m-* is changed into *mi-* given that this is a different category. So, it is not the gender but a more elaborate categorization that is grammatically relevant. Classes are also found in Basque (which has the animate and inanimate classes), in some North American indigenous languages, and various Australian aboriginal languages. Dyirbal, a language from the latter group, has classes, and one of them includes women, fire, and dangerous things. Dyirbal attained global notoriety in the late 1980s when a linguist, George Lakoff, published a book eponymous with this Dyirbal class.

Languages also feature words the use of which seems to be the preserve of one gender. Japanese has a special name for 'feminine words' 女言葉, *onna kotoba*. There are sentence-ending particles, such as わ, *wa*, which is used in the feminine, and ぜ, *ze*, used in masculine discourse (Figure 4.2).

Noble attempts to express linguistic gender equality in making references to people and the professions in which they engage largely exceed the frame of linguistics, being of most relevance in social sciences. Examples include the use of *he/she* or *they* for one person, forms such as *chairperson*, and so on, in English, and the Swedish gender-neutral pronoun *hen* (which stands for either *han* 'he' or *hon* 'she'). German is known for its "in-between I" (*Binnen-I* in German). In German, feminine professions are typically derived from their masculine counterparts. For example, *Lehrer* is 'male teacher' and *Lehrerin* 'female teacher'. The aforementioned in-between I is used to

Figure 4.2 An expert at *onna kotoba* (electravk/Getty Images)

indicate that the feminine form is used to refer to both males and females. So, in job advertisements for teachers, in the word *LehrerInnen*, the I would be capitalized between the masculine stem and the feminine suffix ('female teachers' would be spelled without this capitalization: *Lehrerinnen*).

Canada offers a good example of how gender equality can be pursued in exactly opposite ways (Figure 4.3). Canadian English, or any form of English for that matter, strives to achieve gender equality by removing the gender from the equation (as in *server* for both *waiter* and *waitress*); Canadian French insists on marking the gender, as shown in the way political figures address citizens: *Canadiens et Canadiennes* 'My fellow Canadians, literally: Male and female Canadians.'

As this chapter has demonstrated, gender inequality has a long history, but, fortunately increasingly so, attempts are being made to right the wrongs of the past. Not all traces of gender inequality reflect the current situation in speech communities. Very often they are relics of bygone times. The fate of attempts to remove these relics is yet to be determined: yet another thing that makes languages interesting. The collective habits of language speakers are unpredictable, and one never knows which change will succeed and which will fail.

Figure 4.3 Loonie, a currency of choice for Canadiens and Canadiennes alike (Bloomberg Creative Photos/Getty Images)

5 | *Concepts on the Chopping Block*

Languages differ in the way that they chop up their concepts into words. It is not uncommon to hear native speakers of Slavic languages (Russians, Ukrainians, Poles, and others) say, when speaking English, that somebody stepped on their leg while using public transportation and that their handbag is made of real skin. In their languages, Slavic speakers are indiscriminate when they talk about their bodies. A single word is used to refer to both a foot and a leg. Skin and leather follow suit, and these are not isolated examples. There is a single word for fingers and toes, and likewise for hands and arms. In Russian, even the brain and the spinal cord are technically named the same: *мозг* (*mozg*). However, when referring to the spinal cord, Russian speakers will always say *спинной мозг* (*spinnoy mozg*, literally: 'spine brain'), whereas adding *golovnoy* (as in *головной мозг*, *golovnoy mozg*, literally: 'head brain') is optional and is only used when making a specific reference (Figure 5.1).

But Slavs are more precise in other areas, which causes equally embarrassing errors in English-speaking learners of Russian and Polish. These two languages have four major equivalents of the English verb *to go*, which are described here. Consequently, a learner of Polish will have to make a choice between *iść* (on foot and continuously, without interruptions, e.g., going to a nearby shop once), *jechać* (continuously but using a means of transportation, e.g., going to a distant shop by car once), *chodzić* (on foot, but repeatedly and back and forth, e.g., when going to a nearby shop every other day), and, finally, *jeździć* (using means of transportation, e.g., going to a distant shop by car every other week) (Figure 5.2). These examples show how different cultures chop their concepts into words. Some distinctions are emphasized in one culture, while another culture distinguishes completely different elements.

While it is difficult to say what has caused these differences between languages or groups, some patterns emerge when we compare them.

Figure 5.1 Chopped-up anatomy (appleuzr/Getty Images)

To continue comparing Slavic languages with English, the former are rather imprecise in measures (even when "measuring" one's own body, as seen earlier) and terms of social interaction. A famous example is the word that roughly covers calculations and their results. The word reads *račun* in Slovene, *rachunek* in Polish, and *счём* (*shchot*) in Russian, to name just a few Slavic languages. Its English equivalents are *account* (as in bank account), *bill* (e.g., for water), *receipt* (in a store), *check* (in a restaurant), *calculation*, *calculus*, and *interest* (one's benefit, advantage). English, on the other hand, makes broad references using metaphors from the domestic setting. Bed where one sleeps thus extends to marital relationship, riverbed, bed of flowers, a layer of rock, a foundation (e.g., for a roadbed), and many other meanings. Slavic languages would use separate words for each of those.

Concepts on the Chopping Block 45

Figure 5.2 Planes, trains, and automobiles (MHJ/Getty Images)

The areas where English is apparently "imprecise" show that some of these differences stem from spontaneous development of semantic transfer, mostly metaphorical (as, for example, a bed of flowers looks like a bed for sleeping). These developments simply happen in one language and not in another. Other examples, such as the aforementioned Slavic "imprecision" in measures and terms for social interaction, may be connected to the dimension of collectivism versus individualism, one of Hofstede's dimensions (see Chapter A). Slavic cultures stand on the collectivist end of the scale and English is firmly in the individualist realm. If the culture is collectivist, there is no need to establish precise measures and have sharply divided terms for social interaction.

Another well-known dimension in cross-cultural anthropology that is mentioned in Chapter A is Edward T. Hall's classic pattern of monochronism versus polychronism. In some cultures, time is perceived as one line where the past, present, and future are clearly divided. These cultures are known as monochronic, and mainstream English-language cultures (e.g., the United Kingdom and United States) clearly fall into that camp. Other cultures perceive multiple timelines, where past, present, and future coexist. Slavic cultures generally belong to this polychronic cultural type. This difference might be mirrored in the use of prepositions. English uses fine-grained prepositions for locations. One is *in* the house, *on* the beach, and *at* the concert. So, *in* is used for being inside enclosed physical spaces, *on* for being on top of physical spaces, and *at* for events. Location is where you are, were, or will be – so a kind of present. However, when one talks about the source of movement (the place or event from where you are, where you were, or where you will be going from, so a kind of past) *from* will be used in all three cases (from the house, from the beach, and from the concert). Similarly, the destination (where are, were, or will you be going to, i.e., a kind of future) requires *to* in all three cases (to the house, to the beach, to the concert). So, past and future seem not to be relevant in the present; the distinction is only relevant when talking about locations, that is, in a kind of present. Slavic languages are different. The difference of being inside a physical space, on the one hand, and being atop a flat space or in an event, on the other, is maintained for source, location, and the destination of movement. Slavic speakers, for example those of Serbo-Croatian, have to literally say: I am going *from within* the house (Idem *iz kuće*), I am going *from atop* the beach (Idem *s plaže*), I am going *to within* the house (Idem *u kuću*), I am going *to atop* the beach (Idem *na plažu*), in the same way as *in* the house (*u kući*) and *on* the beach (*na plaži*). So, these distinctions are still important in the past and future of sorts, which may be connected to the polychronic nature of the culture (Figure 5.3).

Concepts on the Chopping Block 47

Figure 5.3 Past, future, and present (porcorex/Getty Images)

An interesting question here is that of which criteria are used in splitting concepts into words. It turns out that the ground for division can be practically anything: relation (as in numerous kinship term differences), gender (as in English *friend* versus Portuguese and Spanish *amigo* and *amiga*), age (English *beef* versus Serbo-Croatian *junetina*, 'young beef', and *govedina* 'older beef'), utility (English *fruit* versus German *Frucht* 'fruit of a tree' – *Obst* 'nutritional category'), manner (English *go* vs. Russian *идти*, *idti*, 'on foot' and *ехать*, *yehat*, 'in a vehicle'), hierarchy (English *school* vs. Serbo-Croatian *škola* 'elementary, middle, and high school' and *fakultet* 'university'), location (Russian *мозг*, *mozg* vs. English *brain* and *spinal cord*), accompanying feature (German *Schnecke* vs. English *slug* and *snail*), exclusion, that is, carving out another more specified word that covers a narrow area of another word (English *field* vs. Hopi: *paasa/paavasa* 'field', and *ōngalvasa* 'field with plants other than corn'), and many others.

Often several different criteria can be applied in dividing the same conceptual field. Let us compare the conceptual field of *deer* in English and Chukchi. According to WordNet, English makes the following two distinctions based on age and gender: *deer*, *cervid* (distinguished from Bovidae by the male's having solid deciduous antlers) => *pricket* (male deer in his second year), => *fawn* (young deer). In Chukchi, the criteria of age, gender, and utility are involved, and there are separate words for calves from birth to one year; fawn from one year and seven months to two years; male from two to three years; female three years and older; breeding bulls (three years and older); castrated oxen; and draft deer. Even more intricate is the North Saami division of the concept of reindeer. It involves sex- and age-related criteria (e.g., the basic term for a 3.5–4-year old reindeer cow is *njiŋŋelas*, a fertile one is *áldu* and one with a calf is *rotnu*, a male reindeer of the same age is *gottos*, a non-castrated one is *heargi*, and a castrated one is *spáillit*), body size, shape, and condition (e.g., *chálggat* 'young animal who is so far advanced that he can accompany his mother even in difficult conditions'), color (e.g., *chuoivvat-gabba* 'white reindeer with a yellowish grey color over its back'), nature of the coat (e.g., *shnilzhi* 'reindeer with quite short hair (just after changing its coat)'), features of the head (e.g., *gierdo-chalbmi* 'dark reindeer with a white ring around its eyes, light reindeer with a dark ring around its eyes'), features of the antlers (e.g., *snarri* 'reindeer with short but very branchy and very bent antlers'), features of the feet (e.g., *sukka-juolgi* 'reindeer with white feet like stockings'), as well as behavior and utility (e.g., *njirru* 'female reindeer, which is very unmanageable, difficult to hold when tied').

As can be seen, speakers of various languages develop their own means of carving the concepts into words. The precision of their carving is determined by the reality in which these languages function, beliefs and patterns found in the cultures that these languages serve, but also random developments in the course of their historical development.

6 | *Unripe Bananas and Ripe Tomatoes*

There are five basic tastes (at least for those who are not culinary critics) (Figure 6.1). Most people will immediately recognize four of them: salty, sweet, sour, and bitter (even when they are combined, as in sweet and sour or bittersweet). The fifth one, *umami*, found among other things in ripe tomatoes, is more elusive. The word comes from Japanese うま味 and it is a neologism coined in the early twentieth century by Kikunae Ikeda, the scholar who brought this taste to our attention. The word is a blend from the 旨い, *umai* 'delicious, yummy' and 味, *mi* 'taste'. Consequent to the lower degree of detectability of the taste itself, it is far less well-known than the other tastes, and many speakers will not be aware of it at all.

Once we go beyond the five basic tastes, we find areas where tastes and textures are expressed much more precisely, as in the worlds of wine and food critics. The former will talk about fruit forward, floral, dry, firm, and light wines; to the latter, the taste of food will be loamy, gamy, minerally, etc. Most other speakers of English will not be that precise.

Speakers of languages will likely develop specific taste names for food items that are prominent in their cultures. Bananas are very prominent in Central Philippines and the word *ap(e)led* is used to describe the taste of unripe bananas. The Mandarin Chinese word 涩 (sè) 'tart, astringent, acerbic' is similar (Figure 6.2).

Words for food and drink will probably be more precise if the item plays an important role in the culture that the language in question serves. Yam is the king of food items in the culture of Maung, an Australian aboriginal language, so the following words refer to it: *kuli, akarnpa, arlamun, rlurrjj, wirlamarr, wulupay, miyulum, pajung, yuwak, wurruwujpiny, mirrwulu, yaltany, artpurrij,* and *akijalk.* Taro is the queen of food in Papua New Guinea, so Kalam, one of its languages, features the following words for it: *adbt, adet, alom, alowmadl, alwag, amlan, apay, apay sup, aweñ, awey, blogow, bomol,*

Figure 6.1 Test tube tastes (Shana Novak/Getty Images)

cabak, caw, cemay, gaywom, glowgogi, gojmay, gomaŋ, gulbalk, jigu, kalŋ, kamej, katol, kek-tŋl, kkp, klbel, kopon, kopon wañs, ksgaŋ, kubagñ, lejp, meleŋ, mlneb, mls, mnop, m ñoŋd magi, molnem, ms, mukut, nem, ñuŋdmagi, olc, pagi, palan, salbad, sanp, sap, sm(u)l, talak, tbep, tlak, tolkom, wañs, weñŋ, wgak, wolpay, yuat, and *yuatp.*

However, one does not have to travel that far to find examples of this kind. The world of mushrooming microbreweries across the United States (and recently around the world) is a case in point. For consumers of industrial lagers, a beer is just a beer, and no further distinctions are used. In the world of microbreweries, not distinguishing between stout and porter, pale, amber, and dark lager, pale ale and IPA, top-fermented and bottom-fermented beer, or even between Hefeweizen and Lambic beer would be an inexcusable transgression.

Unripe Bananas and Ripe Tomatoes 51

Figure 6.2 The spice map of the world (Cavan Images/Getty Images)

Further cultural references are to be found in microbreweries. The British Crown quit India in 1947 (as suggested by Gandhiji). By contrast, India Pale Ale (IPA), thus named because of the extra hops in the pale ale (intended for imperial officers in India) to keep the beer unspoiled during a long trip, lives on. Across the whole universe of microbreweries, it is indeed every hop lover's dream. Of course, many of those hop lovers will have no idea why it is so named, or even what IPA stands for.

The texture of food is another source of cross-cultural and cross-linguistic variation. Japanese scholar Katsuyoshi Nishinari and his colleagues from several other countries have compared food texture terms in English, French, Japanese, and Mandarin Chinese. They studied terms such as soft, crunchy, crumbly, and gooey in English. The number of words for texture and their repertoire turned out to be quite different in these four languages. Some examples include French *caoutchouteux* (rubber-like, springy) of squid (cuttlefish), and the difference between *craquant* (fracturable, cracking, of chips) and *croquant* (crunchy, short, raw carrot, apple); and Chinese 滑嫩, *huá nèn* (slippery and tender, of bean curd), 脆嫩, *cuì nèn* (crisp and tender, of bamboo shoots), and 多孔状, *duōkǒng zhuàng* (multi-holed, of overcooked egg thin soup). The largest number of texture terms is recorded in Japanese, serving a culture and cuisine in which a great deal of attention is devoted to texture. The level of precision of these terms, many of which use sound symbolism, can be seen in examples such as ほくほく, *hokuhoku*, which is used to represent steamed sweet potato that is about to crumble, とろり, *torori*, representing the behavior of thick liquid that does not flow so fast (of stews and melted cheese), トロトロ, *torotoro*, used when a solid has melted and becomes a viscous liquid (of cream soup).

These differences are also apparent when taste is expressed in other languages. In English, both mustard and pepper (capsicum) are *hot* and in German they are 'sharp': *scharf*. In Russian, mustard is 'strong' (сильная горчица, *silynaya garchitsa*) and pepper is 'sharp' (острый перец, *ostriy perets*). Similarly, speakers of Serbo-Croatian use *ljut* 'fierce' for mustard and pepper alike. This brings us to the fact that metaphors describing taste can go both ways. In the aforementioned examples, the direction is from sensations to the taste of food. But there are also examples where words for tastes are used for feelings. For somebody who is angry, Germans say 'sour' (*sauer*). Sometimes things get even more complicated. Serbo-Croatian uses *ljut* 'fierce' not only for the taste of 'hot' лют (*lyoot*) but also the feeling of 'angry', just as Bulgarian uses лют (*lyoot*) and Macedonian лут (*loot*). Etymologically, the meaning of 'angry' came first, but many speakers consider the meaning of 'hot, spicy' to be more basic (Figure 6.3).

The shape of food is also a source of cross-linguistic variation. What is simply 'pasta' in many other languages is divided into very precise categories by Italians, such as *capellini* (hair-like pasta), *spaghetti* (rope-like pasta), *vermicelli* (which look like worms), *linguine* (tongue-shaped pasta), *stringozzi* (shoelace-shaped pasta), *penne* (which look like quils), *farfalle* (butterfly-shaped pasta), *conchiglie* (seashell-shaped pasta), and others.

Words for food and drinks that go bad are also a source of global diversity. Unfortunately, in many languages, English included, more specific terms are being replaced with all-encompassing ones. Rather than saying that their bread is stale, butter rancid, milk sour, meat rotten, tomatoes overripe, etc. English speakers tend to use 'bad' in all instances, which is probably triggered by industrial food production, in which everything has its expiration date.

Figure 6.3 Variety is the life of spices (fcafotodigital/Getty Images)

The famous Latin proverb *De gustibus non disputandum est* 'In matters of taste, there can be no disputes' clearly does not only apply to individuals. It equally applies to different cultures and their languages. Taste starts with the physiology of the tongue, which is shared globally, and is then transformed by myriad global cultures into a diverse patchwork of terms for the taste, texture, and shape of food and drink. In general, heightened interest in any given field leads to higher precision in naming entities within that field.

7 | *Mums and Clocks Mean Death*

More than thirty years ago, chrysanthemums became part of my personal history via a rather unusual instance of a clash of cultures. My son was born in the United States and a big-hearted American colleague came to visit the new mother and baby in the hospital. Of course, he did not come empty-handed – he brought along a bouquet of chrysanthemums. This generous gesture evoked rather unpleasant feelings in us, the parents. In southeastern Europe, from where we hail, at that time chrysanthemums were restricted to one single use – they were cemetery flowers that were not used for any other social occasion. Then, ten years ago, death was part of another curious cultural clash in my personal experience, the only difference being that I was merely an observer rather than a protagonist. A national organization in the United States, with which I was associated at the time, had a custom of gifting a clock to its outgoing president. In this particular instance, the problem was that the outgoing president was a Chinese woman, and in Mandarin Chinese, 钟, *zhong* 'clock' is an inappropriate gift. Gifting it is the equivalent of saying "your time is up; I wish that you die." This grim interpretation could not be any further from the noble intention of the members of the aforementioned organization.

At the opposite end of the scale of life from funerals are baby showers. In southeastern Europe, a similar social gathering takes place, known as *babine* in Serbo-Croatian. However, there is one crucial difference between the two events. The *babine* event happens only after the baby is born, so the baby has to be present at its shower. It would be unimaginable to have it during the mother's pregnancy (as in baby showers), as it may bring bad luck. Assuming that the baby will be born would be interpreted as trying to control something that one does not have control over. Turks have a similar event, which also takes place after the baby is born, where a special drink, *lohusa şerbeti*, is served. In Arabic cultures, similar events are also held only after the baby is born, to avoid bad luck.

Mums and Clocks Mean Death

Figure 7.1 Taiwanese building with no fourth floor (photo by Mladen Šašić)

In mainstream American cultures, where one is always in the driver's seat, bad luck is not a problem at all.

Some numbers evoke certain connotations. For example, the number 13 is unlucky in many languages. So, in some places, room number 13, floor 13, or row 13 is missing. In Chinese and Japanese cultures the unlucky number is four (Figure 7.1). This comes from the fact that the word for number four in Chinese 四 (*sì*) sounds similar to the word for death 死 *sǐ*. On the other hand, lucky number seven is lucky number eight in Chinese and Japanese (eight is the auspicious number). Encountering four crows would be a complete disaster in Japan. These creatures, rather inconspicuous birds in many other countries, are considered dangerous animals in Japan, as they are known to attack passers-by (Figure 7.2). In Russian, an odd number of flowers in a bouquet that is taken to somebody is associated with happy occasions (e.g., birthdays) and an even number with sad occasions (e.g., funerals).

The aforementioned examples show that certain words and the concepts they represent have distinct connotations, that is, typical emotional reactions to them, and cultural scripts related to them.

Figure 7.2 Dangerous Japanese crows (photo by the author)

Languages also differ in how commonly used objects are perceived, that is, in what is considered normal. For example, the prototypical European kitchen table is much taller than its traditional Japanese counterpart, and the same is true for beds. In Japan, as in Arabic countries, food is served at knee level, which is still higher than in India, where it is typically served on the floor. Similarly, when thinking about rooms, Europeans will definitely not imagine paper walls and sliding doors, which is included in the image of a traditional Japanese room. Even a small item such as a can opener can assume different prototypical values. In the United States it has handles and a rotating blade. In the Mediterranean basin, the prototype is more like a miniature knife on the side of a handle, what is known as a military style can opener in the United States. The European concept of dressing is much more elaborate than the Samoan verb *lavalava*, which entails wrapping an eponymous piece of cloth around the hips.

Even closely related languages, such as English and German, exhibit differences in their prototypes. In American English, the prototypical startup company's first venue is a *garage*, which is, in a way, a reflection of the fact that a prototypical American lives in a home with a garage. The equivalent place in German is *Keller* 'basement' (a prototypical German techie lives in an apartment block), which is reflected in the complex lexeme *Kellerwerkstatt* 'basement workshop', which is often used to talk about successful startups. Exactly the same prototype is invoked by *garage* in American English, as in Wozniak, Jobs, and Wayne creating Apple in the garage of Jobs' parents' house.

In many cases, prototypes will be tied to the environment and cultural patterns. The first of these is apparent from the fact that many European languages in the continental climatic band are likely to have the apple as one of their prototypical fruits. The banana is more likely to serve that role in the languages of the tropics. Even in closely related languages, differences in prototypes are based on the environment and culture. In the Slavic realm, the typical alcoholic drink (stretching from northern to southern Europe) is vodka for Poles, beer for Czechs, plum brandy for Serbs, grappa for Macedonians, and wine for Bulgarians. There are also profound differences in which beverages are common and which are not. For most Slavs, *mead* remains equally unavailable as in English-speaking countries, and it has the same association with bygone centuries. However, in Poland, mead is omnipresent in grocery and liquor stores. It is known as *miód pitny*, literally: 'potable honey' and it comes in four main varieties: *półtorak*, literally 'the one and a half parts one' (honey-to-water ratio 1:0.5), *dwójniak* 'the two parts one' (1:1), *trójniak* 'the three one' (1:2), and *czwórniak* 'the four parts one' (1:3), referring to the number of parts (of honey and water in it). In addition to these, there are endless varieties of flavored and cured 'potable honey', for example, *czereśniak* 'flavored with cherry' (*chereśnia* is 'cherry') and *dębniak* 'aged in oak barrels' (*dąb* is 'oak').

These differences in prototypes can also be found in varieties of the same language. In English, prototypical sports are football and baseball for Americans, ice hockey for Canadians (being "the" sport, so much so that it is never called ice hockey but simply hockey), soccer for the English, Australian rules football for Aussies, and rugby for Kiwis (with cricket playing an important role in the last three cases).

The field of food preparation and consumption is full of differences in prototypes that can cause intercultural miscommunication. While the Spanish equivalent of the English word *breakfast* is *desayuno*, the latter is much lighter than the former. *Desayuno* entails juice and jam, rather than bacon and bangers. Prototypical times when meals are consumed are also different – Spaniards consume their evening meal *la cena* (a late supper) at a time when most English people are already in bed.

Eating utensils are another source of differences in prototypes. Knives, which are ubiquitous on the tables of many cultures, were traditionally considered a most inappropriate table item in China and Japan (which may now be changing). They were considered weapons and tools in food preparation, but not food consumption implements. The civilized way of consuming food involves chopsticks, or 筷子 (*kuaizi*) 'quick bamboo thing', as they are known in Mandarin Chinese. Even if "foolish foreigners" (馬鹿外人, baka gaijin, as they are known in Japanese) use chopsticks, they can cause a small scandal by sticking them in the rice rather than laying them down in front of themselves. Such action invokes a funeral, where a similarly shaped incense stick is placed in a bowl of rice and burnt. In Ethiopia, the usual implement is edible – the sourdough flatbread known as *injera* in Amharic and *biddena* in Oromo, which is used to grab various sauces. Similar is the *lepinja*, used in a meal that is very popular across the Balkans – a flatbread stuffed with kebabs (known as *ćevapčići* in Serbo-Croatian and кебапчиња, *kebapchinya*, in Macedonian), and one would traditionally eat the kebabs by grabbing them with a piece of the flatbread and eating them together (Figure 7.3). Needless to say, across the Arabic world, the traditional implement is the eater's right-hand fingers (as the left hand is used in the bathroom and considered dirty).

Languages also differ in what type and degree of processing is needed to render fish and meat as edible. In the aforementioned cuisines of the Balkans, anything short of thermal processing to "well-done" would fail the test of edibleness – a speck of blood would bring unspeakable disgrace to the chef. In contrast, American steaks offer a range of what is considered undercooked in the Balkans – all the way to "rare" (perceived as a plate bloodbath by an observer from the Balkans). Of course, the Italian *carpaccio* and Japanese 刺身, *sashimi* or 寿司, *sushi* with raw fish would fail the Balkan edibleness test, and so would the Peruvian *ceviche* (processed chemically, but, alas, not thermally) (Figure 7.4). To continue with the Balkans, the main course

Figure 7.3 Ćevapčići (photo by the author)

is salty and the desert is sweet and they never mix. So, eating sweet and sour sauce (糖醋汁, *tángcùzhī*), as the Chinese do, or mixing salty turkey with sweetish cranberry sauce, as Americans do for Thanksgiving, would be a no-no. Balkaners find sweet-and-salty peanut butter equally abominable, naming it "that jam" and, of course, not eating it.

There are also cultural prototypes involving the order of eating. In the United States, salad is typically eaten before the main course, but in many European cultures it is taken concurrently with it. During the decades of my life in the United States, I have seen many speakers of Serbo-Croatian fighting with American waiters and waitresses to keep their salad on the table so that they can eat it with their main course. Similarly, while Italians drink cappuccino, caffé latte, or any other milk-infused beverage in the morning, it would be inconceivable for them to consume it after a full afternoon meal.

Differences in prototypes are found far beyond cuisine – in the lofty world of university professors who write letters of recommendation. Prototypical American letters are so supportive and enthusiastic that

Figure 7.4 Raw-fish sushi: all smiles in Japan, all frowns in the Balkans (photo by the author)

continental Europeans, whose letters are far less so, see them as hyperbolae.

Whatever the category is, from birds to fruits and vegetables, to pots and pans, in each language some exemplars are better prototypes for a category than others. To English speakers, some birds, such as the robin, are "birdier" than others, for example, penguins. Similarly, apples are "fruitier" than cranberries. There will also always be questions over where pots end and pans begin. All these intra- and cross-linguistic differences and gray areas in which prototypical roles assigned to various objects and words that represent them are another source of diversity, which makes our world and its languages interesting.

Prototypes and connotations, discussed at the beginning of this chapter, clearly show that words are not mathematical formulae that encapsulate semantic relations. They are much more than that. They are links between languages and their cultural background. What is a commonly held belief or stereotype in the social fiber of society becomes a connotation of a word that is central to that belief. What is typical behavior in a society becomes a prototypical meaning of the word that is central to such behavior. In the field of the lexicon, it is hence impossible to say where words and language end and entities of a nonlinguistic world begin. The two are inextricably intertwined.

8 | *The Past Is in Front of Us and the Future Is behind Our Back*

As St. Augustine observed, "And each hour passes away in fleeting particles. Whatever of it has flown away is past, whatever remains is future." This notion construes time as an invisible axe that divides the past from the future. This basic notion of time needs to be expanded into categories that can account for time as the measure of change, as Aristotle defined it (Figure 8.1). This is known as expanded time. Expanding is based on objective measures (days, years) or those that are purely conventional (weeks, months, centuries). It is also possible to define these units of time based on the similarities of features within a unit of time and their differences with preceding and following units of time. That is how we speak about old, middle, and modern ages. The difference between the notion of time based on a formal calendar and that based on the sequence of relevant historical events is apparent in the disparity between the traditional notions of the nineteenth and twentieth centuries, on the one hand, and Hobsbawm's idea of the long nineteenth century (1789–1914) and short twentieth century (1914–1991), on the other. The latter notion is based on pivotal historical events – the French Revolution, the beginning of WWI, during which major European empires disappeared, and the fall of the Communist Bloc.

The revolutionary French regime tried to change the way we measure time. Between late 1793 and 1805, the so-called French Republican Calendar was used. Each month was divided into three decades, so a "week" had ten rather than seven days. There were ten hours in a day (rather than the conventional twenty-four), one hundred minutes in an hour, and one hundred seconds in a minute. Clocks were even produced to show this new decimal time. This measurement of time was soon abandoned, to be used again during only one other period of condensed and accelerated time: during the eighteen days of the Paris Commune in 1871. French fries eventually turned out to be much more popular than French time.

The Past Is in Front of Us and the Future Is behind Our Back 63

Figure 8.1 A winding clock (DigiPub/Getty Images)

Major historical events are also major markers of time in everyday conversation. For example, in Eastern Europe, where WWII was extremely fierce and completely transformed societies, the phrase *before the war* is commonly used in reference to when something happened. In the Balkans, which underwent another major war in the 1990s, this reference often prompts the question *Which one?* The ambiguity of this reference is that it can refer to the period before WWII or the 1990s wars in the former Yugoslavia.

Returning to St. Augustine and his metaphor of the past being behind and the future in front of us, it is not uncommon to hear such statements in common parlance in the expressions *you have all your life ahead of you* or *to leave everything behind*. However, in the Andean language of Aymara, time is perceived completely differently.

The past is ahead of us, and the future is behind. This seeming inconsistency has a very simple explanation: we lived through the past, so it is known to us; we can see it, so to speak, unlike the unknown future, which is like something behind our back that we cannot see.

In many languages, spatial relationships extend to time, as in the aforementioned example. Some spatial prepositions such as *behind* and *in front* are perceived from the perspective of the observer. If we say that a chair is behind a table, it is influenced by our perspective, that is, the table stands between the chair and us. These are then easily translatable to timelines, as in *to leave everything behind*, which means that a state of affairs is in the past relative to our own position on the timeline of our life.

Languages differ in their methods of transferring spatial relationships into the sphere of time. Hours of the day offer a good example of this. In English, one would say *half past one*, stating that half an hour has passed since the hour was one. So, the marker of time is "behind" the time being stated. Russian, on the other hand, states the same time literally as 'one half of the second (hour)' – полвторого (*polvtorogo* – *pol* 'half' *votorogo* 'of the second'), meaning that one half of the second hour has elapsed, so the marker of the current time is "ahead" of it. Sometimes, these differences are more drastic, as in Swahili, which is spoken around the equator, where the sun invariably rises at 6 a.m. and sets at 6 p.m. The hours of the day are measured against observable phenomena of the transition from darkness to light and light to darkness, as opposed to the variable and not always observable point when the Sun is at its zenith.

The naming of days of the week offers even more beautiful examples of global linguistic and cultural diversity. Some languages are outright boring. In Mandarin Chinese, Monday is 'week 1', that is, the first day of the week (星期一, xīng qī yī), Tuesday is 'week 2' (星期二, xīng qī èr) and so on. Only Sunday is different; it is 'the heavenly day' (星期天, xīng qī tiān). Japanese is much more interesting. Sunday represents the Sun (日曜日, *nichiyōbi* – the Sun day), Monday is the Moon day (月曜日, *getsuyōbi*), and other days are named after substances that represent planets. Tuesday is thus 'fire day' (火曜日, *kayōbi*), representing Mars, Wednesday is 'water day' (水曜日, *suiyōbi*), representing Mercury, Thursday is 'wood day' (木曜日, *mokuyōbi*), representing Jupiter, Friday is 'metal/gold day' (金曜日, *kin-yōbi*), representing Venus, and Saturday is 'earth day' (土曜日, *doyōbi*), representing Saturn.

Japanese day names are modeled after the Graeco-Roman tradition of naming the days of the week after planets and their respective Gods, which has been preserved in most Italic languages. For example, Tuesday is *diēs Mārtis* 'Mars day' in Latin, which is preserved in Spanish *martes*, French *mardi*, Catalan *dimarti*, Romanian *marți*, and many others. Some of this tradition can also be found in English, for example, the name Saturday comes from the Latin *Saturni diēs* (the day of Saturn). In English, and other Germanic languages, *Sunday* and *Monday* are Sun and Moon day, as in most Italic languages. Other days are named after Germanic gods (which correspond to those from the Graeco-Roman pantheon). *Tuesday* is 'Tiw's day', *Wednesday* 'Wotan's day', *Thursday* is 'Thor's day', and *Friday* is 'Frigg's day'.

Rather than using gods and celestial spheres in their names for the days of the week, some languages project their daily activities into these measures of time. Sunday is 'the no work day' in Slavic languages (e.g., *nedeľa* in Slovak), Monday is 'the day after the no-work day' (e.g., *pondelok* in Slovak). Russian is unusual – Sunday is воскресение (*voskreseniye*) 'resurrection day', an obvious reference to Christianity, but Monday is still понедельник (*ponedelynik*) 'the day after the no-work day'. Other Slavic day names are rather less interesting. Tuesday is the second day (e.g., *wtorek* in Polish), Wednesday is the 'the middle day' (middle of the week: *środa* in Polish), Thursday is the fourth day (e.g., *czwartek* in Polish), Friday is the fifth day (e.g., *piątek* in Polish), and Saturday is ultimately borrowed from Hebrew and means 'the day of Sabbath' (for example, *sobota* in Polish). Turkish is another language that projects daily activities into day names. Sunday is *pazar* 'the market day', Monday is *pazartesi* 'the day after the market day', Friday is *cuma* 'the prayer day', and Saturday is *cumatesi* 'the day after the prayer day' (Figure 8.2).

In some cultures, the day of the week determines one's name and, hence, future. In Akan, a Ghanaian language spoken in West Africa, there are so-called day names, names given to boys and girls who are born on a given day. For example, a well-known Akan, Kofi Annan, UN Secretary General from 1997 to 2006, bears the name *Kofi*, which is given to those born on Friday. So he is somewhat of a namesake of Defoe's (*Man*) *Friday*, except that Annan served all nations of the world rather than one colonial intruder. Annan's name is associated with fertility, derived from the root *afi*, and other variants of names given to boys born on Fridays include *Koffi*, *Fiifi*, *Yoofi*, *Afi*, *Afua*, *Afia*, *Afiba*, *Efia*, and *Efua*.

Figure 8.2 An astrological clock in Prague, Czech Republic (Craig Hastings/ Getty Images)

Similar differences, even between related languages, in naming months have already been mentioned, for example, in two Slavic languages *listopad* 'leaf falling (month)' can mean two different things: October in Croatian and November in Polish. But differences in month names can go much further. For example, in Arabic, there are two different systems of months. The first is also used in English, starting with January and officially known as كَانُون ٱلثَّانِي, *kānūn ath-thānī* 'month of resting', but in some regions, names are based on old Latin (يَنَايِر, *yanāyir*) or French names (جانفي, *jānvī*). The second system uses a traditional lunar Hijri calendar, where the year starts with the 'forbidden month' of مُحَرَّم, *muharram*, the months do not correspond with those used in English, and the new Islamic year of 1443 starts in September of 2021. In some cultures, there are no names, but rather periods that coincide with the environmental and agricultural cycle. For example, in the Australian language of Central A̱nangu Pitjantjajara, the season that roughly encompasses January, February, and March is known as *itjanu* or *inuntjji*. It is defined by *utuwari* (overcast clouds), which usually bring rain, food plants that flower, and, if it rains, plenty of fruit and seeds.

We have seen many examples of how space and everything that happens in it get projected into time in myriad different ways. In some cases, the projections turn out to be quite different from reality. A well-known statement during the communist experiment in Russia was that of building a bright future (*светлое будущее, svetloe boodooshcheye*,

The Past Is in Front of Us and the Future Is behind Our Back 67

Figure 8.3 "No future here: Stop! This is the Empire of Death" – written above the entrance to the Catacombs of Paris (photo by the author)

in Russian). Eventually, the future became so bleak that the experiment had to be abandoned. This and many other examples discussed in this chapter point to the need of various languages to make the elusive and abstract notion of time tangible, to situate it in a metaphorical space and give it visible features (Figure 8.3).

9 | *Far and Wide, Here and There*

Languages are embedded in their respective geographical niches. The river that flows through Ljubljana, the capital of Slovenia, is known as *Ljubljanica*. That is in Ljubljana. In the rest of Slovenia, the same river has six different names: *Trbuhovica*, *Obrh*, *Stržen*, *Rak*, *Pivka*, *Unica*, and *Ljubljanica*, each name for one particular segment that flows on the ground (with the underground sections between them), that is, the segment that is visible to the residents of that particular segment of the river. In the Brazilian city of Manaus, there is a place known in Portuguese as *Encontro das Águas* 'Meeting of Waters', where two rivers flow next to each other in the same river bed before they merge into the Amazon river. One of them is black, and it is appropriately named *Rio Negro* (literally: black river). The other is drab, and it is technically the Amazon river, even before this curious confluence. However, the upstream portion of the Amazon River is named *Rio Solimões* (the word of uncertain origin comes from indigenous languages) only in Brazilian Portuguese (Figure 9.1).

A major river in Argentina has a constant surface flow, but in different provinces it is known respectively as *Vinchina*, *Bermejo*, *Desaguadero*, *Salado*, *Chadileuvú*, and *Curacó*. Similarly, the English river *Thames* is known as the *Isis* only in one of its segments in Oxford. In all three cases, for purely visual or historical reasons, speakers divide the entity into distinct segments, which may not be relevant in other languages. A small mountain near the capital of Croatia, Zagreb, is known as either *Medvednica* 'Bear Mountain' or *Zagrebačka gora* 'Zagreb Mountain'. Each name emphasizes one feature of the mountain (Figure 9.2).

Similar, albeit in the lofty heights of religion rather than in the pedestrian world of geographical objects, are the ninety-nine names of Allah in Islam, known collectively as أسماء الله الحسنى (*'Asmā'u l-Lāhi l-Ḥusnā*) 'the most beautiful names of Allah'. For example, two of

Far and Wide, Here and There

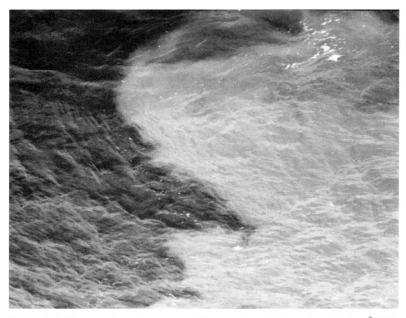

Figure 9.1 The meeting of waters in Manaus, Brazil (photo by Mladen Šašić)

Figure 9.2 Ljubljanica River (photo by the author)

these names form the Quranic invocation: بِسْمِ ٱللَّهِ ٱلرَّحْمَٰنِ ٱلرَّحِيمِ (*b-ismi-llāhi r-raḥmāni r-raḥīmi*) 'In the name of God, most gracious, most merciful'. They are الرحمن (*Ar-Rahmān*) 'the beneficient/all-compassionate/most gracious' and الرحيم (*Ar-Rahīm*) 'the most merciful/ever-merciful/merciful/most clement'. Each name emphasizes a feature of God as seen and recited by believers.

All aforementioned cases exemplify human orientation in geographical space, and, in the last example, in a religious system. Sometimes special opposites are used to refer to a distribution of something, as in left and right, here and there, etc. In some languages, such as Serbo-Croatian, these expressions are extended to convey the meaning of the English *yada-yada-yada*, when used to abbreviate nonessential parts of the story. Expressions such as *tamo-vamo* 'there-here', *lijevo-desno* 'left-right', and *gore-dole* 'up-down' are used for this function. Particularly interesting is the expression for 'disorderly, randomly' (e.g., when various comments are presented without a logical order or sense) in Serbo-Croatian, *zbrda-zdola*, which is literally 'from the hill and from the valley'.

Cities offer examples of cross-cultural differences in spatial orientation. Cardinal directions (a form of geocentric reference) are very common in American English (e.g., the location of a store will be stated as "on the north-west corner of Rural Road and Chandler Boulevard"), but are never used in many other languages, for example, those in the Slavic branch, which use anthropocentric references, such as "on the left-hand side of Rural Road right before you reach Chandler Boulevard." Alternatively, they refer to a common, popular landmark, such as a store, shop, or building. In some languages, this reference to common landmarks extends to distances, as in Nunggubuyu, where there are no units such as 'foot', 'yard', or 'mile'. Distances are expressed by saying that something is as distant as between two known landmarks (e.g., a big tree and a source of water).

Street names and numbers are another source of cross-cultural variation. In the United States, where most cities are built on a grid, the concept of the city block exists (used, among other things, to say that something is three blocks away). The length of a city block varies from city to city between 79 and 200 meters. Street numbers are based on blocks, so the first house of the fifth block is 501, 601 is the first house of the sixth block, etc. Some cities use more than three digits. Even numbers are on one side of the street and odd numbers are on the other, as in continental Europe. However, what is odd about the American system to Europeans is that the numbers are not consecutive, as they are in continental Europe. Thus, if the fifth block has only three houses, there will be a gap between 53 or 503, where the block ends, and 61 or 601, where the sixth block on the street begins. This general principle is also found in the way hotel rooms are numbered, with the first digit representing the floor, which has definitely been gaining some international traction. Even more confusing is clockwise numbering in some parts of the United Kingdom, where numbers run consecutively on the left-hand side of the street, to cross clockwise to its right-hand side at the end of the street. To add to the confusion, some towns feature counterclockwise numbering in some areas and clockwise numbering in others. All this is nothing compared to street numbers in Sapporo, the capital of the Japanese island of Hokkaido. The very term "street numbers" is a misnomer. Rather than naming streets and then numbering them, Sapporoans refer to locations on the street using cardinal directions and a coordinate system. When I was a visiting professor at Hokkaido University, I lived at the following address: 北, *kita 24*, 西, *nishi 12*, which means north 24, west 12. Each location is referred to by the number of street crossings between it and the city center. So, to get from my residence to the center, I needed to cross twelve streets going east and then twenty-four streets going south. This ingenious system not only points to the location precisely but also specifies in which part of the city and how far away the place is (Figure 9.3).

An unusual system of spatial orientation is attested in the Dolakhae dialect of the Newar language, which is spoken in Nepal. The dialect is spoken on steep mountain slopes, so the principal directions of movements are not forward and backward, but rather up the hill (the word *unbho* is used for such movement) and down the hill (using the word *undho*). The nature of the terrain influences the way one speaks about movement.

Orientation in space translates into artifacts such as writing scripts. In most modern languages, lines of text begin on the left-hand side and end on the right-hand side. By contrast, in Hebrew and Arabic, the order is opposite, right to left. In Japan, some texts still use the traditional system going from top to bottom and others have switched to the same order as English.

Another field where spatial orientation is transferred is that of social relations, for example, in the English terms *upper class*, *upper middle*

Figure 9.3 An address in Sapporo, Japan (photo by the author)

class, *lower middle class*, and even *underclass*, or *to climb up the social ladder*, *marry up*, etc. Cardinal directions are also transferred into politics and the economy, for example, across Europe, East and West used to be two poles of an ideological cleavage. Today, they mostly reflect economic disparities of the more developed West and the less developed East, as the South (less developed) and the North (more developed) always were. These associations of cardinal directions are reversed in Australia, where the South and East are the most desirable living places in the country.

Languages also differ as to which areas of their special orientation are finer grained. Thus, Turk and others have shown that in the northeastern Australian language of Yinjibarndi, the word *marnda* covers rock, hill, mountain, mountain chain, and so on, as these are not part of the landscape. By contrast, they distinguish river as water and its flow on one hand, and river as something that stretches in space, on the other. Rivers are not only prominent but also critical for survival.

All this shows that there is an insider and outsider perspective. For example, seeing leaves moving in the rainforest is completely

Figure 9.4 Baldwin Street in Dunedin, New Zealand, known as the world's steepest street (photo by the author)

ambiguous from the ETIC perspective of an outside observer, while it has a distinct meaning (e.g., which bird moves those leaves) from the EMIC perspective of the indigenous population. In the example discussed in this chapter, somebody who is moving forward in the outsider perspective would be moving up or down the hill in the insider perspective of the aforementioned Dolakhae dialect of the Newar language.

Examples discussed in this chapter point to a two-way relationship with the space that surrounds us. On the one hand, we occupy a space of some kind and that space shapes our language. On the other hand, we conceptually and linguistically shape the space around us as we intervene in it physically (Figure 9.4).

10 | Bottles with Throats

Yes, Russian bottles have throats. To be exact, the term for bottleneck is *горлышко бутылки* (*gorlishko bootilki*) 'small throat of the bottle'. The English and Russian metaphors are alike as both of them are based on the human body. The difference is that the English term remains based on sheer visual similarity of the human neck and bottleneck, while its Russian equivalent involves a somewhat more elaborate picture of a liquid (and vodka is the liquid of choice in Russia) flowing through the 'throat of the bottle' (Figure 10.1). Serbo-Croatian follows the Russian pattern, naming it *grlić* or *grlo flaše* 'small throat or throat of the bottle'. In its criminal underworld, a bottleneck broken off from the bottle to be used like a knife in fights is known as *ruža* 'rose'. Elaborate metaphors are ubiquitous in English. One of them can be found in the word *bed*, where the primary meaning of furniture extends into river bed, flower bed, gravel bed, etc., that is, the place where something 'lies'.

All around the world, languages extend 'the Moon' to mean 'month', which makes perfect sense, given the existence of the lunar calendar. Some examples involving words that mean 'moon' and 'month' include Malay *bulan*, Māori *marama*, Turkish, Kyrgyz, and Kazakh *ay*, Swahili *mwezi*, Xhosa and Zulu *inyanga*, etc. Even closely related languages may differ in this regard. Thus, some Slavic languages, such as Russian and Polish, have two separate words for these concepts, while Serbo-Croatian, Czech, Slovak, and Ukrainian link the two meanings in the same way as the previously mentioned global languages.

Some of the metaphors are transparent to us even if they do not exist in our own language. The fact that Erzya, an indigenous language of northern Russia, has the word чи (*chi*), which means 'day' and 'Sun' is very clear (day is when the Sun is up). The same can be said about the Algonquian languages (in central and eastern Canada and the northern United States), where the Moon is named *tibik-kìzis*, literally, the night

Bottles with Throats

Figure 10.1 Assorted spirits sticking out their necks (Chay Chay Chiy Ceriy/EyeEm/Getty Images)

Sun. Then there are cases such as *ikelen'* in the aforementioned Erzya language, which means 'former' and 'future'. The connection here is slightly more difficult to see, but the fact that neither of them is 'current' connects them.

Differences between languages occur when they rely on culture-specific realities. For example, American English and Polish both have a colloquial metaphor for sculpted abs. They are known as a six-pack in American English, as that is the most common way of getting beer from a grocery store. This would not make sense in Poland as beer is purchased by the bottle or crate. The word in Polish is *kaloryfer* 'heating radiator' in reference to the ribs on the classical radiator. This in turn would not make sense for most Americans, where forced-air heating and cooling prevails and most homes do not have radiators.

Some items are like Rorschach's tests. An example is a popular Central European dessert made by separating egg whites and yolks, beating the former into foamy orbs, which are then left to float on the "sea" of liquid yolks mixed with sugar. This delicacy is known as a *floating island* in English, and *islas flotantes* 'floating islands' in

Figure 10.2 A floating island (thelinke/Getty Images)

Spanish. Speakers of German in Germany name it *Schnee-Eier* 'snow eggs', while those in Austria name it *Shneenockerl(n)* 'little snow hills'. Its name in Romanian is *lapte de pasăare* 'bird's milk' and Poles name it *zupa nic* 'nothing soup'. French speakers use both *île flottante* 'floating island' and *œufs à la neige* 'eggs à la snow' (Figure 10.2).

Similar are two related insect families with poetic names. In English, they are known as *dragonflies* and *damselflies*, which is poetic enough, but probably surpassed in the tower of poetry by Serbo-Croatian *vilinski konjic* 'fairy's horsie' and *vodena djevica* 'water virgin'. In Spanish, the word for dragonflies is borrowed from Latin and reads *libellula* 'small level (builder's tool)' as it is in many other European languages: not such a poetic picture. However, the name for damselflies compensates for this as it is *caballito del diablo* 'devil's horsie'. In Slovene, both dragonflies and damselflies are known as *kačji pastir* 'snake shepherd' (Figure 10.3). The term for both species in Swedish is equally poetic: *trollslända* 'troll's distaff'. Navajo is not poetic at all in naming these species; they are simply named *táníil'áí* 'those that swarm out over the water'. In this, as in the previously discussed case of a popular Central European dessert, the same element of reality invokes very different pictures in speakers of various languages.

Figure 10.3 A snake shepherd (photo by the author)

The sphere of slang is where the emergence of new meanings based on semantic extensions of various kinds happens on a daily basis. Years ago, I worked on a Serbo-Croatian–English colloquial dictionary and I found out that over two-thirds of the meanings attested in this dictionary were based on semantic extensions, most commonly metaphors. For example, the word *leš* 'corpse' from the general language is used to mean 'elderly person'. Slang users are youngsters, and from their perspective, anybody older than thirty is already dead. This then extends into using the same word for parent (one's parents are elderly people).

It is interesting that extensions of meaning may be motivated by sound similarity. This happens less often, but it is still present. Thus, in Serbo-Croatian slang, derogatory names for a male gay person include various words starting with the syllable *pe*, not reflecting any semantic connection with each other, but because they share the first syllable with the most common derogatory term for gays. A similar phenomenon is found in rhyming slang in Cockney, where *apples and pears* stand for 'stairs' and *china plate* stands for 'mate'.

In all these examples, the question of all questions is what these cross-linguistic differences can tell us about cross-cultural differences. An even more vexing question is how these connections can be reliably studied: How many of these differences are consequences of random development and how much is reflective of deeper culture-bound patterns. There are no easy answers to these complex questions. However, one thing is for sure: no matter how different they are in various languages, metaphors are extremely powerful mechanisms of extending existing meanings of words in all of them.

11 | *Setting the TV on Fire and Extinguishing It*

The Sun rises every morning and sets every evening. Most people learn in school about Nicolaus Copernicus and his heliocentric model. We are also familiar with various models of the Solar System that put the Sun at its center (hence the name of the Solar System). So, we should know that it is the earth rather than the Sun that does something, but we like to believe our own eyes rather than listen to our teachers. Nobody says that our part of the earth turns toward the Sun in the morning and away from it in the evening. There are also cases where we believe what the scientists have to say and call X, gamma, and other rays so, even if we do not see them as we see rays of light.

Sometimes, previous stages of development are encapsulated in the words we use even if we see something completely different. We are still *dialing* phone numbers and *hanging up*, although our phones do not have dials and hooks on which to hang up the receiver (Figure 11.1).

Serbo-Croatian is interesting in this regard. The verbs originally used for fire, *upaliti* 'to set on fire' and *ugasiti* 'to extinguish', have had a wonderful career, and they are used for anything that can be turned on and off. So, speakers of this language set their lights, cars, computers, and TV 'on fire' and then 'extinguish' them. With lights and cars, one can see the connection – lights used to be lamps, and internal combustion engines are lit in a way. With old radios and TVs and their tubes one can see some connection, as they needed to heat up. With their modern equivalents, computers, and countless other gadgets, the connection is lost but the previous stages of development still live in the words being used. Romanian and Modern Greek use the same verbs for these contexts: in Romanian, *a aprinde* 'to set ablaze/to turn on' versus *a stinge* 'to extinguish/to turn off', and in Modern Greek ανάβω

Figure 11.1 A hang-up phone (PKM2/Getty Images)

(anavo) 'to set ablaze/to turn on' versus σβήνω (svino pronounced zvino) 'to extinguish/to turn off'.

The Serbo-Croatian word for unplugging cables goes even further back in time. The verb is *iščupati*, literally 'to pull out, pluck out' (as with weeds or bird feathers). A common colloquial verb meaning 'to speed' is *nagariti*, literally 'to cover with soot'. This word retains the memory of steam engines, which were covered with soot when speeding.

To continue with Serbo-Croatian examples, most people speaking this language do not engage in animal slaughtering, as their rural ancestors did for centuries. However, the verb *zaklati* 'to slaughter' is used for a rather benign action of cutting watermelon (*zaklati lubenicu*, literally 'to slaughter watermelon'). A darker nuance of the past is contained in the expression for someone who sleeps very soundly – the expression is *spava kao zaklan* 'sleeps as if being slaughtered'. Similar is the expression used to refer to frying an egg, *ubiti jaje*, literally 'to kill an egg.'

Similar examples can be found in English. Someone who is overcharging us is *fleecing* us. Terms motivated by former technologies are also to be found in English. Web pages are opened as if they are newspapers, automobiles are named *cars* (which originally meant 'carriage') and they are *driven* (just like draft animals), motorcycles and bicycles are *ridden*, just like horses. Air navigation has inherited numerous terms from maritime navigation. Some of them still make sense but others do not. The two sides of ships and airplanes illustrate both these cases. *Portside* still makes sense as that is the side of the (air)craft that is parked on the side of the (air)port. *Starboard* has long been overrun by the development of technology. It means 'steering board', which in olden times featured a steering row (quite logically, on the right-hand side of the navigator, given that most people are right-handed). Since then, steering technology has progressed to fly-by-wire, but the memory of the old steering oar still lives in the name for one side of the (air)craft (Figure 11.2).

Games and sports encapsulate a whole feudal world with its states and bloody battles. One attacks and defends, shoots and strikes. There are even languages, such as Serbo-Croatian, where pieces (for example those in chess) are not taken but rather eaten. The game of chess

Saxon Ship—Harold's Ship.—Restored from the Bayeux Tapestry, by H. G. Hine.

Figure 11.2 The starboard side of a Saxon ship (duncan1980/Getty Images)

contains a whole feudal hierarchy with the king and queen on top, all the way down to the pawns, the foot soldiers. There is some degree of variation in how the pieces are named (even in English, *rook* is sometimes called *castle*): *bishop* is *lovac* 'hunter' in Serbo-Croatian, слон (*slon*) 'elephant' in Russian, and *queen* is *hetman* in Polish (which was the title of the second-highest military commander in the fourteenth to sixteenth-century Kingdom of Poland and the Grand Duchy of Lithuania). The very name of the game in Russian, шахматы (*shahmati*), comes from the Persian شاه مات, *shah mat* 'the shah is dead'.

Needless to say, the number of abstract concepts in which older practices of the linguistic community in question still live is countless in any language. In English, ardent enthusiasts will hold fiery speeches awash with flaming remarks (Figure 11.3).

All examples from this chapter show us that the lexicon of any given language serves, among other things, as a repository for our collective memory about past beliefs and practices. This happens even if we are not aware of it. The lexicon of each language contains rich deposits that await discovery by their linguistic archeologists.

Figure 11.3 A fiery speech (akindo/Getty Images)

PART III

How Things Are Done with Words

12 | *Traduttore, Traditore!*

What the title of this chapter literally means is translator, traitor. It is a well-known Italian adage, expressing the same idea as the English phrase *lost in translation*, albeit in a more elegant, euphonic manner. Indeed, there is always a part of the original that is lost in translation, akin to what vintners and distillers call *the angel's share*, part of the batch of wine or spirits that evaporates as they age in barrels.

Situations where the translation outshines the original are quite rare, but they still happen. One such case was the Italian comic book named *Alan Ford*, which was created in 1969. Its glory was short lived in Italy and its Brazilian, Danish, and French editions have failed. By contrast, this comic book was a household name in the former Yugoslavia and it continues to enjoy extremely high popularity and name recognition in all its successor countries (Bosnia, Croatia, Montenegro, Serbia, etc.). This is primarily because of the masterful translation of this comic book into Serbo-Croatian by Nenad Brixy. The unusual choice of words and their combinations in the masterful translation have hugely augmented the comical effect of the original, giving the translated edition a life of its own that unfolds to this day.

Alas, there are also such translations with *the devil's cut* (to continue with a metaphor from vintners' and distillers' terminology, where it refers to the amount of alcohol absorbed by the barrel). A mistranslation of a tiny text of only one word was infamously a source of huge embarrassment in international relations. Back in 2009, in an attempt to improve the relationship of her country under new administration with Russia, Hilary Clinton, the US secretary of state at the time, took to Sergei Lavrov, her Russian counterpart, a mock button with what was supposed to be the word *reset* written in Russian. However, the translation was marred by the devil's cut. Instead of the correct Russian equivalent перезагрузка (*perezagrooska*), the

Figure 12.1 A somewhat rusty reset button (Jupiter Images/Getty Images)

inscription below the button read *перегрузка* (*peregrooska*) 'overload'. This was a very bad omen, as relations between the two countries have remained tense in the years since (Figure 12.1).

My early 2020 testing of a generally available translation engine, Google Translate (https://translate.google.com/), from Serbian into English yielded a colorful bunch of mistranslations (coupled with numerous correct translations). In some mistranslations, it was immediately obvious what the right translation was: *He took a meter out of the tool* instead of *He took a measuring tape from the toolbox*. Others featured a surrealist touch and feel: *We drank wine out of the balloon* rather than *We drank wine out of a demijohn*.

What all these cases of mistranslations have in common is failure to deploy the correct one from multiple English equivalents of the Serbian word. Serbian *metar* is either 'meter' or 'measuring tape', *alat* is 'tool' and 'toolbox', *balon* is both 'demijohn' and 'balloon', etc. Thus, the phenomenon of multiple equivalence, where one word in the source language can be translated by two or more words in the target

Figure 12.2 A less than ideal choice of words in a Chinese-English translation (photo by Mladen Šašić)

language, defines the kind of mistranslations demonstrated in the aforementioned examples (Figure 12.2).

We are not only likely to find mistranslations based on multiple equivalence in a linguist's virtual playground but also in real life. Consider the following example from international marketing. It was reported that a Canadian importer of Turkish shirts destined for Quebec translated into French the label "Made in Turkey." His final translation was "Fabrique en Dinde." The equivalent *dinde* means 'turkey', the bird not the country, which in French is *Turquie* (Figure 12.3).

In his *Lost in Translation: Misadventures in English Abroad*, Charlie Croker lists a range of curious statements in English, mostly literal translations from various languages. There is an elevator that is *out of work*, literally translated from German *außer Arbeit*, which is used for unemployed people and out-of-order devices. Then, there is *Do you wish to change in Zurich? Do so at the hotel bank*! The intended meaning was to recommend tourists to exchange money in

Figure 12.3 A turkey from Turkey (PeopleImages/Getty Images)

their respective hotel banks. German *wechseln* is *(ex)change* (as in currencies, change a course of something, an element of something, etc.) but English change, in one of its meanings, also means changing clothes, for which a completely different verb (*sich umziehen*) is used in German, so the unintended meaning of the English word has escaped the, obviously amateur, translator.

English-language movies are subtitled around the word with local subtitles. The parallel databases of these subtitles aligned with their English originals are rich mines of mistranslations of different kinds. One pattern of lexical mistranslations that emerges is that the translator links an English word with which they are not familiar with a known concept. For example, in Serbian subtitles, one can see that a *pitcher* of beer is translated as *krigla* (which is 'stein, a German-style pint glass'), as pitcher is not much of concept, given that beer is not served in pitchers. A *pitcher* of beer ranges from 1.42 to 1.77 liters and in translation it is reduced to *krigla*, which is typically 0.5 liters. To continue with drinking mistranslations, *rye and Coke* (where rye is rye whiskey) was translated in Serbian as *koktel i kola* 'cocktail and Coke', as the translator was unfamiliar with rye whiskey and chose something that "fits" the situation of ordering in a bar depicted in the movie.

Human beings and machine translation systems tend to create mistranslations, and the consequences range from the entertaining to ones with grave implications. In a very strange way, any mistranslation is actually an ode to the linguistic and cultural diversity of our world. The very existence of mistranslations is predicated on profound lexical and other differences between languages, which concurrently reflect cross-cultural differences.

13 | *May You Suffer and Remember**

The title of the present chapter is inspired by the Yiddish curse זאל ער קרענקען און געדענקען, *Zol er krenken un gedenken* 'Let him suffer and remember'. Yiddish is well-known for such maledictions, some more civil ones include *May all your teeth fall out but one and may that one give you a toothache*; *He should be transformed into a chandelier, to hang by day and to burn by night*; *One misfortune is too few for him*, and many others. One of the strongest ones is יִמַּח שְׁמוֹ *yimakh shemo* 'May his name be obliterated'.

Yiddish is not unique and these curses are nothing new, as evidenced by the following biblical quote, where the curse falls on those who do not obey God.

> [15] and if you reject my decrees and abhor my laws and fail to carry out all my commands and so violate my covenant, [16] then I will do this to you: I will bring on you sudden terror, wasting diseases and fever that will destroy your sight and sap your strength. You will plant seed in vain, because your enemies will eat it. [17] I will set my face against you so that you will be defeated by your enemies; those who hate you will rule over you, and you will flee even when no one is pursuing you. (Leviticus, 26)

An interesting fact in this passage is that the curse projects the agricultural and martial character of the culture from which it stems. The crops will be eaten by enemies and the cursed will be defeated (which at the time was not as benign as losing a soccer game). Some aboriginal languages in Australia have curses such as *May a lightning bolt kill you*, reflecting connections with the environment. Exactly the same curse exists in Serbo-Croatian *Ubio te grom*. The verb in this curse is in the optative form, that is, the wishful-thinking mode, which is structurally related to the past tense. The person who uses this curse is saying something like 'I wish that a lightning bolt has already killed you'.

---

* A chapter with this number is officially not in this book

May You Suffer and Remember 93

Figure 13.1 Interpunction cursing (IntergalacticDesignStudio/Getty Images)

Given strong waves of urbanization ever since the end of WWII, this curse is becoming increasingly obsolete in Serbo-Croatian. Slovene, on the other hand, still has some curses that are embedded in the environment, such as *Naj ti ohrovt zgnije!* 'May your kale rot' (Figure 13.1).

Serbo-Croatian curses used today are very similar to those in English, that is, far less specific. *Drop dead* is pretty general and so is its Serbo-Croatian equivalent *crko dabogda*, literally understood (real etymology will be mentioned further in this chapter) as 'I wish that God allows that you are already dead', as is *choke on it*, when we are annoyed by an upward social comparison (when somebody is better than us or has something we desire), like its Serbo-Croatian equivalent *dabogda ti prisjelo*, literally understood as 'I wish that God allows that you have already had too much of it'.

Actually, according to the Bible, the fact that we have around 7,000 languages on our pale blue dot (as Carl Sagan described our planet) is the result of a curse, described in Genesis 11:1-9.

[1] Now the whole earth had one language and the same words. [2] And as they migrated from the east, they came upon a plain in the land of Shinar and settled there. [3] And they said to one another, "Come, let us make bricks, and burn them thoroughly." And they had brick for stone, and bitumen for mortar. [4] Then they said, "Come, let us build ourselves a city, and a tower with its top in the heavens, and let us make a name for ourselves; otherwise we shall be scattered abroad upon the face of the whole earth." [5] The Lord came down to see the city and the tower, which mortals had built. [6] And the Lord said, "Look, they are one people, and they have all one language; and this is only the beginning of what they will do; nothing that they propose to do will now be impossible for them. [7] Come, let us go down, and confuse their language there, so that they will not understand one another's speech." [8] So the Lord scattered them abroad from there over the face of all the earth, and they left off building the city. [9] Therefore it was called Babel, because there the Lord confused the language of all the earth; and from there the Lord scattered them abroad over the face of all the earth.

This Old Testament curse has not only created separate languages but also all the problems in translation between them discussed in Chapter 12.

Going back to Serbo-Croatian curses, containing the element *dabogda*, which is today understood by speakers as 'may God give' (*da* – may, *bog* – God, *da* – give), things are actually not that simple. That element is in fact an invocation of the pre-Christian Slavic god *Dažbog*, a solar deity. This shows that curses can encapsulate very old phases of language development, given that all Slavs abandoned their own pantheon and accepted Christianity well over a millennium ago, with some of them converting to Islam from the late Middle Ages. Obviously, Christian concepts have also found their way into curses, as in Slovene *Vrag naj go jaše!* 'May devil ride him!' The Irish are also fond of the devil; their curse *Go n-ithe an cat thú is go n-ithe an diabhal an cat* means 'May the cat eat you, and may the devil eat the cat'.

As we all know, curses do not have to be verbalized. Thus, one of the aforementioned Slavic ethnic groups that converted to Islam, Bosniaks, has a tradition of throwing spells known as *sihire* to cause someone harm. The word comes from Arabic سحر, *sihr* 'magic, sorcery, witchcraft' and it is widespread around the Islamic word, all the way to the Indonesian variety of Malay *sihir* with the same meaning. Going back to the devil, apart from being part of a curse (riding someone, as in Slovene, and doing a number of other things), he can also be used to fend off evil. Such is the Italian hand gesture of horns (representing the devil), which is somewhat equivalent to knocking on wood in Slavic and Germanic languages.

A well-known case of nonverbal cursing was registered in Australia in 2004. The prime minister at the time, John Howard, was cursed by a group of Aborigines who turned a kangaroo bone toward him. The curse was not particularly effective given that the aforementioned prime minister remained in office until 2007. No records exist as to why the curse failed, but it might be that the prime minister had one of the anti-curse amulets one finds all around the world. For example, the evil eye (*nazar* in Turkish) and all its curses are very effectively suppressed by *nazar boncuğu*, the lucky eye charm, a blue amulet with an eye on it (Figure 13.2). Arabs and other Near Eastern and North African peoples have a protective hand-shaped amulet known as خمسة (hamsa), which is also the name of the number 5 (representing five fingers on the hand) (Figure 13.3).

Figure 13.2 A *nazar* (photo by the author)

Figure 13.3 A *hamsa* (photo by the author)

Evil can be fended off in a much simpler manner. When something evil (e.g., cancer) is mentioned, Serbo-Croatian speakers move from one place to another (most commonly by moving the chair on which they are sitting) and/or say: *Pomjeri se s mjesta!* 'Move from your place'. The idea is that the person leaves the space inhabited by the bad thing that was invoked in that space by the use of the word for it. Most serious diseases are not mentioned even when a person dies from them. If the cause of death is cancer, a standard formulation in obituaries and media news is that somebody died *nakon duge i teške bolesti* 'following a long and serious disease'. In case of a heart attack, the formulation is that somebody died *nakon kratke i teške bolesti* 'following a short and serious disease'.

People everywhere use words and nonverbal practices to cast spells and fend off evil. Not only do these forms of verbal and nonverbal behavior testify to global diversity, but they also encapsulate earlier phases of development of languages and their respective societies. At the same time, we also do things that we do with words in many other ways (among other things by pointing a kangaroo bone at someone), which shows how intertwined the linguistic and nonlinguistic worlds are.

14 | *I Screw Your 300 Gods*

This chapter will discuss cussing. The title of this chapter is a Serbo-Croatian curse. In the original, it reads *Jebem ti trista bogova*. The number of gods can also be one hundred, which is still high enough. Needless to say, "screw" in the translation is a euphemism; the original uses the f-word. This is just one of many rather curious obscene maledictions in that language. One of the most elaborate literally reads 'I screw one half of you and the other half should be screwed by your crazy father who made you like that'.

The Serbo-Croatian f-word can be combined with practically anything (Figure 14.1). The combinations vary in the level of obscenity and aggression. The gravest ones include mothers and sisters, the two family figures particularly protected in the patriarchal cultures of the region (which makes their mention in the cuss particularly serious). At the other end of the scale is the expression *Jebem ti miša* 'I am f-ing your mouse', which is used as an expression of affection to children (rather than what this combination of words superficially means), especially when they do something naughty but cute. A character in a drama by a well-known Serbian author, Dušan Kovačević, has the following to say about the abundance of profane curses, "I do not know the nation who cusses the Sun more than us ... and along with the Sun, we are cussing out God, bread, and mother."

As in other languages, what is originally a cuss can perform different functions in an appropriate context. Thus, two speakers of colloquial varieties of Serbo-Croatian from a criminal underworld, who are close to each other, can greet each other with *Đe si, jebem ti mater*, literally, 'Where are you, I am f-ing your mother'. This greeting contains *Jebem ti mater* 'I am f-ing your mother', the gravest of all cusses, yet it simply means 'What's up, dawg?'

The cusses in Serbo-Croatian also come in an endless procession of grammatical constructions, for example, May (your) someone/

Figure 14.1 Dropping the F-bomb (JakeOlimb/Getty Images)

something f you, May you f (your) somebody/something, May I f (your) something/someone, I am f-ing (your) something/someone, etc.

Some of this creativity is shared around the globe. While Mandarin Chinese shares its most common obscene curse 肏你妈, *cào nǐ mā* 'F your mother' with Serbo-Croatian, where it reads *Jebi (svoju) mater*, it has a less common one that greatly surpasses it in the level of creativity 肏你祖宗十八代, *cào nǐ zǔzōng shíbā dài* 'F your ancestors to the eighteenth generation'. Going back to Serbo-Croatian obscene curses, among many others, there are two similar varieties with mother: the aforementioned *Jebi svoju mater!* 'F your mother' and *Jebem ti mater* 'I am f-ing your mother'. I once met a shady character, a Polish speaker who in the 1980s made a living from smuggling goods

Figure 14.2 The lightning curse would not have worked on him: Nikola Tesla (Stefano Bianchetti/Getty Images)

from Poland into what was then Yugoslavia. He was so proud of his knowledge of Serbo-Croatian that he bragged to me that he even knew how to cuss. When I asked him to provide a sample of his cussing skills, he readily responded, *Jebem ti svoju mater*. 'I am f-ing my own mother to you'. Some tricksters in Yugoslavia took pleasure in merging the two obscene offenses and teaching the poor Polish soul the hybrid, without revealing the true meaning of the phrase to him.

The language to the north of Serbo-Croatian, Hungarian, is known for its elaborate obscene curses. Some examples include *Basszon agyon a kénköves istennyila!* 'May a sulfurous lightning bolt screw you to death' and *Baszd szájba a büdös kurva anyádat!* 'May you screw your whore mother in the mouth' (Figure 14.2).

To the southwest of Hungary lies Slovenia. Slovene is at the opposite end of the scale of maledictiveness from Serbo-Croatian and Hungarian. Far from being obscene, Slovenian cusses go only as far as to invoke the Devil (actually devils, a lot of them), and even that is done indirectly: *300 hudičev*, literally, '300 bad ones' or *300 kosmatih*

I Screw Your 300 Gods

Figure 14.3 One of 300 Slovene devils (chud/Getty Images)

'300 hairy ones' (Figure 14.3). When Slovenes want to cuss for real, they use either Italian *Porco dio*!, literally 'pig god' or they borrow the Serbo-Croatian f-word.

Further to the north is Polish, which, for some strange reason, is not particularly enamored with the f-word, but uses the w-word (i.e., whore) quite profusely. The word reads *kurwa* and it is used in a variety of situations, often combined with the word for mother, *kurwa mać*, literally, 'whore mother'. But it is equally frequently used on its own. It is found in a range of contexts expressing a variety of emotions, from straightforward offense, such as *Kurwa jego mać*, literally, 'His mother is a whore', actually, 'F him', to the expression of frustration when something goes wrong *Kurwa (mać)*!, literally, 'Whore (mother)', actually, 'F!', to just being a filler word intensifying the statement, as in *On, kurwa, tego nie rozumie*, literally, 'He, whore, does not understand that', actually, 'He does not understand that, all right'.

What is interesting is that the word *whore*, which sounds rather benign in many languages, has a high degree of obscenity in Polish. There are also numerous euphemisms. Among others, *kurczę pieczone*, literally, 'baked chicken', *kurza melodia* 'chicken melody', *kurza twarz* 'chicken face', *kurna chata* 'cabin covered with soot, the one without the chimney', *kurka wodna* 'water hen' are all used as replacements for *kurwa mać*. But that is not all. Numerous other euphemisms exist. For example, the modification of *kurwa* into *kurde* (a non-sensical word) generates a whole range of derivatives with no literal meaning; there are there merely to soften cussing: *kurdebalans, kurdebele, kurdefelek, kurdefiks, kurdele, kurdemol*.

Curious Spanish cusses exploit the s-word, the verb for defecation. They include, but are not limited to, *Me cago en la leche* 'I s on the milk' *Me cago en la hostia* 'I s on the communion wafer'.

The reproductive organs are prolific in obscene phrases all around the world, and English is no exception. In colloquial English, the word for the male member is used directly, combined with the verb *to suck* or, indirectly, being depicted as a bone that is smoked. The word for male member is also used to refer to a stupid or immoral person.

Georgian speakers take it a step further. A stupid person can be called ყლეო (*q'leo*) 'dick' but also ყლეთაყლე (*q'letaq'le*) 'dick of dicks', or ყლისშვილი (*q'lishvili*) 'O'Dick, McDick'. When Georgians do not care about something, they can say that it can go to their dick: ჩემს ყლეს (*chems q'les*) or that it hangs on their dick ყლეზე მკიდია (*q'leze mk'idia*). Georgians move a bit lower down the body when expressing admiration about a baby boy and say შენს ყვერებს ვენაცვალე (*shen q'verebs venatsvale*) 'I admire your balls', testicles being the symbol of strength and virility.

Some utterances obviously have a special status determined by various culture-specific restrictions, testifying again to the inextricable embeddedness of languages in their respective cultures. Maledictions typically come in softer and harder variants, where attitudes in society (or connotations, looking from a linguistic perspective) represent their most conspicuous feature. As can be seen from this chapter, doing ugly things with language is diversified around the globe. This turns the ugliness into the beauty. May a thousand cusses bloom!

15 | *Either He Is Crazy or His Feet Stink*

In 2006, the Italian word *coglione* made world news when Silvio Berlusconi, who was running for prime minister at the time, said that the political left would not win because there were not so many *coglioni* in the country (*coglioni* is the plural form of *coglione*). The word means 'testicle' but its extended meaning used in this context is 'fool'. In this case, fool means someone who does not share the speaker's political views. More broadly, by using the term, the speaker believes that the person to whom it refers is outside the realm of normal and acceptable.

Languages around the world have numerous words and expressions for those that are considered "crazy." One such expression is colloquial Serbo-Croatian *Il je lud il mu noge smrde* 'Either he is crazy or his feet stink'. Although it is superficially meaningless, this expression still has some logic to it. Everybody's feet stink, so it cannot be that. Therefore, it is an ironic way of saying that someone is crazy by offering another impossible option. Serbo-Croatian has many other expressions for "crazy" people. One of them is *lud ko struja* 'as crazy as electricity', probably inspired by the jerky moves of someone who has been electrocuted.

English likes using fruit to describe "crazy" people. They go *bananas* or *nuts*. The latter makes them *nuttier than a fruitcake*, so they are called *fruitcakes*. Animals are also fine. In the southern United States, one is *as crazy as a betsy bug, as crazy as a bed bug, as crazy as an outhouse rat, as crazy as a shithouse rat*, and *as crazy as an outhouse fly*. Southern Europeans, for example, Italians, are similar. One is *pazzo come una cimice* 'as crazy as a bedbug' and *pazzo come una volpe* 'as crazy as a fox'. In French, "crazy" people break something, *péter un cable* 'break a cable', *péter une durite* 'break a hose', *péter un plomb* 'break a fuse' or *péter les plombs* 'break fuses'. The verb 'break' also has the meaning 'to break wind'. In German, "crazy" people spin, *spinnen* 'to spin' is the verb used in in that language. They also have a

Figure 15.1 Going flamingo (RyanLane/Getty Images)

bird (*einen Vogel haben*) and roof damage (*einen Dachschaden haben*) (Figure 15.1).

People who are "stupid," that is, below what is perceived the norm for logical reasoning, are also ostracized around the world. In the Indonesian variety of Malay, they are *kepala udang* 'a shrimp head'. One of the words in German is *Fetzenschädel* 'scrap skull'. English *blockhead* is very similar. Some Polish expressions are very different as they use clothing and furniture. One is *tępy jak noga stołowa* 'as dull as a leg of the table' and *głupi jak but (z lewej nogi)* 'as stupid as a shoe (from the left foot)'. In Russian, stupidity is linked to drinking, somebody is глупый как пробка (*glupiy kak probka*) 'as stupid as a bottle cork'. Czechs are stone-cold: one is *hloupý jako kámen* 'as stupid as a stone'.

Brazilian Portuguese uses stone, as in *burro como una pedra* 'as stupid as a stone' but also the door, as in *burro como uma porta* 'as stupid as the door'. English uses similar references to inanimate objects, as in *dumb as a post* and *dumb as a doorknob*. The very practical and hard-working Dutch like metaphors with useful domestic animals. One is *zo dom (stom) als het achtereind van een varken* 'as stupid as the pig's back' (which also comes in a variety of other forms that include pigs) and *zo dom als een gans* 'as stupid as a goose'.

Figure 15.2 Exploding with anger (John M. Lund Photography Inc./Getty Images)

Darkness (dimwit) is used as the bases for Romanian *prost ca noaptea* and Serbo-Croatian *glup kao noć*, both meaning 'as stupid as night'.

The concept of branding people who do not fit certain perceived norms is closely related to describing conspicuous displays of strong human emotions such as sadness, joy, fear, etc. These emotions fall outside what is considered ordinary. Anger comes very close to the previously discussed cases, as can be seen from English, where *mad* can mean 'insane' and 'angry'. Serbo-Croatian speakers go a step further. An angry person is *bijesan* 'rabid'.

Anger is perceived as a sudden release of energy from a container of some kind. Fire, smoke, explosion, etc. are encountered in many languages (Figure 15.2). In English, one is *bursting with anger*. In Mandarin Chinese, one is 'belching smoke from the seven orifices of the head' 七窍生烟, *qī qiào shēng yān*. In Hungarian, one is all steam, *teljesen begôzölt*. In Japanese, the person is boiling, and this happens either to their intestines (はらわたが煮えくり返る, *Harawata ga nie-kurikaeru*) or the bottom of their stomach (怒りが腹の底をぐらぐら

させる, *Ikari ga hara no soko wo guragura saseru*). In Turkish, anger explodes (*öfkesi patlamak*). Similar expressions are found in numerous other languages.

Languages do not only describe undesirable features. There are many instances of expressions that describe *just the right thing*, *just what the doctor ordered*, such as the English *Goldilocks Zone*, which enabled our existence in this universe. Danes, arguably the happiest people in the world, have the expression *hygge*, which stands for the creation of a pleasant atmosphere and relations that are conducive to enjoying life with good people. The German expression *Gemütlichkeit* comes close to describing the feeling of cheer, coziness, and friendliness. In German, there is also a curious expression for someone who lives well. Such a person lives 'like a God in France' (*wie Gott in Frankreich*). This expression has spread to many languages, including Dutch (*leven als God in Frankrijk*), English (*live like God in France*), and even French itself (*vivre comme Dieu en France*). Yiddish has לעבן ווי גאָט אין פֿרינקרייך (*lebn vi Got in Frankraykh*), but also 'To live like God in Odessa': לעבן ווי גאָט אין אָדעס (lebn vi Got in Odes), referring to Odessa, a city in the Russian Empire with a sizeable Jewish population before 1917. Serbo-Croatian expressions are even more curious. One lives 'like kidney in suet' (*kao bubreg u loju*) or 'their axe dropped into honey' (*upala mu sjekira u med*).

These superficially nonsensical expressions have historic justification. French kings were indeed like Gods. There is a well-known adage of King Louis XV, *après nous, le deluge* 'after us (and royal we is used here) deluge', which clearly shows the attitude of French monarchs. The first Serbo-Croatian expression comes from the practice of eating innards. When lamb is spit-roasted, kidneys are cooked inside a cavity enclosed in suet, as they are anatomically. So, the idea is that everything is where it should be. The expression with the axe and honey comes from the practice of collecting wild honey. One hit trees with an axe until the axe hit honey. When that happens, the person has *hit the jackpot*, as always gambling-ready Americans would put it (Figure 15.3). In Polish and Belarussian, one lives 'like behind God's stove': *jak u Pana Boga za piecem* (Polish) and як у Бога за печкай, *jak u Boha za pechkay* (Belarussian). Behind the stove sounds like the dirtiest part of the kitchen to an English speaker, but in fact this expression refers to a heating stove in the living room, and behind it suggests a cozy, warm nook.

Either He Is Crazy or His Feet Stink 107

Figure 15.3 Hitting the jackpot *(*AdShooter/Getty Images)

In neighboring Russian, the phrase is also rooted in religion. One lives 'like in Christ's bosom' (*как у Христа за пазухой*, *kak u Hrista za pazuhoy*). Going back to French, its speakers also have a peculiar expression for luxurious living, *comme un coq en pâte* 'like a rooster in paste'. The historical reference here is to agricultural exhibitions, where champion roosters were smeared with paste to make their feathers brighter.

Similarities and differences were shown here through the various ways that languages stigmatize outliers and praise desired lifestyles. Similarities (e.g., seeing anger as explosion) stem from general human perceptive mechanisms. Differences stem from divergent cultural developments, which are sometimes rather random (e.g., the practice of beautifying exhibition roosters in France).

16 | *Shoo and Scat*

One of the things we do with words is scare away various animals (Figure 16.1). English is very indiscriminate with its *shoo* (and a newer *scat*), as it can be used for any animal and even people. Turkish is more discriminate; *hoşt* is used for dogs, *kış* for poultry, and *pist* for cats. The same level of precision can be found in Serbo-Croatian; *iš* is used for poultry, and *šic* or *pis* for cats. There is a specific onomatopoeia used to scare away dogs, *šibe*, but it is becoming obsolete. Animals are also called. For cats, English speakers use *here kitty-kitty*, and Serbo-Croatians use *mac-mac*. Russian speakers use кс-кс-кс (*ks-ks-ks*), Finnish *kis-kis*, French bi *biss*, Hungarian *cic-cic*, and Turkish *pissy-pissy*.

Another thing we do with words is imitate animal calls. One would expect them to be similar in various languages, but this is actually not so, as they reflect different phonetics and different perceptive patterns found in each individual language. In some cases, there are visible differences, but there are always languages that break the pattern. Rooster crowing is *kykyliky* in Danish, *cocorico* in French, *kikeriki* in German, *kukuriku* in Hungarian and Serbo-Croatian, кукареку (*kookarekoo*) in Russian, *kukuruku* in Portuguese, and the list of languages with a similar sound pattern goes on forever until we encounter English, and its *cock-a-doodle-do*. Japanese is an outlier of cat meowing. Japanese cats meow: ニャーニャー, *nyan nyan* (Figure 16.2). Countless other languages are exactly the same as English: *miauw* in Dutch, *mijau* in Serbo-Croatian, *miau* in German, Hungarian, and Italian, *miao* in Spanish, etc.

Pigs and dogs are much more diversified. The English *oink oink* is hardly universal, although it is also found in Italian and Spanish. A Japanese pig goes ブーブー, *boo boo*, Polish *chrum chrum*, Serbo-Croatian *grok grok*, and Swedish *nöff-nöff*. Dogs are equally diversified. While English dogs go *woof woof*, their Serbo-Croatian counterparts go *vau vau* or *av av*. Dogs in France go *ouah ouah*, and their German neighbors *wau wau*. In southern Europe, Italian dogs bark

Shoo and Scat

Figure 16.1 Shooing pigeons (aka flying rats) (Qiang Dongliang/EyeEm/Getty Images)

bau bau and their Greek friends ΓΑΒ ΓΑΒ, *gav gav*, the same as their Russian brethren (*гав-гав*, *gav-gav*).

The sounds of African animals are also far from universal. The sound of the elephant trumpet is *baraag* in English, *tööt* in Finnish, *y-y-y* (*u-u-u*) in Russian, and *biaaah* in Spanish. Lions *roar* in English. The sound is *grr* in German, Italian, and Russian (*грр, grr*), while Turkish lions go *uagh*.

What is common with all these examples, shooing and calling animals on one hand, and emulating their calls on the other, is that they utilize unusual combinations of sounds that are generally not encountered in other words. There are many hissing and explosive sounds and their combinations. The technical term for words of this kind is onomatopoeia. It refers to the formation of a word by utilizing the sound associated with the named entity (e.g., a bird call with a bird). Words for animal sounds are more prototypical cases of onomatopoeia, yet the ones mentioned, when used while talking to animals, are borderline cases of this category.

Figure 16.2 Japanese beckoning cats talismans: Bringing good luck without meowing (Yagi Studio/Getty Images)

Words in which the sound plays the central role have long commanded the attention of linguists and anthropologists. Their importance lies in the fact that they may offer insights into the origins of the human linguistic facility. Ever since the late nineteenth century, linguists have proposed hypotheses about the origin of language. In one of the early ones, animal calls play a central role, and onomatopoeias were central in all early proposals. Even the names of these early hypotheses are onomatopoeias.

The great German philosopher, philologist, and encyclopedist Johann Gottfried Herder has proposed that the linguistic faculty stems from imitating animal sounds. This came to be known as the *Bow-wow* or *Cuckoo* theory. The alternative theories are as follows: the *Pooh-pooh* theory, which contended that language has emerged as a means of expressing human emotions, such as pain, fear, surprise, pleasure, etc. The *ding-dong* theory claimed that the early language echoed the natural sound of things. Finally, the *Yo-he-ho* theory advanced a proposal that the human linguistic faculty emerged as a result of rhythmic patterns of collective labor.

Endless other hypotheses have been proposed since these early days. A recent one is known as the *Integration hypothesis*. It was proposed

Shoo and Scat

Figure 16.3 Tweeting (pixelfit/Getty Images)

in 2014 by an MIT professor, Shigeru Miyagawa. The claim is that the sound patterns of bird calls and signs used by nonhuman primates have been integrated into the uniquely human linguistic faculty. The issue of the origin of language remains unresolved.

A record exists that Saint Francis of Assisi preached to the birds. It would be interesting to know how many of his words were tweets. Tweets as in chirps. The tweets of our electronic age are certainly something that condenses our utterances, taking them closer to the onomatopoeias of the early language (Figure 16.3).

Whatever the final answer about the origin of language may be, if it ever comes, onomatopoeias of the kind discussed in this chapter are certainly something that connect us to other animals, our fellow inhabitants of the Earth. Thus, any of us who become a frog, bird, or dog in our next incarnation will already have some experience in making the appropriate calls.

17 | A Dog and Pony Show

Being the best in show, among other things, hinges on the dog's conduct, that is, the way it reacts to the handler's commands (Figure 17.1). Commands for dogs are one-syllable staccato bursts of sounds: *sit*, *down*, *stay*, *wait*, *heel*, *place*, *bed*, *off*, *out*, etc. Commands issued to ponies and other horses are similar. *Whoa* is used to stop a horse, and *giddyap* to urge it to go.

Dog commands in other languages are typically also semantic words that are equivalent to the ones mentioned in English, but even there some degree of variation exists. Thus the heel command is *bei Fuß* 'next to the foot' in German, за мной (*za mnoy*) 'after me' in Russian, and *fot* 'foot' in Swedish. English horse commands are not semantic words but rather onomatopoeias. Those languages that use onomatopoeias in issuing commands to horses have rather different commands, albeit similar to the English counterparts in their shortness. English *giddyap* is *hu*, and English *whoa* is *ho* in French. *Hep* is used to urge a horse in Finnish and *ptruu* to slow it down.

Other languages use semantic words. Italians slow down their horses in the same way they slow down their musicians using the word *piano*. To urge them, *vai* 'go' is used. Russians urge their horses by using пошёл (*pashol*) 'go, literally, you have started to go'. This is a kind of imperative mood that is identical with the past tense. The logic is that by putting the command in the past tense, it has already been executed. This form adds certainty to the obedience and effectiveness of the command. To slow them down, they would use стой (*stoy*) 'stop'. Even closely related languages use different kinds of commands. Russian, as can be seen, uses semantic words, and Serbo-Croatian, another closely related Slavic language, has onomatopoeias. *Giddyap* is *điha*, and *whoa* is *ooo*.

Other than commands, dog and pony shows are great examples of another thing that we do with words, that is, naming and classifying practices. This extends far beyond dogs and horses. Cats, cows, sheep,

A Dog and Pony Show

Figure 17.1 A silent dog command (westend61/Getty Images)

pigeons, and other animals are classified and named after their various features. They are also labeled by their origin. Take pigeons, for example. There is an *English Carrier* and an *English Pouter*, an *Indian Fantail*, a *French Mondain*, an *Old German Owl*, an *American Show Racer*, a *Chinese Owl*, an *Australian Performer Tumbler*, a *Czech Steller Cropper*, and, among many others, a *Serbian Highflyer*. Sometimes languages see different things in the same pigeon. English speakers, see a fan in the *Fantail Pigeon*, in the same way as Serbo-Croatian speakers (where it is *lepezaner*, with *lepeza* being a 'fan'). Bulgarians see a lantern, and the term is фенерлия (*fenerliya*), with фенер (*fener*) being 'lantern'. Czech speakers see it as a 'little peacock', *pávík*. Cats are equally international. Some breeds include Persian, Bengali, Siamese, British Shorthair, American Shorthair, Russian Blue, Siberian, Scottish Fold, Turkish Angora, and Himalayan. To return to dogs, their names in English resemble the international patchwork of societies from the inner circle of English, all of which are in strongly immigrant countries. Not only are the names of their countries of origin featured in many breed names (as in the *Afghan Hound*, the *French Bulldog*, the *Argentine Polar Dog*, the *German Shepherd*, the *Australian Shepherd*, the *Russian Wolfhound*, etc.)

but they also contain words from other languages. Sometimes their pronunciation is modified beyond recognition. Such is the case of the Wiener Dog, which is also known as the *Dachshund*, which is German for 'badger dog' as *Dachs* (pronounced [dahs], *a* as in *bar*) is badger and *Hund* (pronounced [hoont], *oo* as in *book* or *cook*) is dog. It is very difficult to recognize these words in the American pronunciation of this dog breed. However, it is as nothing compared to how *victuals* (pronounced: vidlz) are butchered. Luckily, the word for them is archaic. There are words from many other languages in the names of dog breeds. The name of the breed *Aidi* comes from the Tamazight word for dog. *Akbash* contains the Turkish phrase *ak baş* 'white head'. *Tornjak* means 'sheep-pen dog' in Serbo-Croatian. *Alopekis* comes from the Greek word Αλωπεκης (*Alopekis*) meaning 'fox-like'.

The previously mentioned sausage dog, *Dachshund*, has curious names in various languages around the world. The English *Wiener Dog/Sausage Dog/Hot Dog* is nothing unusual as it can be found in Spanish *perro salchicha* and Portuguese (*cachorro salsicha*) 'sausage dog', in both cases. There are also many other names, such as a name that literally means 'badger dog', *jazavičar* in Serbo-Croatian, patterned after the German word for *Dachshund*. The Poles know it as *jamnik* 'hole dog', which is a variation on the badger hunt. It is *bassotto* 'low dog' in Italian. Russians, Ukrainians, and Belarussians haven't bothered to borrow more than the first part of the German word (*Dachs-*) and they have also changed it beyond recognition, so the name is такса (*taksa*).

Russians have half-borrowed the German word for sausage dog, and the best-known American dog, Balto, has Russian roots. He was the sled dog who led his team to bring diphtheria antitoxin to the sick in Nome, Alaska, in 1925, which earned him a monument in New York City's Central Park. His breed is the *Siberian Husky*. This breed was bred in the Chukchi regions of Siberia, and then introduced to Alaska during the Nome Gold Rush by a Russian fur trader named William Goosak. The first part in the name of the breed is clear, but the second is more obfuscated; it may have come from the word for Eskimo. If true, the name connects the two continents (North America with northern Asia) in the same way as the geneology of the dog.

Russian dogs are no less famous. The first animal in orbit was *Laika*, a Russian space dog, a mongrel, possibly part Terrier and part Husky (the latter would connect her to Balto). *Laika* is also a Russian dog

A Dog and Pony Show

Figure 17.2 The author with faithful dog Hachiko in Shibuya, Tokyo, Japan (photo by Ljiljana Šipka)

breed, which creates some confusion given that Лайка (*Laika*), the space dog, is not a *Laika*. The Russian word is лайка, *layka* (*Лайка*, *Layka* as the proper name), which comes from the verb лаять (*layat*) 'to bark', so the 'barker', 'barking dog'. Other Russian dogs who made orbital flights also had curious names: Белка (*Belka*) 'squirrel or whitey', Стрелка (*Strelka*) 'little arrow', Пчёлка (*Pchyoka*) 'little bee', and Мушка (*Mooshka*) 'little fly', Чернушка (*Chernooshka*) 'blackie', Звёздочка (*Zvyozdochka*) 'little star', Ветерок (*Veterok*) 'light breeze', and Уголёк (*Oogalyok*) 'small piece of coal'.

Perhaps the best-known canine globally is the Japanese dog who waited for his owner as long as nine years after the owner had died (Figure 17.2). In Japan, he is known as 忠犬ハチ公, *chūken Hachikō* 'faithful dog Hachiko'. The name ハチ公, *Hachikō* contains the word hachi, for number 8, an auspicious number in Japanese culture, and the

Figure 17.3 Where bulls and bears live (Mateo Colombo/Getty Images)

endearing particle 公 (-*kō*). The name of its breed, *Akita* (秋田), comes from the eponymous prefecture in the northeast of the central Japanese island of Honshu. In the English-speaking realm, the popularity of *Hachikō* is matched only by the Scottish 'small girl', that is, *Lassie Come-home*.

Not only dogs and ponies find their way into linguistic expressions, as every follower of the stock market knows. The stock market can be *bullish*, when the indices go up, or *bearish*, when they go down. The bull attacks by lifting its horns up and the bear by thrusting its claws down. Hence the symbols (Figure 17.3).

We do different things with words to our nonhuman best friends. We incorporate peculiarities of our respective cultures into the commands we use to control them (with more or less success). We do the same in naming them, starting from expressions such as K-9 (canine) used by the police, reflecting the fascination of armed services with abbreviations. In naming dog breeds, we also engage in international word trade by incorporating names of foreign countries and words from other languages into them. Needless to say, all this is completely lop-sided, given that we are really incapable of fully grasping the ways in which our brothers and sisters from the animal world communicate.

18 | *Blah-Blah-Blah, Yada-Yada-Yada*

Blah-blah, first recorded in English in the early 1920s, has had a great career in many languages, whether spelled with the letter *h* or without (as in *bla-bla* in French, Norwegian, Spanish, Serbo-Croatian, and many other languages). Its success is paramount to the Italian greeting *ciao*. *Yada-yada-yada* is much newer, first recorded in the early 1990s and restricted to English (Figure 18.1).

These two onomatopoeias for meaningless talk show how we reconstruct the sounds of our environment. As every student of Japanese knows, the Japanese language is particularly rich in onomatopoeias of this kind. Comic book buffs certainly know that this form of text cannot be imagined without its *pows* and *booms*. Japanese comic books, *mangas*, are therefore the place where everybody looks for high-quality onomatopoeias for the sounds from our environment.

In Japanese, there are two kinds of onomatopoeic sounds. The first are known as 擬音語 (*giongo*) and they are words that imitate sounds (e.g., ザーザー, *zā-zā* for heavy rain). The second group is 擬態語 (*gitaigo*) and these onomatopoeias describe an emotion, state, or action by means of an associated sound, for example イライラ, *ira-ira* for being irritated.

In both these categories, there are seemingly endless ways to depict realities with sound words and they are abundantly present in the mangas. Weather phenomena are prominent in these onomatopoeias. As mentioned, heavy rain goes *zā-zā*, thunder is rumbling ゴロゴロ, *goro-goro*, a flash of lightning, is ピカッと, *pikatto*, light rain goes パラパラ, *para-para*, things flapping in the wind ぺらぺら, *pera-pera*, humid weather is 蒸し蒸し, *mushi mushi* and the Sun shines ピカピカ, *pika pika*. There is even ぽつぽつ, *potsu-potsu* for rain that has just started to fall.

All this is nothing compared to the richness of Japanese sound words for human actions and feelings. One can walk briskly (スタスタ, *suta suta*) or lazily (ノロノロ, *noro noro*). One can also wander

117

Figure 18.1 An empty talk (Lisa-Blue/Getty Images)

around (うろうろ, *uro uro*). When eating and drinking, one can guzzle (ゴクゴク, *goku goku*), swig (がぶがぶ, *gabu gabu*), slurp (ズルズル, *zuru zuru*), devour food (ガツガツ, *gatsu gatsu*), eat heartily (パクパク, *paku paku*), munch (ムシャムシャ, *musha musha*), and nibble or sip (ちびちび, *chibi chibi*). The latter onomatopoeia *paku paku* gave its name to an early computer game character, Pac-man. The examples for eating shown here are onomatopoeias in English, but their sound is different. The same is true with other languages. For example, slurp is *srk* in Serbo-Croatian, *gulp* is *schluck* in German, *glek* in the Indonesian variety of Malay, and *skil* in Dutch.

Some human sounds, such as heartbeats, the cry of a baby, and laughter are widely spread. The latter sound is very similar (*ha ha* has almost universal traction, but Basque *kar kar* and Batak *kakak* are clear outliers). The other two exhibit cross-linguistic differences. For example, a baby cries *wäh-wäh* in German, *owe-owe* in the Indonesian variety of Malay, *bé bé* in Czech, *kme-kme* in Serbo-Croatian, and *buá buá* in Spanish (Figure 18.2). Heartbeats go *tu-tum* in Finnish, δουκ δουκ *(duk-duk)* in Greek, *boum boum* in French, *tuk tuk* in Latvian and Lithuanian, and *tuks tuks* in Estonian. Some other sounds are universally very similar. For example, the

Figure 18.2 A crying baby – annoying, whatever the onomatopoeia may be (yuoak/Getty Images)

ticking of a clock is either *tick-tock* or *tick-tack* (spelled with the c or without it) in many languages.

What is fascinating about Japanese, which can also be very clearly seen in the mangas, is a wide range of sound words for human emotions, states, and behavior other than walking, eating, and drinking. The sound word ジィー (*jii*) describes someone who stares motionlessly, and オタオタ (*ota ota*) is used for those who are shocked speechless. ソワソワ (*sowa sowa*) describes nervous or excited people. Those who are too tired to think or move are characterized as オロオロ (*oro oro*) and those who have dozed off うとうと (*uto uto*). わくわく (*waku waku*) are those who are excited, and cranky people are つんつん

Figure 18.3 Kaboom: As American as apple pie (zak00/Getty Images)

(*tsun tsun*). Those who loaf around are ゴロゴロ(*goro goro*), and dizziness is くらくら(*kura kura*). It goes on forever.

Japanese sound words for human features are equally rich and fascinating. A skinny person is ガリガリ (*gari gari*), and a muscular person is ムキムキ(*muki muki*). Uncombed hair is ぼさぼさ (*bosa bosa*). Sweating is からから (*kara kara*), and rapid blinking is しばしば (*shiba shiba*).

American comic books are also rich depositories of sound words such as *ktang, pow, ka-boom, kapow, wham, swiff,* and others, that are unlikely to be found anywhere else (Figure 18.3). The page www.comicbookfx.com/fxlist.php, an online project of comic book sounds, lists over 1,000 unique sound effects from *a-aaa-aa* to *zzzzzzzzz*. Many of those are variations of the same sound, for example, whoosh and zzz come in many different versions with a different number of *o* and *z* characters, respectively. One can also find these words in Spanish comic books. A machine gun goes *ra-ta-tá, ra-ta-tá,* a small explosion is *tric* or *tris,* sword fighting is *hischás,* and an explosion is *pataplum* or *cataplum*.

Some onomatopoeias eventually leave their comic book world to become full-blown words and idioms, as in *the business is booming* and *to catch some z's*. The iconic English dish *bangers and mash* contains one such word. The *bang* part in the name for sausage apparently comes from WWI, when shortages forced sausage producers to add various fillers to sausages. Water, one such filler, caused sausages to explode, hence the bang in the name. Movement in the opposite direction is also possible. Phones in comic books and elsewhere go *ring*. This onomatopoeia comes from the verb meaning 'to sound the bell'. Early phones indeed had bell ringers on them, so the extension of the meaning from bells to phones was not a stretch.

Examples in this chapter seem to give some ammunition to the two early theories of the origin of language: the *Pooh-Pooh* theory, which contended that language emerged as the expression of human emotions, pain, fear, surprise, pleasure, etc. and the *Ding-Dong* theory claimed that the early language echoed the natural sound of things. As noted in Chapter 16, many other theories have been proposed since these late eighteenth- and early nineteenth-century attempts at finding the origin of our linguistic faculty. The issue of the origin of language remains unresolved, and it is not clear if onomatopoeias of the kind presented in this book will have a prominent role in the elucidation of this issue. However, that does not take anything from the beauty of their diversity.

19 | Acts of Darkness

Words are used to refer to our reproductive organs and sexual activities. In many languages, anything related to sex is taboo, which causes many words referring to sex to be considered inappropriately direct. There are also replacements for such words. As a rule, these replacements make indirect references to sex, which renders them appropriate. Obviously, some languages and cultures do not consider this field taboo.

Tabooing of the sexual sphere brings somewhat weaker tabooing of the sphere of excretion. This is quite understandable given the polyfunctional nature of the key organs. These spheres are just two of several fields that are typically tabooed. Others include religion, illness, food, clothing, and taboos stemming from etiquette (e.g., not using derogatory names for the boss). Religious taboos can be seen in the modifications of words stemming from one of the ten Christian commandments: "Thou shalt not take the name of the Lord thy God in vain." In American English, *God!* becomes *gosh!* and *Jesus!* becomes *jeez!* German has something similar. The expression of surprise, disbelief, etc. is *herrje*, which is a modification of *Herr Jesu* 'Lord Jesus'. In some dialects of Serbo-Croatian, *Boga mi!* 'I swear to God' becomes *Bora mi!* 'I swear to a pine tree' as *g*, the final sound of *Bog* 'God' is changed to *r*, to make it *bor* 'pine tree'.

The devil is equally tabooed, even in the format of a benign mascot. Arizona State University's athletic teams and students are named Sun Devils, and their mascot is Sparky, a cute little devil with a pitchfork (Figure 19.1). Sparky is prominent on campus and nobody has ever had a problem with it, except for one occasion. In September 1987, the university rented out its stadium for a mass to be celebrated by Pope John Paul II. A condition was attached to the rental – all images and mentions of Sparky needed to be covered, and that is what happened.

Although not fully covered in the English language, references to the Devil are actually indirect. *The Prince of Darkness* is obviously

Acts of Darkness

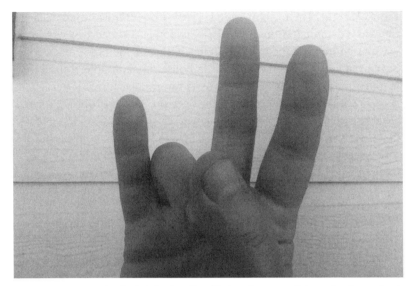

Figure 19.1 Fear the fork: The Sun Devil's hand gesture (photo by the author)

indirect, but the word *Satan* also comes from the Hebrew root שׂטן s-t-n, meaning 'one who opposes, adversary'. The very name *Devil* is also indirect as it comes from the Greek διάβολος, *diabolos* 'slanderer, lit. one who throws something across'. Although Russians have several words for the Devil (дьявол, *dyavol*; чёрт, *chort*; бес, *bes*), a tradition existed among religious people to refer to this creature indirectly as *шут shoot* 'jester', рогатый (*rogatiy*) 'the horned one', лукавый (*lookaviy*) 'the cunning one', or нечистый (*niechistiy*) 'the dirty one'.

Taboos vary from language to language. For example, addressing people by the appropriate address title and last name (e.g., *Ms. Jones*) is a desirable formal form of address in English. Addressing someone by their last name alone (as in *Jones, come with me!*) is restricted to the military, police, and such. In Serbo-Croatian, using the title and the last name is as formal as in English, but using a last name without a title is an unrestricted informal form of address and reference. Any person can refer to a friend by his or her last name, not just those in the military and police. Polish is more curious. Using last names is somewhat of a taboo (a no-no), even if used with the formal form of address. So, if someone is named *Marek Kowalski*, the normal form of address would be *Panie Marku* (literally, Mr. Marek; the name *Marek* is put in a special 'calling form', *Marku*). The form of address *Panie Kowalski* was used in earlier times as a demonstration of force. For example, a supervisor would use it when addressing their subordinates. Some of the taboo restrictions have been loosened in recent years in Polish. For example, it used to be inappropriate to address one's parents informally. Instead, one would need to speak about them in the third person. The appropriate form to ask one's mother if she is going somewhere used to be *Czy mama idzie?*, literally, 'Is mom going?' rather than *Idziesz?* 'Are you going?', but this form of addressing one's parents is becoming increasingly obsolete. In the United States, the previously broadly used *yes, sir* to one's father remains only in small pockets of the US military, Deep South families, and some rural areas.

The word *taboo* (also spelled *tabu*) was borrowed in English from Tongan. It has then spread to countless other languages around the word. The word was introduced into the English language in 1777 by James Cook, who visited Tonga. He noted that the word signifies something that is forbidden. The same word is also encountered in Fijian, and related words are Maōri *tapu* and Hawaiian *kapu*. English, known for its zero derivation (giving words new grammatical functions without changing their form), added to this original adjective a noun (something can be *a taboo*) and a verb (*to taboo* something) (Figure 19.2). Taboo is not the only word Cook brought back from his travel. He is also to be credited for *tattoo* and *kangaroo*.

Borrowing plays an important role in words around acts of darkness. *Penis* and *vagina*, borrowed from Latin, are neutral terms, de facto euphemisms for their domestic equivalents (for example, the c-words in English). The Latin word for the male member comes from the word for tail and its female equivalent from the word for sheath, scabbard. German has the very similar *Schwanz* 'tail' for penis, and vagina is *Schlitz* 'slot, slit'. Some languages share similarities with English. Penis is кур (*kur*) in Macedonian and Bulgarian, and *kurac* in Serbo-Croatian, which comes from the word for 'rooster' (i.e., cock). *Pizda* is the word for vagina with widespread currency in Slavic languages. It is found in Russian, Ukrainian, Polish, Czech, Slovak, Slovene, Serbo-Croatian, etc. It is even borrowed in Romanian, an Italic language. It ultimately comes from the Proto–Indo-European **(e)pi-sed-*, the literal meaning of which is 'upon to sit', meaning the part of the body on which one sits. So, what are today obscene words used to be euphemisms.

Acts of Darkness   125

Figure 19.2 Taboo: Some roads are best not travelled (Adél Békefi/Getty Images)

Meanings of obscene words are also extended and used as derogatory terms. For example, in English, one can say that someone is *such a dick* or *such a prick*. Even closely related languages differ in this regard. For example, Polish is just like English in that one can say that somebody is a *chuj* 'dick'. One can also say that somebody is *kawał chuja* 'a piece of dick' (Figure 19.3). This is impossible in Serbo-Croatian, a Slavic cousin of Polish, as one can only use *pizda*, the obscene word for vagina, which is possible across the board in Slavic languages.

One interesting thing about obscene words is a significant difference between sexual words (e.g., obscene words for copulation and sexual organs) and excretion words (e.g., obscene words for defecation and urination). The former category is considerably more tabooed than the latter in many cultures. I was able to confirm this in two research projects. In the first, I was looking at the distribution of sexual and excretion obscenities in Serbo-Croatian dictionaries. In the 1818 edition of the *Serbian Dictionary* by Vuk Stefanović Karadžić, an autodidact, in which the modern standard variety was inaugurated, both categories were equally present. The idea of the author, consistent with

Figure 19.3 A cocky rooster (GeoStock/Getty Images)

the Romanticist Weltanschauung of the time, was that the literary variety should be identical with the way "the people" spoke. The next edition of the same dictionary, in which another linguist, a trained philologist unlike Karadžić, was involved, established the tradition of listing the excretion words but not their sexual counterparts. This tradition then continued in practically all following Serbo-Croatian dictionaries.

The significant difference between these two groups of obscene terms was also found in a survey of over 200 speakers of Serbo-Croatian. They were offered five terms each in the following categories: obscene curses, sexual obscenities, excretive obscenities, and euphemisms for sexual obscenities. They were asked to rate each of them from 1 (least obscene) to 5 (most obscene). Consequently, the range for the five words was from 5 to 25. The averages for each category were as follows: curses 17.2, sexual obscenities 15.7, excretive obscenities 10.7, and euphemisms 10.5. As can be seen, the difference is colossal, with sexual obscenities being very close to obscene curses, and excretion obscenities practically identical to euphemisms.

Taboos are another field where it is difficult to say where culture ends and language begins. On one hand, languages reflect taboos that exist in their respective cultures. On the other hand, words become taboos. It is not only that cultures and their respective languages differ in what their people consider obscene and euphemistic, but the status of words changes over time. What begins as a euphemism often ends up being an obscenity.

20 | *This for That*

No, *quid pro quo* is not meant here but rather the phrases one would use for an object for which there is no generally available word. For example, most people will not know any of these: *beer comb*, *head cutter*, *foam scraper*, or *foam flipper*. Rather than using any of these synonyms, they are more likely to say *the tool for removing foam from a glass of beer* or something like that.

While teaching in Poland in the mid-1990s I had a former student who had just got a job in a Polish company that produced windows. He was supposed to prepare technical documentation for Serbia, one of the prospective markets of the company. He was calling me for help with finding Serbo-Croatian equivalents for the Polish terms describing parts of windows. Their English equivalents are something like *jamb liner*, *stool cap*, *jalousie security clip*, *Louver link*, *face mount casement window operator*, *inverted tilt balance*, *weep hole cover with clap*, *snap-in tilt latch*, and many others. Not being a home-improvement wizard, I was in some trouble. Eventually, the equivalents were found in various sources of reference and everything went well (Figure 20.1).

The situation described here points to the phenomenon of so-called *agnonyms*, words that are not known to most speakers. Whenever there is a need to refer to something for which we do not know the word, we resort to descriptions of how something looks, to what it is related, or what it is intended for. We will then still be able to do things with words even though we do not know the exact word in question. For example, if we do not know the word *cygnet*, we simply say *young swan*.

There is even a dictionary of *agnonyms* for Russian, where the authors, Morkovkin and Morkovkina (see suggested readings for the source), define this category as inducing one of the following reactions in native speakers of the language:

1. I do not know at all what the word means,
2. I only know that the word refers to some very broad field,

Figure 20.1 A missing piece (JoKMedia/Getty Images)

3. I know that the word pertains to a given class of objects but I do not know how it differs from other words,
4. I know that the word refers to a given entity, but I do not know its characteristics,
5. I know what the word refers to, but I do not know what the entity to which it refers looks like,
6. I know the word from my private or professional experience but I assume that most speakers do not know it.

As can be seen, knowing or not knowing a word is not an on/off switch but rather a gray area between complete unfamiliarity with the word and understanding and being able to use the word.

One interesting phenomenon in practically all languages is the belief among native speakers that they know many more words of their language than they really do. For example, it is estimated that an educated speaker of English commands between 40,000 and 60,000 words. The largest English dictionaries feature over 300,000 entries, which means that most words of our language are agnonyms for us. Even within the minority of words of the language that we command, some lexical areas are an entrance ticket to certain spheres of life. In the United States, the vocabulary section is a significant portion of the SAT test (mandatory to enter undergraduate education) and the GRE test (required for graduate college application). Indeed, our whole life in words is narrowing down the field of agnonyms. Whatever we do, we are not likely to narrow it down significantly, yet it is definitely possible to significantly enlarge the group of words we know, and that is all we really need (Figure 20.2).

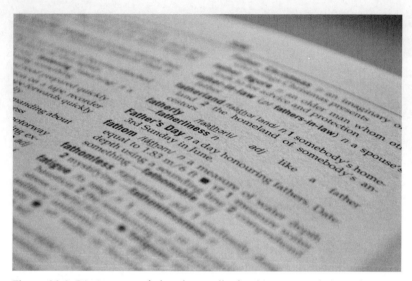

Figure 20.2 Dictionary, a fathomless well of unknown words (Angela May/ Getty Images)

Those of us who are in the business of compiling dictionaries are always faced with the problem known as lexical selection. Aside from the largest monolingual ones, dictionaries always present a selection of words in one or more languages. So, the question is which words to include and which ones to disregard. The issue is most complex. In recent years, frequency in large corpora (collections of various texts) has become increasingly important in lexical selection. However, there are finer points to it. It is perfectly clear that an introductory learner of English needs words such as *socks* and *underwear* and can be perfectly happy not knowing words such as *independence* or *self-determination*. Given that people do not often write about socks and underwear, and that various political terms are very prominent in the press, the corpus data alone present a twisted picture. That is why the frequency data from the corpora need to be matched against the subjective assessment of speakers and their needs. Years ago, I was involved in creating a list of very frequent words to be used in work with Alzheimer's patients. Eventually, the words were included in the list if both corpus data and familiarity scores from the speakers were in agreement that the word is frequent and recognizable enough.

Sometimes, languages miss words altogether. The fact that a language does not have a word for something does not mean that the concept is unknown to its speakers. In English-speaking cultures, there is certainly a concept of a person who leaves daily mundane life to pursue their dream. For example, a corporate executive leaving their job to become a chef or musician. However, there is no word for that person. By contrast, German has the word *Aussteiger* referring precisely to such a person. The metaphor of getting off public transportation is used, as the term comes from the verb *aussteigen* 'to get off (as in public transportation)'. The fact that a concept exists without a word for it has inspired several dictionaries to propose words for these orphan concepts. A book by Adams and Lloyd for English and its German counterpart penned by Böttcher are humorous dictionaries of concepts that are not words yet. Among many other interesting entries, one can find the following example in the English dictionary: *ahenny* (adj.): the way people stand when examining other people's bookshelves. In the German dictionary, there is this, *Alicante*, der Ein Gastarbeiter, der in Lokalen singt. [Alicante – a guest worker that sings in bars, a spoof combining the Spanish town name Alicante, Ali, a common Middle Eastern guest worker name, and the Spanish verb *cantar* 'to sing']. As can be seen, the humorous effect partially relies on the fact that an entity exists, but it is actually not "worth" a concept and its corresponding word in the culture/language in question.

To provide another cross-linguistic example akin to the aforementioned *Aussteiger*, the fifth part of the novel titled *The Book of Laughter and Forgetting* by the famous Czech writer Milan Kundera is titled *Lítost*. The author presents his elaborate observations about this allegedly untranslatable Czech word most succinctly in the following segment of his extended discourse on the topic: "Lítost is a state of torment created by the sudden sight of one's own misery." Although Kundera expressly claims that the Czech word *lítost* is untranslatable, there are those who claim that it is identical with the English word *pity*.

It so happens that words are often borrowed from other languages for concepts without a word in a particular language. For example, English has the concept of malicious pleasure because of somebody's misfortune. However, there was no word for it, so the German *Schadenfreude* was borrowed. It is not only lofty abstract concepts that are imported. The same thing happens with exotic species of flora and fauna and many other things. In explaining these borrowed words, dictionaries link them

Figure 20.3 Doing (im)possible things with words (Isabel Pavia/Getty Images)

to something that is known to its users. In definitions in the Oxford English Dictionary, the phrase *similar to* is used nearly 800 times. For example, the word for the game *camogie* (a borrowing from the Irish *camógaíocht, camóguidheacht, camógaidheacht*) is defined as follows, "Esp. in Ireland: a game similar to hurling, played by women and girls." Similarly, *cavaquinho*, a borrowing from Portuguese, is defined as, "Chiefly in Brazil: a four-stringed musical instrument similar to a ukulele." Unlike *Schadenfreude*, where a word was imported for a known concept, in the two latter cases, the concept was imported along with the word.

What is fascinating about all these examples is that they demonstrate our flexibility to do things with words. First, if the word is unknown to us in our language, or it does not have the word, we can always resort to alternative strategies of doing things with words (Figure 20.3). In other words, we have other words that can be combined to do the trick. Second, even when confronted with an unknown concept, we have the ability to domesticate it by linking it to concepts that are familiar to us.

21 | *Me Tarzan, You Jane*

One thing humans do with words is create new languages. Even those who do not take an interest in languages may have heard of Esperanto, the best-known planned language. Esperanto is also meant to be an international auxiliary language, a language intended for communication between people with different native tongues.

Traditionally, the term used to refer to auxiliary languages is *lingua franca*. Historically, they were just like the English of today, used by native speakers and people who are not core native speakers. These "Englishes" of the past typically were associated with military and commercial might. Greek and Latin have fulfilled this function, as did French, Arabic, Mandarin Chinese, Russian, and many other languages. As it happens with Chinglish, Eurenglish, and other international varieties of English, elements from different languages may be melded into a new variety. The very name lingua franca comes from the Mediterranean Lingua France, which was used in the eastern Mediterranean basin from the eleventh to the nineteenth century. Lingua Franca is the Latin term for "the language of the Franks," and Frank was the term for all Western Europeans. On one hand, it was based on the Venetian, Genoan, Occitan, and Catalan dialects (whence most merchants initially came, with the later inclusion of some Spanish and Portuguese dialects). On the other hand, the original lingua franca included Berber, Arabic, Turkish, and Greek words (the languages of the region), and French, which was gaining importance as an international language.

Mixed languages are known as *pidgins* if they do not have native speakers. There are many English-based pidgins, for example, *Bamboo English*, a post-WWII variety spoken between the members of the US occupying force in Japan and the local population. Once they have native speakers, such languages become *creoles*. An example is *Tok Pisin* in Papua New Guinea, which actually means 'speak pidgin' as the language started as a pidgin, but it now has over 120,000 native

Figure 21.1 Me Tarzan (Zulapi/Getty Images)

speakers. Pidgins typically involve some degree of simplification of the original material, as in the title of this chapter. These words are actually something that the Tarzan actor Johnny Weissmuller said in an interview. The phrase does not appear in the writings of Edgar Rice Burroughs. It can also not be heard in the Tarzan movies. The reason why many people believe otherwise (i.e., that the phrase comes from the 1932 movie titled *Tarzan the Ape Man*) is that it fits the situation in which speakers of other languages speak in an English-based pidgin (Figure 21.1).

Some lingua francas that incorporate elements of several languages have wide geographical distribution. Swahili, which is a native language of the Swahili people (less than two million), is a lingua franca in central East Africa, involving 150 million. It emerged as a language of trade between Arabic merchants and the local Bantu-speaking population. A significant portion of its vocabulary is borrowed from Arabic, and the grammar is characteristic of Bantu languages.

Lingua francas, whether hybrid or non-hybrid, have developed spontaneously. Languages such as Esperanto are different in their planned character. There is an individual or a body of some kind that advances a proposal for a new international language. Esperanto is definitely best-known but not the first of such planned languages. The first such language that gained some currency was *Volapük*. It was created in 1870–1880 in Baden (which is today in Germany) by a Catholic cleric, Johan Martin Schleyer, who claimed that God told him in a dream to create an international language. His proposal was mostly based on English vocabulary with some German and French elements. However, the English words were often modified beyond recognition. The very name of the language contains two words from English: *vol* 'world' and *pük* 'speak'. This language was de facto displaced by Esperanto.

The word *Esperanto* comes from the nom de plume of its creator, under which he published the proposal for this language in 1887. Doctor Esperanto 'hoping doctor' was L. L. Zamenhof, an ophthalmologist, who grew up as bilingual Yiddish and Russian, surrounded by other languages, Polish and Belarussian of his native city (Białystok in today's Poland), and was also exposed to other languages such as French and German, in which his father lectured. The original name of the language was *lingvo internacia* 'the international language' in Esperanto (Figure 21.2). However, Zamenhof's followers liked it so much that the word Esperanto eventually became the name of the language. Originally, Zamenhof proposed 900 word roots based on a mixture of various European languages with a very small percentage of non-European tongues. The list of words grew as the language developed. Esperanto lives on with a broader following around the world than any of the similar proposals, and there were many of them: Ido (reformed Esperanto), Interlingua (based on English, French, Italian, Spanish, and Portuguese), Lingwa de Planeta (based on the World's most populous languages: Arabic, Chinese, English, French, German, Hindustani, Persian, Portuguese, Russian, and Spanish), and many others. One of the selling points is the simple, logical, and consequent grammar, much simpler than that of the European languages from which the word roots come.

Planned languages do not have to be made from scratch. They can also be based on natural languages (Figure 21.3). Such a language is *Basic English*, first proposed by Charles Kay Ogden in 1930 in his book entitled *Basic English: A General Introduction with Rules and Grammar*. It is a simplified subset of English vocabulary (850 basic English words were proposed along with 179 international words) and

Figure 21.2 A monument to Dr. Esperanto in Odessa, Ukraine (Martin Ebner/Getty Images)

Figure 21.3 Raw materials for the words of constructed languages (Catherine Falls Commercial/Getty Images)

grammar that is simpler and much more regular. This proposal has not had much traction, and the same is true of the idea advanced in 2013 by Anna Wierzbicka in the book *Imprisoned in English: The Hazards of English as a Default Language*, where she proposes her Natural Semantic Metalanguage as a lingua franca of sciences.

Not all planned (constructed) languages are created to facilitate international communication and level the playing field for everybody. Some of them have been created for sheer fun. Every Trekkie will be familiar with *Klingon*, the language of the fictional Klingon nation in the Star Trek series. It was created by Mark Okrand but the first impulse came from the actor who played Scotty, James Doohan. In 1984, Okrand published *The Klingon Language*, which sold 300,000 copies and has been translated into five languages. One should say that Okrand is a linguist, a specialist in Native American Languages.

Younger readers may not be Trekkies, but they may remember *Lì'fya leNa'vi*, the N'avi language, constructed by Paul Frommer, a Ph.D. in Linguistics, to be used in the 2008 movie "Avatar." Older readers will certainly remember several languages invented by J. R. R. Tolkien for his novels *The Hobbit*, *The Lord of the Rings*, and *The Silmarillion*.

All constructed languages and all mixed lingua francas are a potent testimony to our ability to do more with words. Many of them come from the need to play with words, which makes them similar to puns and other word plays. They are all going beyond the ordinary, adding new value to our varicolored lexical and, more broadly, linguistic world.

22 | How Many Languages Do You Speak?

The ultimate thing we do with words is that we speak languages, our native tongue(s), and second, third, and so on languages. As the adage goes: without grammar, you speak incorrectly, without words, you do not speak.

Learning new languages, and maintaining and improving those of which I already have some knowledge has been my hobby of sorts. Hence the question that friends and colleagues often ask of me, namely, how many languages do I speak. I always respond with a counter-question, "Could you define what does it entail to speak a language for you?" Indeed, speaking a language can mean anything from being able to exchange pleasantries, introduce oneself, and haggle at the bazar, all the way to being able to deliver a lecture in philosophy or theoretical physics (Figure 22.1).

One thing is certain; climbing up the scale of command in any foreign language takes time. At the University of Sarajevo, Yugoslavia (now Bosnia-Herzegovina), where I worked many years ago, there was a professor by the name of Rikard Kuzmić, who spoke many languages. When asked how he was able to learn all of them, he readily responded, "With my behind. I have sat down and learned them." His laconic response has been confirmed in massive and longitudinal studies at Defense Language Institute, the main language-learning facility of the US Department of Defense. Time on the task is the single best predictor of success in language learning.

For quite some time now, governmental, academic, and corporate venues of language learning have used proficiency scales to assess the proficiency levels of language learners. The scale used in the US government is the ILR (Interagency Language Roundtable) Scale, and it goes from 0 (no knowledge at all) to 5 (highly educated native speakers; most native speakers will score a 3 or 4). The scale used in US academia is the ACTFL (American Council on the Teaching of Foreign Languages), which has the following levels: Novice,

How Many Languages Do You Speak?   139

Figure 22.1 A promo T-shirt of the author's School of International Letters and Cultures (photo by the author)

Intermediate, Advanced, Superior, and Distinguished. The EU uses the CEFR (Common European Framework of Reference for Languages), with levels (from the weakest to the strongest) A1, A2, B1, B2, C1, and C2. Speaking is not the only skill evaluated on these scales. Writing, reading, and listening ability are also assessed. In recent years, intercultural competence was added, as well as two other skills: translation and interpretation. Also, there is a tendency to talk about categories such as interpersonal communication, and presentative and interpretive skills.

Not every language is equally difficult. The closer it is to the learner's first language, the easier it will be to acquire. In the aforementioned Defense Language Institute, longitudinal research has identified four language difficulty categories (LDC) for learners whose first language is English. The easiest, LDC I, encompasses languages such as Spanish, Italian, and Portuguese. German and Indonesian exemplify LCD II. LDC III languages are Russian, Polish, Hindustani, Thai, Hebrew, and many others. The most difficult languages are Chinese, Japanese, Korean, and all varieties of Arabic (Figure 22.2).

Figure 22.2 Hard at language learning (Ian Nolan/Getty Images)

As mentioned, having a certain level of command in a foreign language entails familiarity with a certain number of words. In Mandarin Chinese, one would also need to remember characters, as if attaching a separate picture to words, or more commonly their parts. This is why the study of Chinese is so difficult for all those who do not use these characters in their own language. The Chinese government puts the level of basic literacy at 2,000 characters, which then enables the command of many more words, as many of them are combinations of two or more characters that are also encountered in other words.

American proficiency scales are rather holistic. They describe levels of proficiency in terms of the things one is able to achieve. The CEFR guidelines explain the details of the language machinery. One estimate for the number of words one needs to command in order to be able to understand at each proficiency level defined by this scale is as follows:

A1: Can understand and use familiar everyday expressions and very basic phrases aimed at the satisfaction of needs of a concrete type – 500 words,

A2: Can understand sentences and frequently used expressions related to areas of most immediate relevance (e.g., very basic personal and family information, shopping, local geography, employment) – 1,000 words,

B1: Can understand the main points of clear standard input on familiar matters regularly encountered in work, school, leisure, etc. – 2,000 words,

B2: Can understand the main ideas of complex text on both concrete and abstract topics, including technical discussions in his/her field of specialization – 4,000 words,

C1: Can understand a wide range of demanding, longer texts, and recognize implicit meaning – 8,000 words,

C2: Can understand with ease virtually everything heard or read – 16,000 words. Of course, there are other estimates, and the question is what a word is.

Which words we need to know varies greatly from person to person. This is particularly true about lower proficiency levels. Where we live, what family members we have, and what we do for a living all influence the words we need to be able to speak about ourselves.

The speed with which we acquire a new language also exhibits individual variation. Some people have a higher language learning aptitude. The aforementioned Defense Language Institute administers the so-called DLAB (Defense Language Aptitude Battery) to its prospective students to then assign those with high aptitude to the most difficult languages. The fact is that if we speak another foreign language, that too influences the speed with which one progresses. Some estimates are that knowing an unrelated second language reduces the acquisition difficulty of the third language by 30 percent and that the command of a related language can cut that time by as much as 50 percent.

All this being said, there are no magic wands in language learning. The claims that one encounters in the media about lightning quick language learning facilitated by technological advancements are sheer charlatanism. Languages have been, and for the foreseeable future will be, studied with our behinds. We need to sit down and learn them. Time on the task is the single best predictor of success. Sitting down is not to be understood literally, as we are clocking time on the task in all situations in which we are exposed to the language – from literally sitting down and reading to asking for directions when lost in a foreign city (Figure 22.3).

Figure 22.3 No language knowledge can be found in this hat (Sean Gladwell/Getty Images)

23 | *Harmful and Shitty People*

Learning a similar tongue is an express lane of language learning. However, there are some potholes on that road. They are known as false cognates or false friends of the translator (as in French *faux amis de traducteur*). They are words that sound alike in two languages but have completely different meanings. These false cognates make us do unwanted things with words.

There is a story, perhaps apocryphal, about a Yugoslav representative in Moscow, Soviet Union (now Russian Federation), during the 1948 conflict between the two countries. He said the following in one meeting, Знаете, мы маленький народ, но вредный и поносный (*Znaete, my malenkiy narod, no vredniy i ponosniy*). In his native Serbo-Croatian, this sentence would read, *Znate, mi smo malen narod, ali vredan i ponosan*. So, the words are all very similar in these two closely related Slavic languages, yet their meaning is completely different. In Serbo-Croatian, the meaning is 'You know, we are a small nation, but hard-working and proud'. This is what he intended to say. By contrast, the meaning in Russian is 'You know, we are a small nation, but harmful and covered with diarrhea'. That is what his Russian interlocutors understood (Figure 23.1).

Another example, again, possibly apocryphal, of Serbo-Croatian–Russian false cognates was registered in the US military. The increased need for Serbo-Croatian linguists during the war in the former Yugoslavia in the 1990s was met by a course titled Turbo Serbo, where Russian linguists were cross-trained into Serbo-Croatian. One of the commands that they used was *Stoj da pucam!* In Serbo-Croatian, this means 'Stop, so that I can shoot you'. The comic effect comes from the conjunction *da*, which in this context means 'so that' in Serbo-Croatian, and in Russian it means 'or else' (Figure 23.2).

There are such false cognates where the two meanings are polar opposites, as in German *Gift* 'poison' versus English *gift*, or completely unrelated, for example, German *Tag* 'day' versus English *tag*.

Figure 23.1 A monument to Joseph Stalin, the leader of the Soviet Union at that time – collateral damage to false friends (Craig Pershouse/Getty Images)

However, more commonly the two meanings are much closer to each other, as they are connected in some way. French *crayon* is 'pencil', which is a writing implement, as is the English *crayon*. French *demander* is 'ask for' and, when one is *demanding* in English, that is a not-so-nice manner of asking. French *college* is 'high school', which is an institution of learning, as is *college* in English. The Spanish *idioma* is a 'language', and English *idioms* are part of the language system. Sometimes the link is not so obvious, as in Spanish *actualmente* 'currently' and English *actually*. However, at a deeper level what is currently happening is real. It is precisely these false cognates that are related in their meaning that are particularly dangerous, as it is not

Harmful and Shitty People 145

Figure 23.2 Stop so that I can shoot you (by_nicholas/Getty Images)

very clear from the context that something is wrong. Thus, if a French speaker says that their sister goes to college, they may mean 'high school' but their English interlocutor will not notice anything fishy.

It is also very common that the two languages may share some senses, but not all of them. Thus, in the English–Macedonian pair *conductor: кондуктер (kondukter)*, both these languages use this word to refer to the person who controls tickets on public transportation, but Macedonian does not use it for a musical conductor, using *диригент (dirigent)* instead. Similarly, both English *engineer* and Slovene *inženir* refer to a person with a degree in engineering (electrical, mechanical, civil, etc.), but the Slovene word does not refer to a person who operates an engine. They use *strojevodja* for that sense, a word that literally means 'the operator of the engine' (or even more literally, 'leader of the machine').

In my academic career, I have compiled two dictionaries of false cognates. The first involved Polish and Serbo-Croatian, two Slavic languages that have developed from the same source, the Proto-Slavic language. The other was an English–Serbo-Croatian dictionary, where the two languages are not directly related (although they have common Indo-European heritage), but they share the Greco-Roman cultural sphere. The data from these two projects show that in more closely related languages, the main generator of false cognates is the split of the root from the ancestor language. In less related languages, they are mostly generated by new meanings of the words borrowed from the classical Greco-Roman stock. Between Polish and Serbo-Croatian, 91 percent of cases were caused by the Slavic root split (see suggested readings for the sources of these data). For example, *jutro* is 'morning' in Serbo-Croatian and 'tomorrow' in Polish. The link is obvious – tomorrow starts in the morning. To move onto a Slavic–non-Slavic comparison, between English and Serbo-Croatian, Latin roots are responsible for 51 percent of the cases (e.g., *honoraran* 'part-time' versus *honorary*). The other major factors include borrowings from other languages (24 percent, as in Serbo-Croatian *akademija* 'academy, college, commemoration' vs. English *academia*), and the development of new meanings in English words borrowed in Serbo-Croatian (22 percent, as in *spiker*, which means 'announcer' and *speaker*).

False cognates can be found between variants of the same language. For example, the Spanish word *concha* has a number of meanings, principally 'shell'. However, among other senses, the Spanish Royal Academy Dictionary lists one that is found only in Argentina, Bolivia, Chile, Guatemala, Peru, Paraguay, Peru, and Uruguay, namely the obscene term for vagina.

The varieties of English are a rich source of intralingual false cognates. One can find them even in terminologies. Along with the all-English *back-of-the-envelope calculation*, for a rough, informal estimate (as if a calculation made on whatever is in front of us), Americans use *back-of-a-napkin calculation*, while Britons also have *back-of-a-fag-packet*, in which the informal word for cigarettes is certain to raise a few eyebrows in America (Figure 23.3). General language is not

Figure 23.3 Back of an envelope waiting for a calculation (kyoshino/Getty Images)

different: American *suspenders* are *braces* in British English, and British *suspenders* are *garters* in North America. British *pants* are *underwear* in America, and American *pants* are *trousers* in England. German is similar; in Germany, *Fahrausweis* is a riding pass, as on a train, and in Switzerland, it is 'driver's license'.

Yes, false cognates are likely to make us do funny or even stupid things with words. What looks easy on the outside turns out to be hard when we scratch the surface. However, we are equally likely to eventually notice the problematic nature of such words. The process may be long and even painful, but we are learning languages "not because it is easy, but because it is hard," to quote JFK's famous words about space exploration.

PART IV

How Words Are Born

24 | Cars with Tails and Leadfooted Drivers

Americans love their cars, which is quite understandable, given that in most parts of the country large distances make life without a car impossible. Cars are still perceived as draft animals – they are *driven* (just like *oxen*), and they have *heads* and *tails* (as in *headlights* and *taillights*) (Figure 24.1). And this goes on. American highways have *shoulders*, and impatient drivers have *lead feet*.

In naming new technology, or new concepts in general, extending existing words is one way to go. It is also possible to combine existing roots into new words. Germans are the uncontested champions of that discipline. Mark Twain noticed this in his essay titled *The Awful German Language*, citing, for example, *Unabhängigkeitserklärungen* (one word) in German versus *independence declarations* (two words) in English and *Generalstaatsverordnetenversammlungen* 'general assembly of state representatives' and then commenting, *These things are not words, they are alphabetical processions*. An extreme example of this is the recently dropped German law named *Rindfleischetikettierungsüberwachungsaufgabenübertragungsgesetz*: the English equivalent is *law for the delegation of monitoring beef labeling*. This law, the name of which was a 63-letter word, was introduced in 1999 in the German state of Mecklenburg–West Pomerania. It was subsequently abandoned in the process of unifying the EU legislation in this field. Right now, the longest German word is for minimum-coverage car insurance, *Kraftfahrzeughaftpflichtversicherung* lit. 'obligatory insurance of a motor vehicle'.

A well-known case in which new technology is named using a combination of metaphors and word formation is the WWII Navajo Code Talkers Dictionary, where airplane carrier was TSIDI-MOFFA-YE-HI 'bird carrier', armor was BESH-YE-HA-DA-DI-THE, 'iron protector', and pyrotechnic was COH-NA-CHANH 'fancy fire'. The way in which the words for new technology have developed in Mandarin Chinese is very similar. For example, computer is 'electronic brain': 电脑 (*diàn nǎo*).

151

Figure 24.1 Lights are lit, but the head and the tail are in the dark (Michael Duva/Getty Images)

The first sign represents electricity; one can see that it looks like a plug. The second sign stands for the brain. The term electronic brain has had a career in English, spiking in usage in the early 1960s to then be generally abandoned. The term for computer in Mandarin Chinese is part of a broader system of terms. TV is thus 电视 (dianshi / diànshì) 'electric watching', a movie is 电影 (dianying / diànyǐng) 'electric shadow', and phone is 电话 (diànhuà) 'electric voice', etc. (Figure 24.2) Many other terms are similar. For example, airport is 飞机场 (fēijīchǎng). The first sign represents flying, the second a machine, and the third is space. So, airports are 'spaces for flying machines'. Mandarin Chinese creates its own terms for everything.

Japanese is different, as speakers often resort to borrowings. Computer is コンピューター (konpyūtā), television テレビ (terebi), and radio ラジオ (rajio) – all direct borrowings from English. The word for computer, which is used even more frequently than konpyūtā is パソコン (pasokon – paso 'personal', and kon 'computer'), a pseudo Anglicism.

Figure 24.2 Electric hands (Yagi Studio/Getty Images)

In naming new technology, languages can differ in in that one language features a full form of a complex lexeme or an idiom while its counterpart has an abbreviated form as its equivalent. For example, colloquial American English uses the designation *cell phone*, and so does Afrikaans (*selfoon*). In contrast to these languages, where a full form is used, there are languages that use an abbreviated form in colloquial use. In Albanian, *celulari* is used (abbreviated from *telefoni celular*), and colloquial Czech uses *mobil* (abbreviated from *mobilní telefon*).

Coming back to American cars, another term that shows how existing realities are projected into naming new concepts is the North American term for side collision. The term is T-bone collision after the T-bone in T-bone steak, a common food item. In many other cultures, even those where beef is consumed, this would not be much of a concept, given that meat on both sides of the bone (a smaller filet mignon and a larger strip steak) is served separately and the bone is discarded in the process of cutting, so regular eaters would never see a T-bone steak (Figure 24.3).

American cars have had *cruise control* and *air conditioning* for a long time – no wonder, given the long distances and unfriendly climate.

Figure 24.3 A T-bone steak (Diane Labombarbe/Getty Images)

The former term is a naval metaphor – your car cruises with the device on and the device controls it (keeps it at a constant speed). The latter is a textile manufacturing term. The initial air conditioners regulated the amount of moisture in the air in the aforementioned process. In many continental European cultures these two devices started to be used much later and with them the need to name them. Many languages, such as German and Polish, have created a new word for cruise control by combining a Latin root *tempo* 'tempo' and a Greek-based αυτοματον, *automaton* (which comes from αυτοματος, *automatos* 'acting of itself'), so the term is *Tempomat* in German and *tempomat* in Polish. In some languages, such as in Danish *Fartpilot* 'trip pilot', the device is personified. Moving on to the second term, air conditioning, Germans name it *Klimaanlage* 'climate system', which is then literally calqued into *klima uređaj*, or just *klima* 'climate' in Serbo-Croatian, so speakers have a climate of their choice in cars. French *climatisation* and Slovak *klimatizácia* are very similar. Some languages have simply translated the English term 'air conditioning' as in Russian кондиционирование воздуха *(konditsionirovanie vozdooha)*, Danish and Swedish *Lutkonditionering*, etc.

In this brisk review of terms for new technologies, the three main mechanisms of their creation can be seen: extending existing meanings, combining existing roots into new words, and borrowing a word from another language (either the word itself or its translation). One can also see the diversity of these terms and how the realities of the culture in question shape the naming process, pointing yet again to unbreakable ties of language and culture. The topic of how the new words and their meanings emerge was briefly discussed here. The discussion will continue with a closer look into individual cases of naming new concepts.

25 | *Monkey, Dog, Worm, Snail, i.e., "Crazy A"*

The at sign (@) is an interesting case of how names of new concepts (or concepts that have suddenly been released from relative obscurity) project mental images, which differ between languages. One should say that they were actually different in the mental lexicons of those who have coined the term or helped popularize it. This sign lived in the secluded world of ledgers, meaning 'at the rate of'. It is first attested in a mid-fifteenth century Bulgarian chronicle as the initial of the word *amen* (амин, *amin* in Bulgarian). It is later found in Spanish and Portuguese *arroba* (the amount a donkey could carry), which was twenty-five pounds in Spain and thirty-two pounds in Portugal. It then lived in the obscure world of accounting and invoicing for many years. Enter e-mail, and the use and familiarity of the @ sign exploded (Figure 25.1).

In English, the word *at* came first and the sign simply left the obscurity of ledgers for the bright world of e-mail addresses. In many other languages that would not make sense, as the word for 'at' does not begin with an *a*. The continuation of accounting would not make sense for an additional reason. In many languages, it was pronounced simply as an *a*, which is unrelated to 'at'. Speakers of these languages (most likely computer nerds who were the only ones with e-mail addresses in those early days) needed to come up with names for this suddenly popularized concept.

One possibility that was utilized in various languages is borrowing from English. Turkish has *et* (that is how the pronunciation of English *at* is perceived by Turks) and Georgian ეტ -ი (et-i) (-i is the nominative case suffix). Another common way of creating new words for the *at* sign is resorting to metaphors. There is a whole menagerie of global names for the @ sign.

Monkey or small monkey is found in Polish *małpa* 'monkey' and German *Äffchen* 'small monkey' (which was also borrowed by Slovenes as *afna*). Russians call it a dog (собака, *sobaka*) and

Monkey, Dog, Worm, Snail, i.e., "Crazy A"

Figure 25.1 The @ seal (Laurent Hammels/Getty Images)

Belarussians use snail *(сьлімак, slimak)*. It is small mouse in Mandarin Chinese (小老鼠, *xiǎo lǎoshǔ*), worm in Hungarian (*kukac*), and duckling in Modern Greek (παπάκι, *papaki*).

Sometimes only part of an animal is used. Trunk (as in elephant trunk) is used in Danish (*snabel-a*'trumpet a'), cat's tail in Finnish (*kissanhäntä*), and monkey tail in Afrikaans (*aapstert*) and Dutch (*apestaart*). In some languages, the name is based on culinary products. It is баница (*banitsa*) in Bulgarian (which is a roll of cheese-stuffed filo dough pastry, a staple of Bulgarian cuisine). Hebrew speakers call it a שטרודל (*strudel*), and Slovaks use rollmops (*zaviná*č).

Serbo-Croatian is an interesting case. One can use et, borrowed from English, but there is also the expression *majmunsko a* 'monkey a', and a third option; one can call it *ludo a* 'crazy a'. Using the concept of craziness in the name of the at sign is very similar to the practice of cattle branding in the American Southwest. The brand for a *P* ranch was a regular P, a *crazy P* ranch would have an upside-down P, and *lazy P* is a P that lies on its back. It is remarkable how the two languages, a century apart and miles away from each other, use very similar metaphors. This connection is certainly not all hat and no

Figure 25.2 All hat and no cowboy (photo by the author)

cowboy: it is rooted in the universal human cognitive capacities of creating mental images with words (Figure 25.2).

In general, the democratization of computing was a worldwide laboratory of lexical creation. English resorted either to word formation, as in *computer* = *comput(e)* + *-er*, or semantic extension, as in *printer*, initially typesetter, a person, and this extends to the device that performs similar tasks. Other languages have these two options plus an easy one – borrowing from English. Some languages have two options for many terms. In Serbo-Croatian, one can say *kompjuter* or *kompjutor* (borrowed from the English *computer*), but *računar* or *računalo* can also be used (derived from the verb *računati* 'to count, to calculate'). The former set of terms is more colloquial, and the latter more bookish, but generally, all of them have been in use for many years now. Even neighboring and closely related languages have taken different paths in creating their computing terminology. Among Slavic

Monkey, Dog, Worm, Snail, i.e., "Crazy A" 159

Figure 25.3 A computer at the time when its name became relevant (Weerayut Renmai/EyeEm/Getty Images)

languages, Slovene uses *računalnik* (from the verb *računati* 'to count, to calculate') like Czech, which has *počítač* (from the verb *počítat* 'to count, to calculate'), although *komp* or *kompl* is used colloquially (back-clipped from the English *computer*, as the colloquial English *puter* is front-clipped). Further to the north, Polish uses *komputer* and Russian компьютер (*kompyooter*), both of which are borrowings from English (Figure 25.3).

An interesting case is the Croatian variant of Serbo-Croatian (for more about variants of Serbo-Croatian, see Chapter 37). An established tradition of replacing borrowed words with those of Slavic origin has prompted the quest for replacements for hardware and software. These English terms were calqued (directly translated), so *otvrđe* and *omečje* were proposed, containing the words *tvrd* 'hard' and *mek* 'soft', respectively. However, speakers have never accepted these new terms, and borrowings from English, *hardver* 'hardware' and *softver* 'software', are used to this day. The fate of these two terms was shared with various other proposals, only a few of which are broadly used in today's Croatian. This story shows a very important aspect of the birth of words. There are always individuals, members of linguistic elites or those that are simply connected to the new concept in some way, who give an initial impulse for the birth of a word. For the word to live, this is not enough. If speakers do not accept it, the word is stillborn.

The lexicon of any language is on the one hand a result of its spontaneous development, or, from another angle, of spontaneous changes in the habits of its speakers. On the other hand, and especially in the field of newly introduced concepts that need to be named, it is a result of negotiations between linguistic elites and the majority of speakers. There is a well-known Latin adage *Non Caesar supra grammaticos*. 'The emperor is not above the grammarians', emphasizing that political authorities should not interfere in issues of language. One should also add that grammarians are not above speakers of their language.

26 | Rovers and Ski-Rolls

Rovers, as in Land Rovers and Range Rovers, are known to be rather pricy vehicles. However, in Poland they can be had for a very reasonable sum of money. The word for bicycle in Polish is *rower*, derived from the British company Rover, which produced and distributed them in Poland in the early twentieth century. The birth of the bicycle generated many interesting words in various languages. The English *bicycle* is a Latin borrowing, meaning 'two circles', that is, 'two wheels'. It is found in numerous other languages, Turkish *bisiklet*, Italian *bicicletta*, Occitan, Catalan, Portuguese, and Spanish *bicicleta* (colloquially abbreviated to *bici* in Spanish), Basque *bizikleta*, Tagalog and Ilocano *bisikleta*, Albanian *biçikleta*, Esperanto *biciklo*, Swahili *baisikeli*, and many others (Figure 26.1).

The French *vélocipède* (from the Latin words *velox* 'rapid' and *pes* 'foot', so 'rapid foot') has also had a global career. It was borrowed in Russian велосипед (*velosipet*) and then from Russian into various other languages of the former Soviet Union, among others, Georgian ველოსიპედი (*velosipedi*), Bashkir, Chuvash, Kazakh, Tatar *velosiped*, and Yakut *belisipiet*. There are also other languages that have adopted the French word, such as the Bulgarian and Macedonian велосипед (*velosipet*).

Then there are languages where domestic lexical means were mobilized in naming bicycles. Japanese call it 自転車, *jitensha* 'self-rolling vehicle'. The term was coined in the Meji era (1868–1912), when bicycles came to the country on a broader wave of modernization. Mandarin Chinese has 自行车, *zìxíngchē* 'by oneself land vehicle'. Modern Greek uses ποδήλατο (*podilato*) 'foot move'.

Using the local word for the wheel seems to be exceptionally popular in many languages. Vietnamese has *xe đạp* (*xe* – 'wheeled vehicle', *đạp* – 'pedal'). German has *Fahrrad* 'riding, travelling wheel', colloquially *Rad* 'wheel'. It is precisely that the same in Czech (*jízdní kolo*, shorter *kolo*). Many other languages follow suit. Bicycle is named *kolo*

Figure 26.1 A modern "woodcycle" (photo by Mladen Šašić)

'wheel' in Slovenian. Colloquial Macedonian borrowed the Serbo-Croatian word for wheel *точак* (*tochak*), which is how it refers to the bicycle. Estonian names it *jalgratas* 'foot wheel'. The Hungarian word for bicycle is *kerékpár* 'a pair of wheels'. Lithuanians name it *dviratis* 'two wheels'. The latter two are calques, that is, literal translations of the word bicycle. Obviously, many languages have several options, such as ביציקל (*bitsikl*), ביציקלעט (*bitsiklet*), וועלאָסיפעד (*velosiped*), and ראָווער (*rover*) in Yiddish.

The bicycle was introduced a long time ago. More recently, we have witnessed the introduction of various other self-propelled means of locomotion, from scooters to roller blades. The English word for scooter, kick or push scooter, more recently electric scooter, has had a global career (Figure 26.2). The word was borrowed in Japanese スクーター (*sukūtā*), Korean 스쿠터 (*seukuteo*), Malay *skuter*, Czech *skútr*, Catalan *escúter*, German *Scoooter*, and Danish, Dutch, French, Italian, Spanish, and Norwegian *scooter*. These borrowings generally refer to motorized scooters. In some languages, such as Japanese, the word can also be used for the kick scooter, although there is a more

Figure 26.2 Waiting to scoot away (Brian Bumby/Getty Images)

precise term, キックスケーター *kikkusukētā*. For kick scooter, Dutch has borrowed the English word, but not scooter. One Dutch term for this means of locomotion is *step*. Russians name it самокат (*samokat*) 'self-ride'. Before the French borrowing велосипед (*velosipet*) prevailed in Russian, *samokat* was the term for bicycle. Speakers of Polish name it *hulajnoga* 'carousing foot'.

The French word *trottinette* comes from the verb *trotter* 'to trot, to amble'. It is also possible to say *patinette* in French, which comes from the verb *patiner* 'to skate'. The first French word was borrowed by Serbo-Croatian and Macedonian speakers as тротинет (*trotinet*), Bulgarian тротинетка (*trotinetka*), Dutch *trottinette*, etc. The second is to be found as *patinete* in Galician, Portuguese, and Spanish. Another word used in Serbo-Croatian is *romobil*, from *rolati* 'roll' and *(auto)mobil* '(auto)mobile'. Hungarian is similar; it simply uses *roller*. Italian has *monopattino* 'one skate'. It is 'sliding land vehicle' (滑板車, *huábǎnchē*) in Mandarin Chinese. Swedes say *sparkcykel* 'kick cycle'. In Iceland, it is *hlaupahjól* 'running wheel'.

The history of words for skating gear in English is interesting to show how new concepts are formed by adding modifiers to words for known entities. *Skates* were first. Once the variety with wheels in the

Figure 26.3 Roller skaters rocking and rolling (Flashpop/Getty Images)

four corners of the base was introduced, they were named *roller skates* (Figure 26.3). Once the four wheels were aligned, the term *inline skates* was born. A similar process can be seen in the life of the construction concept *board* (as in 'plank'), which moved into the sphere of recreation to live happily on in *surfboards, bodyboards, skateboards*, and *snowboards*.

Naming of all these new nonmotorized means of locomotion shows an interesting patchwork of finding solutions in lexical borrowing, semantic extensions, and recombination of lexical material. New concepts trigger the need for naming, and the community of speakers readily responds using naming mechanisms at their disposal. It is often so that words for new concepts start as the act of one person (e.g., a journalist that reports about a new vehicle). It is then diffused in the speech community and eventually either accepted or displaced by an alternative word.

27 | *Extra Crispy Soccer Players*

Athletic terms were another real-life laboratory of the emergence of new words. They also include numerous examples of the usage of metaphors based on athletic terms in other spheres of life, such as politics, economics, etc. The most popular sports today are relatively new, mostly a little more than one hundred years old. One such term in Polish, the term for offside in soccer (aka association football), lent the title to this chapter. The term is namely, *na spalonym*, literally 'on the burnt'. The word for offside itself is *spalony* 'burnt'. In the neighboring and related Russian and Ukrainian, the term is surprisingly literal and long. It is положение вне игры (*polozhenie vnye igri*) in Russian and положення поза грою (*polozhennya poza groyoo*) in Ukrainian, both meaning 'position outside of the game'. Similarly dry are Slovenes, who name it *prepovedani položaj* 'forbidden position'. Bulgarians are much more colorful, as they say засада (*zasada*) 'ambush'. In the Croatian variant of Serbo-Croatian, the term is *zaleđe* 'behind-the-back-ness'. Macedonians have simply borrowed the English word; the term is офсајд (*ofsayd*), which is an additional option in other Slavic languages too. All these are Slavic languages that have developed from the same source, the Proto-Slavic language that disintegrated between the second and fourth centuries AD Centuries later, when soccer was introduced, they had been separate languages for a long time, so the repertoire of terms for offside shows the same level of diversity in naming that exists between unrelated languages.

Soccer seems to be the ultimate modern surrogate for medieval battles. There are two clearly defined sides of the battlefield, offensive operations and defensive maneuvers. It is no wonder that there is a position named *striker* in English or *Stürmer* 'stormtrooper' in German. Russians name it бомбардир (*bombardir*) 'bombardier', drawing on more recent wars. There are even executions on the battle field in some languages. For example, the expression for the penalty kick in Serbo-Croatian is *najstroža kazna* 'capital punishment',

Figure 27.1 Capital punishment with no life lost (Image Source/Getty Images)

literally, 'the most rigorous punishment', the same phrase that is used for executions (Figure 27.1). War references in soccer are found even in the names of the stands from which the fans watch games. Thus, the Second Boer War Battle of Spion Kop in 1900 gave its name to stands at various English stadiums, most famously to the (Spion) Kop at Anfield in Liverpool. Spion Kop was a steep hill where the aforementioned battle took place. Steep spectator stands resembled the hill in South Africa, which was very much in the public eye because of the battle His Majesty's armed forces fought.

Soccer is all about battles and wars between two well-defined sides. It is then no wonder that soccer fans worldwide find baseball hopelessly boring. The action takes place around a diamond and in its middle without sides having a clear territory of their own.

Chess, a much older game, is another surrogate of a medieval battle, much less violent than soccer, at least in its physical aspect (Figure 27.2). The terms used themselves are still very violent. English is benign, as one only takes the opponent's chess piece. Polish speakers are somewhat more violent, as they 'beat the chess piece down'. The verb is *zbić* (*z* – out of, *bić* – beat, strike). This is still as nothing compared to Serbo-Croatian, where the verb is *jesti* 'to eat'.

Extra Crispy Soccer Players 167

Figure 27.2 The Conquistador side of a Brazilian chess set (photo by the author)

Chess pieces themselves are less violent but characterized by a similar degree of variation (Figure 27.3). Take the *queen*. Many languages name the piece in that way. It is *reina* in Spanish, *kraljica* in Slovene and Serbo-Croatian, *koroleva* in Ukrainian, βασίλισσα (*vasilissa*) in Greek, etc. Many more languages, including some of the aforementioned ones, use the word for 'dame'. It is *dama* in Portuguese, *dame* in French, *Dame* in German, дама (*dama*) in Macedonian, *dáma* in Czech and Slovak, and *damo* in Esperanto. As mentioned, many languages use 'queen' and 'dame' interchangeably, for example, Spanish *reina* and *dama*, Finnish *kuningatar* and *daami*, and Serbo-Croatian *kraljica* and *dama*. There are also some outlier languages. In Polish, this chess piece is known as *hetman*, which was the word for the second-highest military commander rank in the fifteenth- to eighteenth-century Polish and Lithuanian Commonwealth. Turks name it *vezir* 'vizier' after a viceroy or high government minister. It is *vezér* 'leader' in Hungarian. The Russian term ферзь (*fers*) is a borrowing from Persian فرز (*ferz*), meaning 'vizier' or 'field commander'.

Figure 27.3 The Indigenous side of a Brazilian chess set (photo by the author)

In naming the *rook*, languages mostly name it a 'tower'. This is found in German *Turm*, French *tour*, Italian *torre*, Greek πύργος (*pirgos*), Czech *věž*, Slovak *veža*, and Polish *wieża*. However, there are different solutions: Hungarian *bástya* means bastion, rampart, and Turkish *kale* means 'fortress', and it is *top* 'cannon' in Slovene and Serbo-Croatian. All these are connected – there are towers on bastions and fortresses and cannons in them. Russian ладья (*ladya*) 'boat' is somewhat more distant.

The *bishop* is much more diversified and the English naming style for it is rather rare; one can find it, for example, in Icelandic *biskup*. The term 'runner' is much more widespread. The term is *Läufer* in German, *goniec* in Polish, *loper* in Dutch, etc. Czech uses *střelec* 'shooter', Serbo-Croatian names it *lovac* 'hunter'. The most curious names are found in Russian and Ukrainian слон (*slon*), and Turkish *fil*, which all mean 'elephant'.

English *knight* is also rather lonely, as is Hungarian *huszár* 'hussar'. Most commonly, this chess piece is known as 'horse', 'rider', or 'springer'. The first naming convention is found in Russian конь (*kon*), Catalan *cavall*, and Italian *cavallo*. The second can be seen in Latin *eques*, French *cavalier*, Czech *jezdec*, and Slovak *jazdec*. Finally, German has *Springer*, Norwegian *springer*, Polish *skoczek*, and Serbo-Croatian *skakač*, all meaning 'springer'.

King is king with almost no exceptions. *Pawn* is almost universally named a 'foot soldier, a pedestrian'. This interesting case shows how all languages maintain connection between medieval battles and the game of chess, but the exact way that this is done varies from language to language.

Athletic terminology reflects phenomena from the cultural history of its society. However, this is not a one-way street. Some terms leave the realm of sports to get a new life in their respective societies. A good example is American English, and its most beloved sport, baseball. In business, one *pitches* ideas or makes a *pitch*. A strange idea comes *out of left field*. Something successful is *hit way out of the park*. Achieving success is also *hitting a homerun*. A rough estimate produces *a ballpark figure*. *Strike one* and *strike two* are warnings that you did something wrong. *First*, *second*, *third base*, and *homerun* have each a distinct meaning in love affairs. Other sports also have similar terms, as in *slam dunk* from basketball and *Monday morning quarterback* from football.

The case of athletic terminology shows how words are born. It also shows how they are reborn, returning to other realms of social life. The metaphor of a sport competition as a battle has populated athletic terminology with numerous words initially used for battles in bygone times. The metaphors of business, political, and other competitions as sports have brought many concepts back into the non-athletic sphere. Overall, metaphor seems to be pivotal in linking the linguistic and nonlinguistic worlds.

28 | Chinglish and Eurenglish

One of the things we do with words is communicate with those who do not share our native tongue. In such situations, one would normally resort to a lingua franca, a third language that serves as a bridge between speakers of two languages. Many languages have played and still play that role regionally: Mandarin Chinese, Arabic, Russian, Spanish, Portuguese, and French. Globally, the role of English today is akin to that of Latin in the past (with the only difference that at the time of Latin, classic and medieval, the known world was much smaller). Now, English is used as the principal language of global communication.

On one hand, the choice of English is a function of colonialism and the wide global spread of the British Empire. On the other hand, it is a result of US global political, economic, military, and popular cultural influence since WWII. A language that acts as a lingua franca becomes diversified over time. This has been happening with English, hence the superficially confusing term *World Englishes*, coined by the Indian-American linguist Braj Kachru, with English in plural still disliked by spell-checkers. Kachru advanced a theory of three circles of English. The inner circle is composed of those countries one normally associates with English speakers: United States, United Kingdom, Australia, New Zealand, Canada, etc. The outer circle encompasses countries where other languages are native, but English plays or played the role of an official language. These are countries such as India, Pakistan, Bangladesh, Nigeria, Kenya, etc. Many words from this circle, such as *karma* from Sanskrit and *safari* from Swahili, have entered English and then many other languages around the world. Finally, there is an expanding circle of English, where English does not have a history of official use, but has been widely used as a second language. This circle encompasses most of Europe, Japan, China, Russia, and today almost the entire globe.

Chinglish and Eurenglish

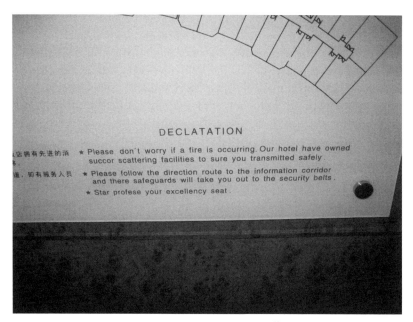

Figure 28.1 Chinglish gone wild (photo by Mladen Šašić)

The varieties of English in the aforementioned outer circle, such as Chinglish and Eurenglish, are developing their own features, grammatical and lexical (Figure 28.1). My son, who holds dual bachelor's degrees in global studies and information technologies, did his internship in an international organization in Belgrade, Serbia, several years ago. Among other things, he was charged with correcting texts in English written by local employees of the organization. Pointing out how difficult his work was, he made the following comment about these Serbenglish texts, "Words are in English, but sentences are in Serbian."

Indeed, various grammatical features are very prominent in the expanding-circle varieties of English. However, new words have been born in these varieties.

Jeremy Gardner, a senior EU translator and a student of Eurenglish, has published a dictionary of words and phrases, in which he writes the following, "Like 'foresee', 'in the frame of', meaning 'in connection with', 'in the context of' or 'within the scope of' corresponds literally to an expression found in a number of other languages (Italian '*nel quadro di*', German '*im Rahmen von*', French '*dans le cadre de*' etc.). Unfortunately, this expression does not exist in English." At another place in the dictionary, he has the following entry, *hierarchical superior*, meaning 'boss', 'manager', 'director', etc. in Eurenglish. The entry is equipped with the following explanation, "In English, this term is used almost exclusively in the ecclesiastical context, and even 'hierarchy' and 'hierarchical' may be seen as difficult words by many readers."

There are many other books of this kind (see suggested readings for bibliographic information). Fletcher and Hawkins' book, titled *Denglish for Better Knowers*, contains a nonexistent English calque (direct translation) of the German expression *Besserwisser* 'better knower'. Zoya Proshina addresses Rusenglish. In it, she finds Russian culture-bound words, such as *дача* (*dacha*) 'second home' and *квас* (*kvas*) 'fermented bread drink', and also calques (direct translations) from Russian, such as *heroine mother*, for mother with many children, *social work* to mean 'volunteering', and new coinages, such as *shop-tour* 'shopping trip abroad', etc. Rusenglish was also prominently featured in a lovely book titled *Everything Is Illuminated: A Novel* by Jonathan Safran Foer (Figure 28.2). Alex Perchov, one of the two lead characters in the book, keeps using an imaginary English verb *to bile* following the Russian pattern *жёлч* (*zholch*) 'bile': *жёлчить* (*zholchit*) 'to gall, to irritate, literally, 'to bile'.

Scholars have written about expanding-circle Englishes in Japan, Korea, East and West Africa, etc. However, Chinglish remains the most prominent variety of these Englishes. Not only does it command the interest of scholars but it has an extremely high degree of recognition in the general population. Its notoriety in the latter group is simply unparalleled and it has been generating myriad memes and web pages on this subject. Many of them are simply boring and tasteless, as they focus on simple blunders with sexual or excretion references. However, in the sea of dullness, there are some islands of wit. A 2010 *New York Times* article titled "Shanghai Is Trying to Untangle the Mangled English of Chinglish" mentions various trivial cases, such as naming extra-large clothing sizes *fatso*, and using words such as *urine district* for public toilets. Then there are more subtle points. The following Chinese equivalents of *Keep off the grass* were mentioned, *The little*

Chinglish and Eurenglish 173

Figure 28.2 The Motherland Calls – a monument in Volgograd, formerly Stalingrad, Russia (Victoria Sedykh/Getty Images)

grass is sleeping: Please don't disturb it or *Don't hurt me: I am afraid of pain*. Examples like this show how cultural patterns of societies in the expanding circle are being incorporated into respective varieties of World Englishes.

The birth of new words in Eurenglish, Chinglish, and other World Englishes seems to justify the following verse from Leonard Cohen's *Anthem*, "there is a crack in everything, that's how the light gets in." (Figure 28.3) World Englishes are indeed a crack in the global domination of English. Obviously, the ultimate bulwark that protects linguistic and hence cultural diversity is the use of languages other than English.

Figure 28.3 Cohen's crack (Slavi Korchev/EyeEm/Getty Images)

29 Comrade, Sir

An interesting case of the birth and eventual death of words and forms to address other people was recorded in the former Eastern Europe and some other countries that participated in the communist experiment. When comrades took over, they enforced their title on the general population. The level of acceptance varied during different times and from country to country (Figure 29.1).

The previous history of equivalents of the word *comrade* was similar to that of English. The English word comes from the French word *camerade*, which in turn comes from Spanish *camarada* 'chamberful', that is, 'chamber fellow', 'chamber mate', 'chum', which is the original meaning of the English borrowing, which then evolved into 'fellow soldier' (as they typically shared chambers), hence *comrade-in-arms*. This then extended into those who fight the common fight, especially socialists and communists, as a prefix to the name. While the original 'chum' meaning was attested in the late sixteenth century, the prefix usage only appeared three centuries later.

As mentioned, languages of former communist societies used the word *comrade* in this way, with the difference that, on the establishment of communism, it became a generally used prefix to first, last, or full names. Another difference was the etymology of the word for *comrade*. German is particularly interesting in this regard. The term is *Genosse*, as in *Genosse Honecker* 'Comrade Honecker', in the title of the long-serving leader of the German Democratic Republic. The noun comes from the verb *genießen* 'to enjoy'. So, comrade is the one with whom one enjoys something. So, in German, communist convictions were not just shared but also enjoyed. After all, this ideology is a German invention. Russians were first to practically implement this lofty German idea, so the etymology of their term is more pedestrian. The Russian communist title *товарищ* (*tovarishch*), comes from Turkic languages, and it includes the words *tovar* 'property, goods,

Figure 29.1 A comrade quartet (Dina Alfasi/EyeAm/Getty Images)

cattle' and *esh* 'exhange, swap'. Initially, this word was used for merchants who traded in similar goods. It then expanded to those who were pursuing similar political goals.

As communism was exported to other Slavic countries, the Russian word for 'comrade' enjoyed a limited international career. It was adopted in Slovene (*tovariš*), Ukrainian (*товариш*, *tovarish*), and Polish (*towarzysz*). Other Slavic and some non-Slavic languages went with the word for 'friend', as in Serbo-Croatian *drug*, Macedonian and Bulgarian *другар* (*drugar*), and Albanian *shok*. Some went with the similar 'fellow friend', as in Czech *soudruh* and Slovak *súdruh*. Asian communists were more creative; the title in Chinese is 同志, *tóngzhì* 'those of the same will', which was then borrowed in Vietnamese as *đồng chí*. The Cuban Spanish *compañero* 'companion' is similar to the English term. It ultimately comes from Latin, and its deeper origin reads, 'fellow bread eater'. So, sharing bread rather than sharing chambers, both of which were done by fellow soldiers. Hungarian *elvtárs* (*elv* 'principles' *társ* 'companion') seems to merge the Chinese and Cuban ways of creating this name prefix.

Figure 29.2 This sir is present but nowhere to be seen (Sean Gladwell/Getty Images)

These name prefixes were not the only change introduced with the advent of communism. There were some attempts to change the form of address more broadly. Polish was an interesting case in this regard. The pre- and post-communist name prefix for males is *pan*, as it also is in Lower Sorbian and, in the form *pán*, in Czech and Slovak. In Polish it also means 'gentleman, lord, master'. It is 'mister' and 'sir' in one word (in the latter usage it has inflectional endings, as in *proszę pana* 'excuse me, sir' (Figure 29.2). Moreover, this word is used in any formal form of address. So, to say 'Would you like to have something to drink, sir?' one needs to say *Czy pan czegoś się napije?* literally, 'Is sir going to drink something?' In other words, the person is addressed in the third person form ('he' or 'she' rather than 'you').

This is how it is normally done in Poland. When communist rule was established, there were attempts to replace this traditional addressing formula with the Russian way: *wy* in Polish, after Russian *вы* (*vi*), which is the same in French, that is, a person is formally addressed by the plural you, similar to *y'all* or *yous*, but part of the standard language rather than dialectic. This address formula renders the aforementioned sentence 'Would you like to have something to drink, sir?' as *Czy napijecie się czegoś?* literally, 'Are y'all going to drink something?' That really did not fly, even during the time of hardcore communism, except in the military and police force. Once communism was abandoned in 1989, this peculiar usage disappeared even from these organizations. In a similar manner, other languages reverted to their pre-communist form of address, for example, *господин* (*gospodin*) 'mister, sir' in Bulgarian, Macedonian, and Serbo-Croatian.

The military is the last current bastion where Russian *товарищ* (*tovarishch*) lives. It is still used in the Belarussian and Russian Armed Forces. In Ukraine, its use was replaced with *пан* (*pan*) in 2018. Russians actually do not have an ideologically neutral equivalent for *товарищ* (*tovarishch*). Once it was abandoned, they switched from using *tovarishch* along with the last name, to the first name and the patronymic (middle name derived from one's father's name) without any name prefix. So, while he was still in the KGB, the main civilian intelligence agency in the Soviet Union, the current Russian president was addressed as *товарищ Путин* (*tovarishch Putin*). Once Communism collapsed and he transferred to public administration, he was addressed by *Владимир Владимирович* (*Vladimir Vladimirovich*) '*Vladimir* – his first name, *Vladimirovich* - the son of *Vladimir* – his father's name'.

Words are born, then they die, and then they are reborn. Some language-specific forms of using name prefixes have not changed no matter their ideological background. Polish is quite interesting in this regard. It has a varied system of name prefixes for various professions. *Pan* is a general 'Mr.' and *Panie* a general 'Sir!'. Then there are specific titles for various professions. A priest is *ksiądz*, not *pan*. Professor is *profesor*. Dean of any kind is *dziekan*. Attorney at law is *mecenas*, literally, 'benefactor'. Every journalist is *redaktor* 'editor'. While working at a university in Poland a German colleague visited. In German, a university dean is *Dekan*, and associate and assistant deans are *Prodekan* (the prefix *Pro-* comes from Latin and it means 'for, on behalf of'). In official titles, this distinction is maintained in Polish

Figure 29.3 A dean (or perhaps an associate dean) hard at work (andresr/ Getty Images)

(*dziekan* versus *prodziekan*). However, when addressing people, Poles "elevate" the real title (just as all journalists are "promoted" to editors) and call everybody a dean (*dziekan*) (Figure 29.3). My German colleague was most confused when he was introduced to three "deans" of the same school.

Terms of address and titles, that is, name prefixes, are one of the fields where doing things with words has visible social consequences. These linguistic elements reflect the configurations of power in society and testify to social relations. These relations change with the flow of time, either abruptly or gradually, which is then reflected in the language.

30 Beer and Whiskey Mighty Risky

The English adage in the title continues as follows, *beer and wine, mighty fine*. This piece of advice is rather indiscriminate compared to the following German saying, *Bier nach Wein trinkt nur Schwein, Wein nach Bier das rat ich dir*. 'Only a pig would drink beer after wine; wine after beer, that is something I can recommend to you.' There are also several other variations of this German saying. The Dutch (who brought gin, aka protestant courage, to England, which then became associated with Englishness, all gin lanes notwithstanding) have something similar, *Wijn op bier geeft vertier; bier op wijn geeft venijn*. 'Wine on beer gives you pleasure, beer on wine gives you poison.'

Russians are even more specific, as they also prescribe the correct tempo. They say, *Между первой и второй – перерывчик небольшой* (*Mezhdoo pervoy i vtoroy – pererivchik nebolyshoy*) 'between the first and the second (shot of vodka, of course) there is a short pause' (Figure 30.1).

Well, one may argue that the order and the tempo are less relevant. The main thing was discovered by Old Romans, namely that the truth is in wine (*in vino veritas*). When I was a student in Sarajevo, Yugoslavia, now Bosnia and Herzegovina, there was a health-awareness campaign against student drinking. Its slogan went like this, *In vino veritas, u jetri ciroza* 'The truth is in wine, cirrhosis is in your liver'. This was a more elaborate Serbo-Croatian variant of the US highway signs, *Drive hammered, get nailed*, with medical rather than legal consequences being highlighted.

Prototypical drinkers are also different around the world. In English, these are sailors. A well-known sea shanty, aka chantey and chanty, asks what we shall do with one of them. In Serbo-Croatian, these are Russians (*pijan ko Rus* 'dead drunk', i.e., 'as drunk as a Russian'), and in French, the Poles (*saoul comme un Polonais* 'dead drunk', i.e., 'as drunk as a Pole').

Beer and Whiskey Mighty Risky

Figure 30.1 Are they going to heed the Russian voice of reason? (Izabela Habur/Getty Images)

Drinking cultures around the world do not only produce sayings of this kind. They are also home to the birth of new words, and, equally commonly, revival and spread of previously relatively obscure concepts and words for them. Some of the processes were so convoluted that they lend themselves to be described by the following Russian adage, *Тут без бутылки не разберёшься* (*Tut bez bootilki nye razberyoshsa*) 'You cannot figure that out without a bottle.' Needless to say, the bottle in question is filled with vodka.

The art of mixology is responsible for scores of new multiword units, from *White Russian* to *Corpse Reviver*. The very origin of the word *cocktail* is uncertain, despite the fact that everybody will recognize the separate words in its first part (*cock*) and second part (*tail*) (Figure 30.2). One credible theory is that the original meaning was 'non-purebred horse' because their tails were customarily docked. The meaning then extended to the beverage given that a spirit is diluted with something else, as if not "purebred." Cocktails may not be purebred drinks, but their names come with a pedigree of high-shelf inventiveness. Sometimes these names encapsulate a piece of cultural history of the language in question. An example is the German (or, to be

Figure 30.2 An orange-tail cocktail (Jordan Lye/Getty Images)

precise, Bavarian) term *Radler* 'shandy, a 50:50 mixture of beer and lemonade', literally 'cyclist'. The name does not make any sense without knowledge of its origin.

The story goes like this. One Franz Kugler, an early twentieth-century innkeeper in Deisenhofen just outside Munich, created a cycling path from Munich to his establishment, and made a hefty profit from selling beer to thirsty cyclists. On one occasion he was running out of beer, so he decided to go with the mix. That is how *Radlermaas* 'cyclist liter' was born, which was then abbreviated to *Radler*. *Maas* is a standard beer stein in Bavaria amounting to one liter, that is, about two pints (slightly less in imperial pints and a bit more in US pints). It used to be that reputable Bavarian watering holes would never pour less than a *Maas*, except as a *Schnitt* 'cut', the last drink one orders before leaving the pub. Alas, things have changed recently, so one can also order a half *Maas* at any point.

While this cannot be confirmed in relevant sources, while living in Munich (i.e., Minga, as it is properly called in Bavarian), I heard an alternative story about the origin of *Radler*. The legend has it that letter carriers on bicycles would stop by people's homes, having a standard-issue *Maas* at each of them. This caused many lost letters and pensions,

Figure 30.3 A meeting of the Maases (Westend61/Getty Images)

so eventually they were ordered to have their beer diluted, which solved the problem (Figure 30.3).

Bavarians also have the *Russ* 'Russian', a mixture of wheat beer and lemon soda. One of several theories about this mix is that it was created during the economic crisis of the 1920s to make beer cheaper. According to this theory, the name comes from the popularity of the drink with Russian guest workers in Bavaria at the time. Well, it is certainly easy to believe that there were Russian guest workers in Bavaria. However, the claim that they exhibited affinity for diluted alcoholic drinks is somewhat of a stretch.

Names for some beer cocktails are self-evident. *Diesel* is popular in many parts of continental Europe. It is a mix of beer and cola. The name was created in the second half of the twentieth century, when Diesel engines still roamed freely on European roads, and when it was easy to connect the color of the fuel in the pump to that of this mix.

A *White Russian* is made with vodka, hence Russian, and with cream, and so kind of white. But this is not all there is to it. Белый русский (*Beliy roosskiy*) 'White Russian' in Russian, where the name came from, also refers to a member of the White Army, anticommunist royalists during the civil war in Russia in the early twentieth century.

So, aside from the obvious, there are some subtle facetious cultural references in the name. The previously mentioned *Corpse Reviver* is much more straightforward. It is a hangover cure cocktail, like a *Bloody Mary*, which is somewhat more intricate. The bloody part is clear, the cocktail is tomato red, but who exactly Mary was remains unresolved. Was it Queen Mary I of England or Hollywood actress Mary Pickford? There is even a theory that invalidates even the "bloody" part. It claims that the real name of the cocktail is the Russian name *Vladimir*, and that *Bloody Mary* is the butchered Anglo pronunciation of that name.

The American beer microbrewing revolution of the late twentieth and early twenty-first century was all about revival. Before the revolution, beer was just beer, and, in the United States, it mainly referred to industrial lagers, which were brewed with a very limited amount of hops, as their clientele was mostly inherited from the producers of sodas.

Microbrewing has been generating new words, such as *craft beer*, *microbrewery*, *nanobrewery* (a scaled-down version of a microbrewery with one entrepreneur and a limited batch of beer), and *brew pub* (a pub that brews its own beer). Much more than that, the microbrewing revolution has revived many concepts, from *farm(house) brewery* (a brewery on a farm), which has been around for centuries, but it became generally used and en vogue on the wave of the microbrewing revolution.

Similarly, countless varieties of beer that lived their lives in the dark corners of English, German, and Belgian pubs are now household items. Around US microbreweries one can find *Kölsch* 'Cologne beer', as in Cologne, Germany, and the variety from its rival city of Düsseldorf, *Altbier* 'old beer'. There is Belgian *Lambic* 'alembic, that is, alchemical still'. Needless to say, there are numerous *Scottish Ales*, *Irish Stouts*, and *English India Pale Ales (IPAs)*. Aside from the English, IPA comes in numerous other varieties: *East Coast IPA*, *West Coast IPA*, *Session IPA*, *Double IPA*, *Triple IPA*, *Black IPA*, etc. In American microbreweries, you may even find a *Black and Tan* (a mix of pale ale and stout) poured, which would be impossible in Ireland, were the only appropriate designation for that beer mix is *half and half*. The reason is that Black and Tan was the nickname for the Royal Irish Constabulary Reserve Force, which was sent to Ireland in early 1920, an event that does not evoke positive emotions in today's Republic of Ireland.

For every new or revived drinking word there is a story that accompanies it. Words are inextricably connected to their social and cultural background. This is true even (or, perhaps, especially) in the moment when they are born. Many cultures are drinking cultures. There are also many dry cultures. This chapter was about the former cultures, which does not mean that what is found in them is universally applicable.

31 SOFs and SOWs

Working as a *SOF 'terp* will earn you the *FLIP* according to the *SOW*. To a great number of *GIs*, this sentence will be perfectly understandable. For those who are not Government Issued, to be comprehended the sentence would need to be expanded into Working as a Special Operation Forces interpreter will earn you the foreign language incentive pay according to the statement of work. Militaries around the world are champions at creating and using acronyms and abbreviations.

Military English is awash with numerous other acronyms, such as *CO* (*commanding officer*), *NCO* (*non-commissioned officer*), *AAA* (*anti-aircraft artillery*), and *DOD* (*Department of Defense*), to name a few. There are also more colorful ones, such as *SNAFU* (originally, 'status nominal: all f-word up', today interpreted as, 'situation normal: all f-word up'). Using acronyms creates new words out of necessity for brevity. Military, police, and similar services are organizations where succinctness is highly prized, so it is no wonder that a high number of acronyms and abbreviations compared to other spheres of life are used. The aforementioned US military is not an exception. Military and police organizations around the world do the same. Criminal police in German is *Kripo* (abbreviated from *Kriminalpolizei*). In the former Yugoslavia, conscripts of the Yugoslav People's Army (1941–1992) cleaned the barrels of their rifles with *DRNČ* (*Deterdžent za ručno čišćenje naslaga čađi* 'detergent for manual cleaning of sediments of soot'). This acronym contained too many consonants even for a language that has numerous consonant clusters.

Russian and earlier Soviet Armed Forces have also been high achievers in this field. There were even rules on how to create and spell acronyms in the military. There are three prescribed manners of their creation. They can be made from initials, as in *vrhr – vzvod radiatsionnoy i hemicheskoy razvedki* 'radiation and chemical reconnaissance platoon'. Initial letters of the parts of compound words can also be used, *msd - motostrelkovaya diviziya* 'motorized infantry division'. Initial syllables can also be used, as in *medsanbat* – *mediko-sanitarniy batalyon* 'medical and sanitary battalion'.

There were even rules on how to avoid ambiguity, which is certain to arise, given the massive number of acronyms. Two strategies were deployed. One relied on differentiating using lowercase and uppercase characters, as in *TR* – *takticheskaya rota* 'tactical company' versus *tr* – *tankovaya rota* 'tank company'. The other used initial letters in one member of the pair and syllables in the other. This can be seen in *rr* – *razvedivatel'naya rota* 'reconnaissance company' versus *remr* – *remontnaya rota* 'maintenance company'. Both principles can be deployed in a single pair, *PO* – *peredovoy otryad* 'forward squad' versus *pogo* – *pogranichniy otryad* 'border squad.'

Aside from military and police forces, it seems that totalitarian regimes show a clear affinity for the creation of acronyms and abbreviations. The dark legacy of the *Nazi* regime (abbreviated from *Nationalsozialist* 'national socialist') lives in numerous abbreviations and acronyms, such as *Gestapo* – *Geheime Staatspolizei* 'secret state police', *KZ* – *Konzentrazionslager* 'concentration camp', *NSDAP* – *Nationalsozialistische Deutsche Arbeiterpartei* 'National Socialist German Worker's Party'. The massive practice of abbreviating continued to the end of the regime, as one can see from the names of *V1 flying bomb* and *V2 rocket*, a series of two 'revenge weapons' (*Vergeltungswaffe* – that is where the V comes from) used toward the end of WWII.

Obviously, acronyms and abbreviations are used in other spheres of life. It is a common practice in English to create an acronym that coincides with an existing word, often to drive an educational point home. Thus, *SMART* describes the desired way to set project goals, *specific*, *measurable*, *achievable*, *relevant*, and *time-bound*. There are also those created just for fun, such as in James Bond novels and movies, *SPECTRE* (*SPecial Executive for Counter-intelligence, Terrorism, Revenge and Extortion*). In some cases, the convenience of abbreviating defies logic. In downtown Sydney, there is a harbor named *Circular Quay*. Australians have simply abbreviated its original name, *Semi-Circular Quay*, which is, give or take, the actual shape of the quay. In consequence, many a foreigner has been left wondering as to how a circular quay would be possible.

On the other hand, there are acronyms where most speakers will not even be aware of the full name. *Radar* comes from *radio detecting and*

Figure 31.1 A R.A.D.A.R. (Vyacheslav Arenberg/Getty Images)

ranging and laser from *light amplification by stimulated emission of radiation* (Figure 31.1). *Scuba* is abbreviated from self-contained underwater breathing apparatus. Most native speakers of English will be unable to expand these three acronyms. They now function as "regular" words. Even fewer speakers will be aware of the fact that ZIP as in *ZIP code*, postal code in the United States, comes from *Zone Improvement Plan*, which was the campaign in which these codes were introduced in 1963 (Figure 31.2).

Acronyms and abbreviations often have expiry dates. During the years of socialist Yugoslavia (1945–1992), the country practiced the model of worker's self-management, introduced in the 1950s. This practice has generated a number of acronyms. The government was not simply government in Serbo-Croatian, but rather *SIV – Savezno izvršno vijeće* 'Federal Executive Council'. Companies were not just companies, but rather *OOUR – Osnovna organizacija udruženog rada* 'the basic unit of associated labor', and bigger ones were *SOUR – Složena organizacija udruženog rada* 'the complex organization of associated labor'. Even commercials were not commercials, but rather *EPP – ekonomsko propagandni program* 'the economic propaganda program'. Once capitalism was reintroduced in the early 1990s, these acronyms were forgotten very quickly.

Figure 31.2 FYI, this is an acronym (Melinda Podor/Getty Images)

Figure 31.3 Information-age acronyms (Vladimir Godnik/Getty Images)

Capitalism is not free from acronyms. The corporate abbreviation *PR* – *p*ublic *r*elations has had an interesting life in Russia. It is not only that it is borrowed from English as *piar* (the way it is pronounced) but it also spawned derivations such as *samopiar* – self-advertising, and *popiarit'sya* – to spend some time in self-advertising.

The birth of acronyms and abbreviations is not very different from that of nonabbreviated words. It always reflects the realities of the social and cultural background in which it happens. Similarly, some creations lasted longer and others were short-lived (Figure 31.3).

PART V

Where Words Live

32 | Old-Lady Torturers, Horse Killers, and Bad Mornings

The connection of languages with the historical and cultural fiber of the societies in which they are spoken is prominently featured in first and last names of their speakers. In some regions of the world, last names are a relatively new phenomenon. This is so in the Balkans. Serbs, Croats, and Bosniaks were perfectly content using something such as *Nikola Petrov* 'Nicholas, son of Peter' to differentiate people who had the same first name. Things were done at the level of a village, and the society is patrilocal and patrilineal, hence the father's name. When last names were introduced, some of them, especially in the regions of Herzegovina, Krajina, and Lika near the military border between the Austrian and Turkish empires, were quite peculiar, to put it mildly. Examples include *Mučibabić* 'old-lady torturer', *Ubiparip* 'horse killer', *Zlojutro* 'bad morning', and many others of that ilk (Figure 32.1). All these last names are still around. There is also a story, possibly apocryphal, as to how these came to be. The story goes that the Austrian Empire, which ruled over the region, was conducting a population census. One version of the story tells that the locals were stating nicknames to the census takers, as they did not know what last names were. Of course, in a Spartan rural culture that never sugarcoated anything, these nicknames were somewhat less than laudatory. Another version of the story is that they gave purely invented names just to spite their Austrian overlords.

Interestingly enough, the tradition of referring to a person by their father's names has been retained in Icelandic last names, which are de facto patronymics, as previously discussed in Chapter 3. This is rather curious given that today's Icelandic society is far from being traditionally patriarchal. It illustrates a well-known fact that words, including names, encapsulate earlier periods in society. Russians are somewhere between Icelandic and languages that use separate last names. They have the patronymic, a middle name based on one's father's names. So, in *Фёдор Михайлович Достоевский* (*Fyodor Mikhailovich*

Figure 32.1 A bad morning (sturti/Getty Images)

Dostoevsky), *Fyodor* is the first name (the English equivalent being *Theodor*), *Dostoevsky* is the last name, and the patronymic *Mikhailovich* means 'the son of Michael', as *Mikhail* (*Michael*) was the name of his father (Figure 32.2).

Illegitimate children are another interesting story. The Old French word *fitz* 'the son of' was used in English in that precise meaning and as a part of the last name (as in *FitzRolf*) from the Norman Conquest in the eleventh century all the way to the fourteenth century, to then be abandoned. It was then revived in the Stuart Era (seventeenth and early eighteenth century), to be used, primarily if not exclusively, for illegitimate sons of kings, princes, and aristocrats, for example, *FitzRoy* '(illegitimate) son of the king', *FitzJames*, (illegitimate) son of King James II, etc. Something similar is recorded in Russian history. Grigory Potemkin (1739–1791), who gave his name to the phrase

Figure 32.2 A memorial plaque in Saint Petersburg, Russia, on a house where Dostoevsky lived (photo by the author)

Potemkin village, allegedly had an illegitimate daughter with Catherine the Great, whose name was Elizabeth Grigorieva Temkina. Her last name was a front-truncated version of her father's last name. So, while English aristocrats were adding sounds to characterize illegitimate paternity, their Russian counterparts were subtracting them.

On the subject of gender relationships in last names, there used to be, but now increasingly less frequently, a tradition in Serbian of expressing whether women were married or not in their last names. So, if somebody's last name was *Marković*, and the person was an unmarried woman, the form *Markovićeva* was used. If the woman was married, the form *Markovićka* was used. This practice is being abandoned, and the last name is typically used in the same form as masculine last names, that is, *Marković*, with the only difference being that most female last names are not inflected, and their masculine counterparts are. For example, to note the object case, in this case one would change *Marković* into *Markovića* for males, and leave it unchanged for females, as in *Vidio sam Petra Markovića* 'I saw Petar Marković' as opposed to *Vidio sam Mariju Marković* 'I saw Maria Marković'. The last bastions of marking marital status of women by their last names are sport sections. In relations to athletic events, journalists refer to female athletes as *Markovićeva* if their last name is *Marković*. For this, there is no fact-checking. Every female athlete is assumed to be single.

Last names have different origins. In addition to being derived from first names, as in *Jones* (being John's son), last names are often based on various professions, in that they keep the memory of the previous stages of development in their respective societies. Blacksmiths, or any other smiths, are extremely rare in Europe and North America alike. However, last names derived from the word for a smith are extremely frequent in many languages of these two regions. *Smith* is as common in English as *Jones*. Equally frequent is German *Schmidt (Schmied* being 'smith'), French *Lefebvre*, with variants *Lefèbvre, Lefèvre, Lefeuvre,* and *Lefébure*. It is derived from the Latin *faber* 'craftsman', which evolved into smith. The Occitan *Fabre, Favre, Faure, Favret, Favrette,* and *Dufaure,* Corsican *Fabri,* Italian *Fabbri* and *Fabri* have the same origin. Slavic languages are no exception; *Kowalski* ('smith' is *kowal*) is one of the most frequent in Polish, as is *Kovačević (kovač* is 'smith') in Serbo-Croatian. Russian has two popular last names derived from the two synonyms for 'smith', коваль (*kovaly*) and кузнец (*kooznets*), so Ковалёв (*Kovalyof*) and Кузнецов (*Kuznetsof*).

Numerous other professions are encapsulated in last names, which is not even registered by native speakers. For example, there is the last name *Baručija* in Serbo-Croatian, which comes from *barut* 'gunpowder' + *-džija* '-er', so *barutdžija*, which changes into *baručija* 'gunpowder quartermaster'. Most speakers will definitely not connect the last name with the underlying word for gunpowder, let alone the military title.

When gunpowder was in use, the terrors of Christian Europe were the Janissaries, elite Ottoman Turkish armed forces, founded in 1363 anddisbanded in 1836 (Figure 32.3). Their name in Ottoman Turkish was یکیچری *yeñiçeri*, literally 'new troop, new soldier'. These troops were created from Christian boys, forcibly separated from their families in faraway parts of the empire, who were then trained and

Figure 32.3 Sixteenth-century Janissaries (duncan1890/Getty Images)

converted to Islam in the heart of the empire. The idea was that through their training their loyalty would be to the troops only, unlike the corrupt old force that was local and had their own interest above everything else. The symbols of loyalty to the new force were a copper cauldron and a ladle (used in their common meals). The ranks were accordingly based on the kitchen hierarchy. High commanders had the rank of *çorbacı* 'soup chef' (soups were made in the cauldron). Below him were *aşçıbaşı* 'chef', *aşçı* 'cook', *çörekçi* 'baker', and *gözlemeci* 'flatbread baker', all the way to *karakullukçu* 'scullion'. So, if somebody's last name is *Çörekçi*, it is hard to say if it comes from the cooking or martial profession.

First names are equally interesting. Many of them have a protective function. The best-known writer from Germany, the land of poets and thinkers, as Germans like to say, is *Johann Wolfgang von Goethe*. The second part of the first name means 'wolf's gait'. The popularity of the name Wolfgang grew until the mid-twentieth century, when it was among the most popular German names, and then its popularity started to diminish, with the name now being around rank 200. Another wolf-based name is infamous rather than famous. The name *Adolf* comes from Old High German *Adalwolf* 'noble wolf'. This name was among thirty most popular German names from the end of the nineteenth century. With the political rise of Adolf Hitler, it became even more popular. With his demise, the name became extremely unpopular, as it remains to this day.

American English speakers are rather possessive about their names. One is often asked to spell their name. Taking interest in one's name and pronouncing it correctly belongs to elementary decency. There are even phrases meant to be demeaning, such as *what's his name* or *If I could only remember her name*, etc. By contrast, speakers in Slavic cultures could not care less about their names. My first name, *Danko*, is rather infrequent and there is a much more frequent name, *Darko*. It is often the case that various people, even those who have known me for years, call me *Darko*. They do not care; I do not care. This might be one of many consequences of the individualism versus collectivism dimension of cross-cultural variation. It is natural that individualistic American culture cares about names of individuals much more than collectivist South Slavic cultures. If this link between language and culture is true, one's name is considered a treasured personal possession in individualistic societies, which put emphasis on individuals rather than on communities. This is not the case in collectivist societies.

This story about last and first names shows how linguistic elements remain inseparable from their respective societies, including the history of those societies. Names reflect past events, and new events can influence them. This is true not only of first names and surnames. Other proper nouns, such as names of geographical objects, are a rich depository of cultural and historical information still waiting for language archeologists.

33 | A Fleeing Bus

When speakers of some Slavic languages miss a bus, the phrase they use is literally 'The bus ran away from me' (*Pobjegao mi autobus* in Serbo-Croatian, and *Uciekł mi autobus* in Polish). It is as if the only purpose of the bus was to flee and run away from the person in question. Needless to say, the phrase absolves the person from responsibility for being late. This is very different from the English equivalent *I missed the bus*, where the blame is clearly assigned (Figure 33.1).

This is just one of many phrases where English and Slavic languages differ significantly. English speakers are almost always in the driver's seat when they talk about their feelings, preferences, disposition, sensations, etc. The phrases are something like, *I am bored*, *I like or do not like something or somebody*, *I feel like doing or not doing something*, *I am cold*, etc. The way in which all these are expressed in Slavic languages is rather different. The patterns are literally, 'Boring to me it is', 'It/he/she likes itself/himself/herself to me', 'It does not want itself to me', 'Cold to me it is', etc. For example, 'I am cold' is Ладно ми е (*Ladno mi e*) in Macedonian, *Hladno mi je* in Serbo-Croatian, *Jest mi zimno* in Polish, Мне холодно (*Mnye holodno*) in Russian, and *Je mi zima* in Czech and Slovak, literally, 'Cold to me it is'. Similarly, 'I do not like winter' is Не ми се допаѓа зимата (*Ne mi se dopagya zimata*) in Macedonian, *Ne dopada mi se zima* in Serbo-Croatian, *Nie podoba mi się zima* in Polish, Мне зима не нравится (*Mnye zima nye nravitsya*) in Russian, and *Nelíbí se mi zima* in Czech, literally, 'Winter does not like itself to me.'

Even when being imprisoned, English speakers are *doing their time*. They are actively doing something, unlike their Slavic counterparts. In Slavic languages they sit (as in Russian сидеть в тюрьме, *sidet v tyoormye*, and Polish *siedzieć w więzieniu*, both meaning 'to sit in prison') or lie, as in Serbo-Croatian *ležati u zatvoru* 'to lie in prison'. Of course, one can also find English synonyms, such as *rot in prison*, which go against this attitude of being in the driver's seat.

Figure 33.1 A fleeing bus (ljubaphoto/Getty Images)

While one needs to be very careful about making claims about the links between predominant cultural patterns in a given society and the language spoken in that society, some hypotheses can still be advanced. In English-speaking cultures, especially in those in North America, there is genuine optimism about forging our own destiny. Stemming from Protestant work ethics, the American Declaration of Independence mentions three birthrights that the Creator has given us, which should be protected by the government: *Life, Liberty, and the Pursuit of Happiness*. Pursuit, that is, a chance, an opportunity, is a key word here and it is up to each individual to forge his/her own destiny.

In Slavic cultures, on the other hand, there is a feeling that some mysterious forces rule our lives and that we are but straws in the wind. The proverb Человек предполагает а бог располагает, *Chelovek predpolagaet a boh raspolagaet* (lit. 'Man assumes, God distributes') in Russian, *Człowiek strzela, Pan Bóg kulę nosi* (lit. 'Man shoots, God carries the bullet') in Polish, and *Čovjek snuje, Bog odreduje* (lit. 'Man dreams, God determines') in Serbo-Croatian, is well-known in all those cultures, and seems to encapsulate this attitude. The same kind of feeling can be found in numerous writers in Slavic languages,

Dostoevsky being best known and most prototypical of this attitude. But the proverb is not restricted to Slavic languages, as German has *Der Mensch denkt, Gott lenkt* (lit. 'Man thinks, God turns') and English features *Man proposes, but God disposes*, all of which (including the proverbs in Slavic languages) are translations of the Latin phrase *Homo proponit, sed Deus disponit* from Book I, Chapter 19, of *The Imitation of Christ* by the German cleric Thomas à Kempis.

This proverb points to two important issues about the relation of words with their cultural and social environments. First, something that looks as if it could have originated in one culture may in fact be triggered by a random event, a line in a work of literature, etc. Second, although not indigenous to a given culture, certain linguistic elements can be more frequent in them and thus possibly point to an underlying way of thinking. Indeed, the level of familiarity people in Slavic countries have with this proverb and the frequency of their use of it is considerably higher than in German- and English-speaking societies.

While one should be careful about establishing causal relationships between language elements used to express feelings, sensations, etc. and predominant views and attitudes, it is still very clear that some coexistence between the two can be established. English-speaking cultures are not any different in the link between language and culture. They are strongly individualistic. One can see this in the concept of *privacy*. Translating it into many other languages, those from the Slavic family included, is a bit of a problem. Yes, one can find the local equivalent, but it is definitely not going to convey the same idea, and the very word sounds rather unnatural in those languages. The point is that in much more collectivist cultures, privacy is not much of a concept. Over the years, I have witnessed cultural conflicts between Slavs and Americans over privacy. Americans would consider Slavs inappropriately intrusive for asking very personal questions of people they barely know. Slavs would consider Americans arrogant for not asking the same questions. In reality, each of them acts appropriately according to the norms of their respective cultures. Differences along the lines of individualism versus collectivism can also be seen in the way media report on shooting victims. In English, the phrase is that someone was shot. The equivalent in Slavic languages is that someone was wounded, that is, the attention is not on what the shooter did but rather the suffering of the victim. In a way, solidarity with the victim is being expressed in the latter pattern found in Slavic languages.

Figure 33.2 Privacy requested (Image Source/Getty Images)

The word privacy is a clear case, but what about the following. Verbs such as *have*, *take*, and *give* are extremely prolific in English compared to Slavic languages. One is *having breakfast* in English, one "breakfasts" in Slavic languages (e.g., *zajtrkovati* in Slovene, *zajtrk* is 'breakfast', *-ovati* is a suffix used to make verbs from nouns). One is *having a fight* in English, one 'beats each other' (e.g., *tući se* in Serbo-Croatian). English speakers are *having a good time*, and Slavic speakers are 'spending time well' (e.g., хорошо провести время, *harasho provesti vremya* in Russian), etc. One can ask if this has anything to do with a stronger emphasis on individual possessions in individualistic societies. There are certainly no simple answers to questions of this kind (Figure 33.2).

This brings us back to that fleeing bus from the beginning of this chapter. I always have to warn my students of Serbo-Croatian about one phrase that is easy to recognize for them, but extremely difficult to understand. The phrase is *nema problema* 'no problem', which students with even very limited skills will be able to recognize. What the phrase actually means when somebody is giving assurances that

A Fleeing Bus 203

Figure 33.3 A piece of cake: No problem (ArxOnt/Getty Images)

something will be done is one thing. If that something will actually be done, is a completely different story. On average, in English, this means that the person is actually going to do it. With most speakers of Serbo-Croatian, the concept of responsibility is somewhat more relaxed, to put it mildly, so assurances of that kind do not actually mean a lot. I always tell my American students to expect problems of all kinds when then hear *nema problema*. This difference in punctuality and adhering to obligations brings us back to Edward T. Hall's difference between monochronic and polychronic cultures, mentioned in Chapter A. English language cultures are predominantly monochronic, and Slavic language cultures are primarily polychronic. One should add, however, that links between cultural and linguistic patterns are easy to spot and intuitively grasp, yet finding consistent proofs for such links is extremely difficult (Figure 33.3).

34 | *I Wish That You Enjoy in What You Have Deserved!*

The title of this chapter is the way one congratulates in Nahuatl. The original is as follows, *mah xicmopaquiltilia in motlamacehualiz!* There is no word for 'to congratulate' in Nahuatl, so the way one goes about congratulating is somewhat circumlocutory. Chinese and Japanese do have a compact way of congratulating and praising someone. However, the way one responds to praise in those cultures is substantially different than in cultures where English is the first language (Figure 34.1). It would be absolutely unacceptable to thank someone who praises you, as in English. One is supposed to vehemently deny that praise is in order. In Mandarin Chinese, the response to praise is never 谢谢, *xièxiè* 'thank you' but rather 哪裡, 哪里, *nǎlǐ, nǎlǐ* 'not so, not true'. Japanese is similar. When somebody pays a compliment, the answer is not ありがとうございます, *arigatoo (gozaimasu)* 'thank you (very much)' but rather 'no, no, not really' (いえいえ、それほどでも, *īe, īe, sorehodo demo*). This construction can also be found in Argentine Spanish (more specifically in Buenos Aires), where a common response is ¡*No, por favor!* 'No, please', as if saying, give me a break.

The requirement of Chinese and Japanese cultures is that modesty be expressed in words, which is not the case in English. The sociocultural context of languages influences linguistic differences between them even at the most elementary level. This is noticeable in the very early stages of language learning. I studied Mandarin Chinese for a year. Among other things, the book that was used in my course taught me to say 'Pleased to meet you'. The phrase was: 认识 你 很 高兴, *rènshì nǐ hěn gāoxìng!* Several years after taking the course, I went to China and used the phrase. My interlocutors were rather confused and did not repeat the phrase, as I expected them to do. My first thought was that I butchered the tones so badly that I was actually saying something else. In the evening of the first day, I double-checked the tones, and they were fine. The next day I made a conscious effort and pronounced

I Wish That You Enjoy in What You Have Deserved!

Figure 34.1 Congratulations are in order (Luis Alvarez/Getty Images)

all tones perfectly. The reaction from the new people I met (or lack thereof) was the same. On inquiring further, I came to realize that people in China actually do not use the equivalent of 'Pleased to meet you'. They introduce each other, shake hands, and that is it. The authors of my book followed the English cultural script, so they had to put something for 'Pleased to meet you', which exists theoretically, but not in practice.

The English word *congratulation* comes from Latin. The ultimate Latin origin is a word composed of the prefix *com* 'together', and *gratulari* 'give thanks, show joy'. This, in turn, comes from *gratus* 'agreeable'. The idea is that the person congratulating shares some joy with the one being congratulated. The French congratulation formula *félicitations* also comes from Latin, but from a different verb, *felicitari*, which is derived from *felix* 'happy', 'fruitful'. Spanish *felicitaciones* have the same origin. In German, one would use German words and say *Herzlichen Glückwunsch*, literally, 'heart-felt wish for happiness/luck'. The South Slavic congratulation formula, *čestitam* in Slovene and Serbo-Croatian, честитки (*chestitki*) in Macedonian, and честито (*chestito*) in Bulgarian, is derived from the word чест (*chest*) 'honor, respect', which is not different from the informal English congratulating formula *Respect!* On the other hand, some other

Figure 34.2 A nonverbal approval (Kiyoshi Hijiki/Getty Images)

English greetings may sound very strange to non-English people. Take *Good for you!* The strangeness of this type of congratulation to many other speakers is that the congratulating person does not participate in the joy of the person being congratulated. For them it is as if they hear "Good for you, and I do not really care about it." (Figure 34.2)

Wishing well is also encountered in greeting people. In Macedonian and Serbo-Croatian, an informal greeting (akin to the English *hi*) is *здраво* (*zdravo*). It is *здравей* (*zdravej*) in Bulgarian, and *здравствуй* (*zradstvooy*) in Russian. They all come from the adjective *zdrav(iy)* 'healthy'. So, the wish included in the greeting is 'may you be healthy'. Slovene *živijo* 'may you live' is similar. Speakers of Southern German (Bavarians, Austrians, etc.) are so well-intentioned that they offer themselves as servant to their interlocutors. A very common greeting is *Servus!*, which comes from Latin *servus* 'servant, slave'. Hungarians have the same greeting; they just spell it differently, as *Szervusz!* The Italian *ciao*, which has achieved enormous global popularity (as it can be found among others in Spanish, French, Romanian, Dutch, English, German, Latvian, Maltese, Japanese, and all Slavic languages), is of a similar origin. It is abbreviated from Venetian *s-ciao*, which comes from *sciavo*, and represents a shortened form of the phrase *s-ciao*

I Wish That You Enjoy in What You Have Deserved! 207

vostro 'your slave', where the ultimate origin of the word *sciavo* is the Latin noun *sclavus* 'slave'.

Nations and peoples around the world differ as to when their new year starts. However, what they have in common is that good wishes are expressed for the new year. Slavic languages are interesting in this regard. Using the same word for 'happy' and 'lucky', they wish you both happiness and luck for the new year. So, it is a two-in-one combo. The phrase is 'Happy/lucky new year' and it is rendered as *Srečno novo leto* in Slovene, *Sretna nova godina* in Serbo-Croatian, Среќна нова година (*Srekyna nova godina*) in Macedonian, *Szczęśliwego nowego roku* in Polish, *Šťastný nový rok* in Czech, Счастливого Нового года (*Shchastlivovo novovo goda*) in Russian, etc. Some Germanic languages have the same construction. *It is Gelukkig nieuwjaar!* in Dutch, and *Glückliches neues Jahr!* in German. Among alternative ways of extending New Year's wishes, Germans have an interesting one, *Guten Rutsch!* 'Good slide'. There is this mental image of sliding into a new year, which makes sense given that the expression has emerged before global overheating, when late December and early January were freezing cold in German-speaking lands.

There are numerous other situations in which good wishes are extended. Those speakers of English who sneeze frequently can count their blessings, unless their interlocutors are less religiously minded, in which case they will hear the German borrowing *Gesundheit!*, which simply means 'health'. The idea is that sneezing will improve your health. A similar formula is also used in Slavic languages, as in *na zdrowie* in Polish and *nazdravlje* in Serbo-Croatian (*na* means 'onto' and *zdrowie* or *zdravlje* means 'health'). The idea is that sneezing will land on your health, that is, be healthy for you. The same phrase can also be used when drinking, to mean 'cheers'. The idea is the same. The drink will end up being healthy for you. It does not really matter that modern medicine has demonstrated that there is no such thing as healthy consumption of alcohol (Figure 34.3).

When it comes to showing respect, Koreans are world champions. Korean is well known for its many speech registers reflecting varied degrees of formality and politeness. These levels go like this: High levels, *Hasoseo-che* (very formally polite), *Hasipsio-che* (formally polite); Middle levels, *Haeyo-che* (casually polite), *Hao-che* (formally neither polite nor impolite), *Hage-che* (Neither formal nor casual, neither polite nor impolite); Lower levels, *Haera-che* (formally

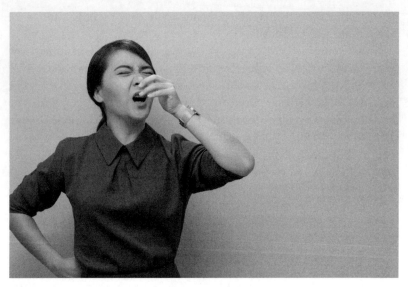

Figure 34.3 Onto your health! (Teeramet Thanomkiat/EyeEm/Getty Images)

impolite), *Hae-che* (casually impolite). Each one is used in very specific social situations.

This chapter was a cursory review of a very small fragment of the situations in which people wish each other well (whether they really mean it or not). In the variety of ways of doing this, there is one thing in common. All lexical formulas for well-wishing stem from the human faculty of empathy. To wish well, if one is doing it honestly, requires that one has a feel for a fellow human's needs and desires.

35 | *Happy Hunting Ground*

I have been calling the American Southwest my home for roughly twenty years now, but my first impressions of the region were formed much, much earlier than that. The culprit is one Karl May, a German writer known for his novels about the American Old West, which he wrote without ever setting foot on American soil (one should say that he did pay a visit long after his novels became enormously popular in central Europe). His novels were a staple of young adult fiction in the former Yugoslavia, where I grew up in the 1960s and 1970s (Figure 35.1).

Along with his fictitious representation of the Old West, Karl May brought to the former Yugoslavia, and its major language Serbo-Croatian, the phrase *vječna lovišta* 'eternal hunting grounds'. This is a translation of the German term introduced by Karl May, which reads *Ewige Jagdgründe* 'eternal hunting grounds'. Other languages where Karl May was popular have something similar, *večna lovišča* in Slovene, *věčná loviště* in Czech *kraina wiecznych łowów* 'land of eternal hunts' in Polish, *Eeuwige jachtvelden* 'eternal hunting grounds' in Dutch, etc.

It seems that May has merged a common German reference to death *ewige Ruhe* 'eternal rest, literally: peace, quiet' and the phrase *happy hunting grounds*, which he probably found in James Fenimore Cooper's novel *The Last of the Mohicans*. The phrase itself comes from the beliefs of several tribes from the American Great Plains, including the Lakota, and their mental image of the afterlife.

These happy or eternal hunting grounds are used as a tongue-in-cheek reference to where somebody went. As death is something unpleasant, it is rarely mentioned directly, and much more commonly using indirect references. The Islamic concept of the afterlife is known as الآخرة, *akhirah* in Arabic. Religious Bosniaks (also known as Bosnian Muslims) have borrowed the word as *ahiret*. So, when somebody dies, they say that he or she has moved (as if changed the place of residence, the verb is

Figure 35.1 The Old West straight from a Karl May novel (Matthias Clamer/ Getty Images)

preseliti). This is abbreviated from *to move to the akhirah*. A different picture is found in the Slovenian language. The phrase is *posloviti se* 'to say goodbye' and that is how they report deaths of prominent people in the mainstream media, for example, *Poslovil se je predsednik* 'The president passed away', literally, 'said goodbye'. Russians say *Его/Её не стало* (*Yevo/yeyo nye stalo*) 'He/she passed away', literally, 'Him/her stopped to exist', and at a deeper etymological and historical level, *стало* (*stalo*) comes from the verb *стать* (*stat*) 'to stand'. So, eventually, someone stopped standing (Figure 35.2).

Happy Hunting Ground

Figure 35.2 They have all said goodbye (nokee/Getty Images)

Both the Slovene and the Russian phrases are formal. Sometimes, even closely related languages differ substantially in the domain of application of terms referring to death. Macedonian has the verb *почине* (*pochine*), which can mean either 'get rest' or 'decease'. The verb is formal, and media will report something like *Почина претседател* (*Pochina pretsedatel*) 'The president passed away', literally, 'got rest', but it is also possible to say in a private conversation *Почина ми другар* (*Pochina mi drugar*) 'My friend died'. In neighboring Serbo-Croatian, the formal media reference to somebody's passing is made using the verb *preminuti*, where *pre* means 'over' and *minuti* means 'pass'. However, unlike in Macedonian, the use of this verb is restricted to formal texts, such as media reports, and it cannot possibly be used in informal conversations. Macedonians are definitely world-best nonnative speakers of Serbo-Croatian, yet even the best among them may miss this very subtle detail. The Serbian variant of Serbo-Croatian has another, even more specialized, verb for dying, namely *upokojiti se*, literally, 'in-peace oneself', which is used for clergy.

Not all words and phrases for dying are this respectful. There are also those that approach this somber event in a less serious vein. English is no exception. There are expressions such as to *push up the daisies* (obvious reference to being *six feet under*), *to bite the dust* (in which there is a picture of falling down, as in a Wild West shootout), to croak (the connection is to raven's croaking as a bad omen, enforced by the act of gasping for air while leaving this world), and *to kick the bucket*. While the etymology of the latter is not confirmed, one likely explanation is that it comes from hanging as a form of execution, and the prisoner kicking the bucket on which they were forced to stand. An alternative explanation is that it may be related to stretching one's legs in the moment of death. Spanish has an expression that is directly related to that action, that is, *estirar la pata* 'to stretch one's legs'.

Serbo-Croatian has the same expression, but with a twist. The expression is *otegnuti papke* 'to extend one's hooves'. It follows a general pattern of talking about somebody's death disrespectfully by equating that person with an animal. Such is also the verb *crći* 'to die, of animals', which becomes offensive when used about people, rather than neutral, as it is when used about animals.

When somebody dies, *condolences* are in order. They are all about empathy. That is true even at the etymological level. The word *condolence* comes from the Latin *con* 'with' and *dolere* 'grieve, suffer'. The same concept is found in many European languages, either borrowed from Latin or calqued (directly translated). Thus, French has *condoléances*, Italian *condoglianze*, Maltese *kondoljanzi*, Romanian *condoleanțe*, Portuguese *condolências*, Spanish *condolencias*, etc. Unlike all these that have borrowed from Latin, many languages create calques after the Latin word. All the following have the meaning of 'grieving with somebody': German *Beileid*, Slovene *sožalje*, Croatian *sućut*, Serbian and Bosnian *saučešće*, Macedonian *сочувство* (*sochuvstvo*), Russian *соболезнование* (*soboleznovaniye*), etc.

Talking about the end of life is not very different from talking about anything else. Some things are universally human; others are delightfully culture- and language-bound (Figure 35.3).

Figure 35.3 Cat condolences (Benjamin Torode/Getty Images)

36 | *A Language Is a Dialect with an Army and Navy*

Words ultimately live in languages. In some cases, it is difficult to say if something is a separate language or just a variety of a language. The quip that lent itself to the title of this chapter is Yiddish, and it reads: אַ שפּראַך איז אַ דיאַלעקט מיט אַן אַרמיי און פֿלאָט (*A shprakh iz a dialekt mit an armey un flot*). It has been ascribed to a Russian Jewish scholar of Yiddish, one Max Weinreich (or in the full Russian version of his name, *Мейер Лазаревич Вейнрейх, Meyer Lazarevich Veynreykh*), but there are some who question the veracity of this ascription. Yiddish is just one of many languages to which this saying can be applied. Some other examples include German, Spanish, Portuguese, and definitely English.

While there is consensus today that British, North American, Australian, and so on, English are geographical (or, more precisely, national) varieties of the English language rather than separate languages, some alternative theories previously existed. In 1919, the celebrated American journalist H. L. Mencken, known by his nickname "The Sage of Baltimore," published a book titled *The American Language*, in which he advanced the claim that American (what we today know as American English) is a separate language. Obviously, words different from those used in British English were at the crux of his line of argument.

In addition to documenting the peculiarities of American English (i.e., the American language), he also documented the influence of American English on other immigrant languages in the United States at the time. The second supplement to the book discusses "Non-English Dialects in America." There are Germanic languages, such as German, Dutch, Yiddish, and Swedish; "Latin" languages, such as Italian and French; Slavic languages, such as Polish and Russian (with Lithuanian, a Baltic language erroneously in the mix); Finno-Ugrian languages (Finnish and Hungarian); Celtic languages (represented by Gaelic); Semitic languages (Arabic); Greek; "Asiatic" languages

Figure 36.1 Boomerang (photo by the author)

(Mandarin Chinese and Japanese); and Miscellaneous (Armenian; Hawaiian; and "Gipsy," i.e., Romani).

Years later, in 1945, Sidney J. Baker published *The Australian Language*, with Chapter I titled, *The New Language*. Again, the words make Australian special. He mentions words from the environment, such as *kangaroo*, *billabong*, *bush*, etc. Then, there are artifacts that natives would use, *budgeree*, *boomerang*, and such (Figure 36.1). The next group encompasses words stemming from the new rural conditions of life, such as *bushranger*, *stockman*, etc. Finally, there are words related to new tastes and habits as the cities of Australia grew. These are words such as *larrikin* and *wowser*.

Needless to say, claims concerning separate languages for the varieties of English are now dead and buried. Pragmatism is highly valued in the mainstream English-language cultures. It is unnecessary to translate or interpret between geographical varieties of English and it would be equally unreasonable to have speakers of one variety learn another English-language variety as a foreign language. What sense would it then make to speak about separate languages. However, the two aforementioned books, along with various dictionaries, have contributed to gaining recognition for varieties of English other than RP (received pronunciation, i.e., standard British English). Back in 2014, while a visiting professor at The Australian National University (marked, among other things, along with The Ohio State University, with the unusual use of the definite article in its name), I visited The

Figure 36.2 The author at the Australian National Dictionary Centre (photo by Ljiljana Šipka)

Australian National Dictionary Centre. My conversation with colleagues revealed a very clear sense of the important place of Sidney J. Baker in efforts to emancipate the Australian variety of English (Figure 36.2).

To return to Mencken, one of the Slavic languages for which he documents the English influence in the immigrant community is Serbo-Croat. Mencken shows words borrowed from English that differ from those used "in the old country," such as *haus* (house), *kičen* (kitchen), *šat of viska* (a shot of whiskey), and *vurkati* (to work). He even mentions *Džulajevo*, the word for the Fourth of July (US Independence Day), derived from *džulaj* (borrowing from the English July), and the Serbo-Croatian suffix *-evo*, used in the names of holidays, for example, *Vartolomejevo* 'St. Bartholomew's Day'.

Serbo-Croatian has variants, in the same way as English. The linguistic differences between the two main ones, Serbian and Croatian, are fewer than those between British and American English. However, their political status is completely different. Linguistically, it is one language, just like English. However, there are three political languages, Serbian, Croatian, and Bosnian. In public administration, schools, media, and courts, if one is a Serb, the language is known as Serbian, Croats name it Croatian, and Bosniaks (formerly known as Bosnian Muslims) know the same language as Bosnian. There are also some who name their variant of the language Montenegrin (a relatively new development), but the majority of Serbo-Croatian speakers in Montenegro still name their language Serbian.

This disconnect between linguistic and political status of the language has led to a rather curious situation in Croatia. A 1989 Serbian movie titled *Rane* 'Wounds', a rather gritty drama about the underworld of the Serbian capital Belgrade, was to be shown in Croatian movie theaters. The Croatian distributor decided to subtitle the movie, as is customary with other foreign languages. The result of this decision was that viewers in Croatia were bursting with laughter while watching a very serious movie. Most of the time the "translation" looked like close captioning for the hearing impaired. Viewers found this funny, just like those instances where there were some differences between the two varieties – even in these cases the word from the Serbian variety was perfectly comprehensible. Imagine watching a British movie subtitled in "the American language." Needless to say, this Croatian movie-theater subtitling was done once and never again.

In the end, we can say that the comparison of English to Serbo-Croatian brings us back to Weinreich's quip from the beginning of this chapter. Indeed, what one considers a language is often a political decision that may be blind to linguistic facts. The subtitling story shows that political power still has some limitations. Talking the talk about separate languages at a symbolic level is one thing. Walking the walk is an entirely different issue. Speakers will generally be inclined to

Figure 36.3 A T-shirt with Aussie expressions (photo by the author)

reject absurd solutions that affect their daily lives. Most words know in which language they live. With some of them, there may be disputes. However, words move from one variety to the other (e.g., from colloquial to formal standards), and, even more commonly, from one language to another. From this point of view, it is not really crucial to know if something is a separate language or a variety of a broader language (Figure 36.3).

PART VI

A Word After

At the end of this journey around the world in thirty-nine chapters (including the A, B, and C ones), and less than half of the number Phileas Fogg needed to complete his voyage (and less that forty to avoid the ominous number of 4), we can relax a little and reflect (tongue-in-cheek, of course) on the age-old question of what makes us human. Language is often proposed as the key feature that makes us human. Human languages are indeed considerably more complex signifying systems than those found in other animals. It is therefore unclear how much came through when St. Francis of Assisi preached to the birds.

The chapters of this book were about words and their meanings, the elements of language architecture that are most directly and intimately connected to its cultural background. Languages serve as tools of their respective cultures. Words and their meanings are introduced and they disappear depending on the needs of members of those cultures. Cultures, in turn, are rooted in their respective space and time. Consequently, making and negotiating meaning bears an indelible mark of that space and time. In each language and in each culture, that mark is different.

We have seen a variety of ways in which various languages carve out their words and meanings of these words. A great variety also exists in the way things are done with words. When new words and their meanings are needed, speakers of various languages have different ways of coming up with them. Finally, how words and their meanings interact with their respective languages and cultures is very different around the globe.

With all this in mind, one can say that what makes us human is also what connects us most strongly to the rest of the natural world. The diversity in human languages is a kind of adaptation to the cultural niche every language occupies, just as plants and nonhuman animals adapt to their biological niche. Different ways in which we humans name colors, wish each other good or evil, come up with new words for means of locomotion, or shape our last names (if we use them at all) are akin to birds having different feathers, or plants bearing fruits of different shapes and locations.

In the *Introduction*, I stated the following: The cases of cross-linguistic differences presented here are a testimony to the diversity of the human condition, thought, and its linguistic expression. This richness should be cherished – a world in which one language prevailed would be as boring as the natural world with only one kind of tree and animal. This book is thus meant as a small contribution toward preserving the richness of human linguistic diversity. I have nothing more to add.

PART VII
Words about Words

Selected Chapter Readings

A What Is a Word

The definition of culture is found in Hofstede and Hofstede (1994:5), and Hall's classic patterns are described in Hall (1959) and (1966). The original Hofstede dimensions are explained in Hofstede and Hofstede (1994), with two additional dimensions presented in Hofstede (2020). Definitions of the word can be found in lexicography textbooks such as Lipka (2002), Jackson (2007), Halliday and Yallop (2007), and Taylor (2015).

B The Internal Affairs of Words

Lexical semantics is discussed in Cruse (1986) and Geeraerts (2010), and general semantics in Palmer (1976), Lyons (1977), Cruse (2011), and Altshuler et al. (2019). Goddard (2008) addresses cross-cultural aspects of semantics, and Zgusta's model of meaning can be found in Zgusta (1971). Approaches to metaphorical transfer are discussed in Steen (2007), while cross-cultural variation in metaphorical transfer is addressed in Lakoff and Johnson (1980), Lakoff and Johnson (1999), and Kövecses (2005). Wittgenstein (1922) and Wittgenstein (1953) offer further discussion of family resemblance. Rosch (1973) brings attention to prototypes in linguistics, and Frege 1882 (Frege 1948 is the English translation) addresses the difference between sense and reference.

C The External Affairs of Words

The following lexicology textbooks offer excellent reviews of lexical relations: Lipka (2002), Jackson (2007), Halliday and Yallop (2007), and Taylor (2015). Wordnet (2020) is where lexical relations of English words can be explored. Haspelmath and Tadmor (2009) offer a solid introduction into lexical borrowing, and one can browse fascinating cases of borrowings in various languages in Haspelmath and Tadmor (2020).

Chapter 1 1 = 2, 5, 6, or 7

Menninger (1969) offers a cultural background of worldwide number systems. There are also analyses of the systems of numerals in particular language families, such as Ndimele and Chan (2016). Yang and Regier (2014) discuss broader communication ramifications of the systems of numerals in various languages. The classic work about the grammatical category of numbers is Corbett (2000), which provides a thorough review of this category in various languages, along with a discussion of theoretical implications of these differences.

Chapter 2 Beer Eyes and Wine-Dark Sea

Berlin and Kay (1969) is the most authoritative work about color words in world languages. Hardin and Maffi (1997) offer further insights into color categories in language and thought, and Winawer et al. (2007) discuss how color words may affect cognitive processing. Loreto et al. (2012) address the origin of basic color terms, while English color terms are discussed in Casson (1997). Wilford (1983) talks about Homer's wine-dark sea. Pavlenko et. al (2017) discuss color references in multilingual speakers.

Chapter 3 Second Cousins Twice Removed

Schusky (1983) proposes a methodological framework for the study of kinship systems around the world. Nogle (1974) offers further methodological and theoretical considerations about semantic and broader cognitive aspects of kinship terminologies. McConvell et al. (2013) present a number of studies about changes in the systems of kinship and techniques for the reconstruction of previously used systems.

Chapter 4 I Have Three Sons and a Child

Hellinger and Bußmann (2001, 2002, 2003) and Hellinger and Motschenbacher (2015) present a wide selection of papers about various aspects of gender in language. Issues around Slavic gender linguistics are addressed in papers edited by Mills (1999). Lakoff (1987) is where women, fire, and dangerous things are discussed, and linguistic aspects of sexism are discussed by Mills (2008). Corbett (1991) offers an excellent review of the grammatical category of gender across the world's languages.

Chapter 5 Concepts on the Chopping Block

Šipka (2015a) offers a general framework to account for lexical and conceptual differences in the world's languages, and Geeraerts (2010) provides a theoretical account of approaches to those differences. Further theoretical insights can be found in Goddard (2008). Magga (2006) offers excellent examples of diversity in Saami terminology.

Chapter 6 Unripe Bananas and Ripe Tomatoes

Hardach (2019) discusses language-related issues of expressing tastes, and O'Mahony and Manzano Alba (1980) provide a comparison of taste descriptions in Spanish and English. Nishinari et al. (2008) provide an excellent review of food texture terms in English, French, Japanese, and Chinese. Simner and Ward (2006) offer an interesting discussion about synesthesia, that is, the crossing of the senses. Croimans and Majid (2016) address the language of wine and coffee experts.

Chapter 7 Mums and Clocks Mean Death

Sharifian (2011, 2017) offers an accessible review of differences in cultural scripts and cultural conceptualizations in various languages, and Allan (2007) discusses the effects of connotations. Zhu (2010) addresses cross-cultural miscommunication stemming from different cultural conceptualizations.

Chapter 8 The Past Is in Front of Us and the Future Is behind Our Back

The St. Augustine quote is from St. Augustine (2006: XV,20). Hobsbawm (1995, 1996) presents a different understanding of the nineteenth and twentieth centuries in common parlance and his approach. Hall (1959, 1966) demonstrates how the perception of time can have broader implications for cultural conceptualizations. Fuhrman and Boroditsky (2010) provide experimental results about cross-cultural differences in mental representations of time, and Núñez and Sweeser (2006) discuss the peculiar perception of time in Aymara.

Chapter 9 Far and Wide, Here and There

Space in language and cognition is discussed in Levinson (2005). Dase and Mishra (2010) address spatial orientation, discussing also Dolakhae (pp. 98–99). Mark (2011) includes a number of papers on construing landscape in various languages, and Mark and Turk (2003) provide an excellent example of how geographical categories are conceptualized differently in English and Yindjibarndi.

Chapter 10 Bottles with Throats

Lakoff and Johnson (1980, 1999) provide a fascinating theoretical account of the role of metaphors in languages, illustrated by a range of interesting examples. Kövecses (2005) offers an excellent review of cross-cultural variation in metaphors, and cross-cultural aspects of figurative language are discussed by Dobrovol'skij and Piirainen (2005).

Chapter 11 Setting the TV on Fire and Extinguishing It

Grzega and Schöner (2007) discuss the models of lexical development, and Liberman (2009) offers an excellent accessible guide to the study of word origins. Cresswell (2010) presents origins of over 3,000 English words and phrases.

Chapter 12 Traduttore, Traditore!

Pym (2010), Bassnett (2011), and Malmkjaer (2011) offer extensive reviews of translation studies, and Macdonald (2015) provides an interesting review of major mistranslations. Matsuzaki et al. (2016) present results of experiments with erroneous machine translations. Crocker (2007) shows examples of mistranslations, and Džamić (2017) explains the phenomenon of the Alan Ford comic book.

Chapter 13 *May You Suffer and Remember*

Austin (1962) is the groundbreaking classic work on doing things with words, which is relevant for this and most other chapters in this part of the book. Hrisztova-Gotthardt and Aleksa Varga (2015) offer an introduction to the study of proverbs, an interesting cross-linguistic comparison of which may be found in Weber et al. (1998). The background of Yiddish curses is discussed in Shai (1978).

Chapter 14 *I Screw Your 300 Gods*

Jay (2000) explores neurological, psychological, and social background of cussing, and the same author (Jay, 1992) provides an analysis of American English cussing in courts, movies, schoolyards, and on the streets. Pinker (2008) has chapters titled *Pottymouths and Five Ways to Cuss*. Šipka (2000) includes a full repertoire of Serbo-Croatian f-word cusses in its "jeb" section.

Chapter 15 *Either He Is Crazy or His Feet Stink*

Cowie (1998) includes a range of papers covering theoretical and practical aspects of the study of idioms. Granger and Meunier (2008) present papers discussing theoretical, corpus-linguistic, cultural-linguistic, lexicographic and natural-language-processing aspects of idioms, and Skandera (2008) includes papers addressing cultural aspects of English idioms.

Chapter 16 *Shoo and Scat*

Herder (2007) offers insight into his theories about the origin of language, while Simone (1995) includes papers discussing the phenomenon of iconicity of relevance in this and the next chapter. Further elaboration of the phenomenon can be found in the papers included in Zirker et al. (2017). Florencia Assaneo et al. (2011) look into the phonological aspects of onomatopoeias. Friedman (2015) provides interesting examples of cross-linguistic differences in onomatopoeias. Pinker (2008) discusses sound symbolism in the chapter titled: *Bling, Blogs, and Blurbs: Where Do New Words Come from?*

Chapter 17 A Dogs and Pony Show

All references mentioned in Chapter 16 are also relevant here.

Chapter 18 Blah-Blah-Blah, Yada-Yada-Yada

All references mentioned in Chapter 16 are also relevant here. Hamano (1998) discusses Japanese onomatopoeias.

Chapter 19 Acts of Darkness

Allan (2018) includes papers discussing the role of taboo in language, and euphemisms and dysphemisms are addressed in Allan and Burridge (1991). McEnery (2006) explores various social parameters of obscene words in English. Further exploration of "bad language" in English can be found in Wajnryb (2005).

Chapter 20 This for That

Morkovkina (1996) provides further information about the concept of agnonyms. D'Anna et al. (1991) tackle the issue of vocabulary size, and Aitchison (2012) offers an accessible guide to the mental lexicon.

Chapter 21 Me Tarzan, You Jane

An account of planned languages is provided by Blanke (2018), and Peterson (2015) discusses the process of creating languages for artistic purposes. Falk (1995) addresses international auxiliary languages. Mackenzie (2014) discusses the role of English as a lingua franca, and Holm (2000) provides an introduction into pidgins and creoles.

Chapter 22 How Many Languages Do You Speak?

ILR (2020) offers an insight into the Interagency Language Roundtable scale, an early language proficiency gauge. ACTFL (2019) describes the skills that are expected at each proficiency level and in each of the skills. Leaver et al. (2005) provide an excellent insight into all relevant parameters of language acquisition, and Liddicoat and Scarino (2005) explore intercultural aspects of language learning.

Chapter 23 Harmful and Shitty People

Domínguez and Nerlich (2002) provide an insight into theoretical aspects of the study of false cognates. O'Neill and Casanovas (1997) discuss the role of false friends in lexical acquisition. Šipka (2015b) compares false cognates in a closely related language with those in a less related language.

Chapter 24 Cars with Tails and Leadfooted Drivers

The following readings are relevant in this and the next three chapters. Pinker (2008) has a chapter titled: *Bling, Blogs, and Blurbs: Where Do New Words Come from?* Words typically emerge in three ways: by word-formation, semantic transfers, or borrowing from other languages. Plag (2012) and Štekauer and Liebe (2005) provide a review of word-formation mechanisms (one of the ways new words are created). Geeraerts (2010) offers a review of semantic mechanisms (another common mechanism of naming new concepts), and Kövecses (2005) addresses the metaphor, the most common of all semantic processes. Borrowing, the third common way of naming new concepts, is addressed in Haspelmath and Tadmor (2009). Talmy (1985) discusses general parameters of lexicalization. Bodle (2016) reports on the emergence of new words in English, while a more thorough analysis of those words can be found in Fischer (1998).

Chapter 25 Monkey, Dog, Worm, Snail, i.e. "Crazy A"

All readings mentioned in Chapter 24 are relevant here.

Chapter 26 Rovers and Ski-Rolls

All readings mentioned in Chapter 24 are relevant here.

Chapter 27 Extra Crispy Soccer Players

All readings mentioned in Chapter 24 are relevant here.

Chapter 28 Chinglish and Eurenglish

Kachru (1986) is the classic work where the concept of the three circles of English and world Englishes has been introduced. Bolton and

Kachru (2006) and Kirkpatrick (2012) offer reviews of world Englishes. Schreier et al. (2020) provide a collection of chapters on world Englishes. Gardner (2016) offers numerous examples and thorough analysis of Eurenglish, and Jackobs (2010) shows examples from Chinglish. Fletcher and Hawkins (2014) talk about Denglish, while Proshina (2012) discusses Slavic Englishes.

Chapter 29 Comrade, Sir

Sociolinguistics is reviewed in Hudson (1996) and pragmatics in Levinson (1983), the two fields relevant in the study of forms of address. Various aspects of forms of address are discussed in Dickey (1997). Farese (2018) offers a comparison of forms of address between English and Italian, and Lagerberg et al. (2014) address Russian address forms.

Chapter 30 Beer and Whiskey Mighty Risky

Curtis (2010) provides some background about cocktails, and Acitelli (2013) offers more information about the American beer brewing revolution. McKenna (2005) provides in-depth information about drunken sailors.

Chapter 31 SOFs and SOWs

Fayndrich (2008a, 2008b) discusses mechanisms involved in the creation of acronyms. Malenica and Fabijanić (2013) explore English military abbreviations. Jones (1968) addresses Soviet acronyms, and Young (1991) provides an analysis of totalitarian languages.

Chapter 32 Old-Lady Torturers, Horse Killers, and Bad Mornings

Hough (2016) presents a collection of chapters about names and naming by various authors from around the world. The principles of onomastics, the scholarly study of names, are presented in Nuessel (1992). W3C (2011) discusses the issues that the global variety of surname formats create in documentation. The following document also provides information about variety in naming practices www.fbiic.gov/public/2008/

nov/Naming_practice_guide_UK_2006.pdf. Öney Tan (2016) explores the unexpected link between military ranks and cooking.

Chapter 33 A Fleeing Bus

Lado (1957) offers a range of interesting examples relevant in this and the next two chapters. Wierzbicka (1992, 1997) addresses various culture-specific language forms, and Sharifian (2011, 2017) provides various examples of culture-specific conceptualizations. Palmer (1996) discusses culture-specific imagery.

Chapter 34 I Wish That You Enjoy in What You Have Deserved!

Brown and Levinson (1987) discuss politeness in language use, and Leech (2014) explores the pragmatics of politeness in English. The role of greetings in teaching is addressed in Folarin Schleicher (1997).

Chapter 35 Happy Hunting Ground

Rundstrom Williams (2006) looks into the pragmatics of condolences, and Gladkova (2010) compares Russian and English condolences. Metaphorical aspects of talking about death are addressed in Sexton (1997). Crespo-Fernández (2006) explores Victorian English euphemisms for death.

Chapter 36 A Language Is a Dialect with an Army and Navy

Weinreich (1945) is where the language versus dialect quip was mentioned. Maxwell (2018) offers an analysis of Weinreich's quip. Various issues about the relations between languages and dialects are addressed in Cheshire and Stein (2014). Pereltsveig (2012) provides an interesting review of the global linguistic variety. Baker (1945) talks about the Australian language and Mencken (1919) discusses the American language.

Pronunciation Respelling

Words from languages that use non-Latin scripts (other than Mandarin Chinese) are transcribed using English pronunciation respelling. This means that the closest English sound is given when possible. Sometimes, this sound stands for two sounds in the source language. For example, *i* as in *bit* stands for two Russian sounds, *u* – a regular *i* and *ы* – pronounced further back in the mouth and sounding a bit darker. Similarly, most Russian consonants will have soft and hard versions, so here t stands for both a hard т and a soft ть. When no corresponding sounds are available in English, the pronunciation of the sound is explained in nontechnical terms.

The present table is not meant to be a comprehensive account of all sounds in the languages mentioned in this book but rather a guide that enables pronunciation of the examples used here.

- ‾ (line above the vowel), ā, ē, ī, ō, ū – the vowel is pronounced longer than its counterpart without the line

    ʻ – ʻayn, sound in Arabic with no English equivalent pronounced by creating friction in the throat

a – as in c**a**t
b – as in **b**oy
ch – as in **ch**at
d – as in **d**ay
dh – as in **th**is
g – as in **g**o
h – as in **h**ide
ḥ - in Arabic, h pronounced in the throat in
i – as in p**i**t
j – as in **j**oy
k – as in **k**ilo
l – as in **l**emon
m – as in **m**om
n – as in **n**o
o – as in p**o**t
oo – as in t**oo**k
p – as in **p**art
r – as in **r**ay
s – as in **s**it
sh – as in **sh**op
t – as in **t**ip
th – as in **th**in

ts – as in blitz
u – as in but
v – as in vector
y – as in yes
z – as in zebra
zh – as in pleasure

Language-Specific Latin Characters

All languages that use Latin-based scripts, along with Mandarin Chinese, of which the standard pinyin transcription uses a Latin-Based script, are presented in the script they use. For Mandarin Chinese, pinyin Latin transcription was given along with the original rendering in Chinese characters. Only those special characters encountered in the examples used in this book are explained here. This is by no means a comprehensive pronunciation list for the languages mentioned in this book.

- ā á ǎ à – the signs over the *a* or any other vowel (*e, i, o, u*) represent 1st (flat), 2nd (rising), 3rd (falling and rising), and 4th (falling) tone in Mandarin Chinese. The vowel without the diacritic has a neutral tone.
- á – the sign over the *a* or any other vowel (*e, i, o, u, y*) in Czech, Slovak, and Hungarian means that the vowel is pronounced longer than its counterpart without the sign
- äu – oy, o as in pot, y as in yes
- ą – o as in hot but pronounced together with passing the stream of air through the nose, as if pronouncing the n sound very shortly after the o sound
- aa – long a as in father
- ay – ey, e as in bet, y as in yes (in French)
- č – ch as in cheese, in Polish and Serbo-Croatian, which also have a ć, the tongue is more tense than in the English ch
- c – ts as in blitz (most languages), k as in kit (in French, Italian, Spanish when before of a, o, u or a consonant), s as in sit (in French, Italian, Latin American Spanish, when in front of e, i), th as in that (in European Spanish, when before e, i), dzh – d as in day, zh as s in pleasure (in Turkish)
- cci – ch as in chip (in Italian)

ch – h as in hit (in German and Polish), ch as in cheese (in Spanish)
ć (spelled ci in Polish before a vowel) – ch as in cheese, with tongue being more relaxed
e – e as in bet (most languages and positions), silent (at the end of the word in French), e as in higher (in German before a consonant at the end of the word)
ě – ye, y as in yes, e as in bet (in Czech)
ę – e as in pet, but pronounced together with passing the stream of air through the nose, as if pronouncing the n sound very shortly after the o sound (in Polish)
ei – ay, a as in apple, y as in yes (in German)
eu – e as in bet, with lips rounded as when pronouncing o in ore (French), oy, o as in off, y as in yes (in German)
eux – e as in bet, with lips rounded as when pronouncing o in ore (in French)
d' – j as in Jack with the tongue being more relaxed
đ – – j as in Jack with the tongue being more relaxed
dź (spelled dzi before a vowel) – j as in Jack with the tongue being more relaxed
gh – g as in go
gli – ly, l as in list, y as in yes
ie – ee as in bee (in German)
ı – e as in over (in Turkish)
j – y as in yes (most languages), h as in hit (in Spanish)
ll – y as in yes (in many Latin American varieties of Spanish) ly, l as in list, y as in yes (in European Spanish), l (in Italian, German)
ł - w as in word
ń, spelled ni before vowels – ny, n as in no, y as in yes (in Polish)
nh – ny, n as in no, y as in yes (in Portuguese)
ó – oo as in look
öő - short and long version of the sound where the lips are set to pronounce o as in pot, but then e as in bet is pronounced
ou – oo as in book (in French)
q – k as in kit (in most languages), ch as in chip (in Albanian)
ř – a sound between r as in rip and s as in pleasure (in Czech)
rz – s as in pleasure
s – s as in set (most languages) z as in zip (in German), sh as in ship (in Hungarian)
st – sht, sh as in ship, t as in tip (in German)

ß, ss – s as in sit (in German)

sz – s as in sit (in Hungarian), sh as in ship, with the tongue being more tense (in Polish)

sch – sh as in ship (in German)

š – sh as in ship

ś, spelled si before vowels – sh as in ship, with the tongue being more relaxed

ş – sh as in ship

t' – ty, t as in tip, y as in yes

ţ – ts as in blitz

tsch – ch as in chip (in German)

ü, ű – short and long version of the sound where the lips are set to pronounce oo as in book, but then i as in bit is pronounced

v – v as in vat (in most languages), f as in fat (in German)

w – v as in vat (in Polish and German)

y – a sound between i in sit and e in bet (in Polish), i as in sit (in Czech, Slovak, Hungarian)

z – z as in zip (in most languages) – th as in this (in Spanish), ts as in blitz (in German)

ż – s as in pleasure, with the tongue being more tense (in Polish)

ź, spelled zi before vowels – s as in pleasure, with tongue being more relaxed (in Polish)

ž – s as in pleasure

zz – dz, d as in day, z as in zip

References

Acitelli, Tom. 2013. *The Audacity of Hops: The History of America's Craft Beer Revolution*. Chicago: Chicago Review Press.

ACTFL. 2019. *NCSSFL-ACTFL Can-Do Statements. Progress Indicators for Language Learners*. Alexandria: ACTFL, www.actfl.org/publications/guidelines-and-manuals/ncssfl-actfl-can-do-statements (accessed January 14, 2020).

Adams, Douglas and John Lloyd. 1983. *The Meaning of Liff*. London: Pan Books.

Aitchison, Jean. 2012. *Words in the Mind: An Introduction into Mental Lexicon*, 4th ed. New York: Wiley.

Allan, Keith. 2007. The Pragmatics of Connotations. *Journal of Pragmatics* 39(6), 1047–1057.

  (ed.). 2018. *The Oxford Handbook of Taboo Words and Language*. Oxford: Oxford University Press.

Allan, Keith and Kate Burridge. 1991. *Euphemism and Dysphemism: Language Used as Shield and Weapon*. Oxford: Oxford University Press.

Altshuler, Daniel et al. 2019. *A Course in Semantics*. Cambridge: MIT Press.

Assaneo, María Florencia, Juan Ignacio Nichols, and Marcos Alberto Trevisan. 2011. The Anatomy of Onomatopoeia. *PLOS ONE*, December 14, 2011, https://doi.org/10.1371/journal.pone.002831.

Augustine. 2006. *Confessions*. Indianapolis: Hackett Publishing.

Austin, John L. 1962. *How to Do Things with Words*. Oxford: Clarendon Press.

Baker, Sidney J. 1945. *The Australian Language*. Sydney and London: Angus and Robertson.

Bassnett, Susan. 2011. The Translator as Cross-Cultural Mediator. In: Malmkjaer, Kirsten and Kevin Windle (eds.) *The Oxford Handbook of Translation Studies*. Oxford: Oxford University Press, 94–107.

Berlin, Brent and Paul Kay. 1969. *Basic Color Terms: Their Universality and Evolution*. Berkeley: University of California Press.

Blanke, Detlev. 2018. *International Planned Languages*. New York: Mondial.

Bodle, Andrew. 2016. How New Words Are Born, *The Guardian*, February 14, www.theguardian.com/media/mind-your-language/2016/feb/04/english-neologisms-new-words (accessed March 16, 2020).
Bolton, Kingsley and Braj Kachru (eds.). 2006. *World Englishes*. London and New York: Routledge.
Böttcher, Sven. 1999. *Der tiefere Sinn des Labenz. Das Wörterbuch der bisher unbenannten Gegenstände und Gefühle*. Frankfurt am Main: Rogner & Bernhard.
Brown, Penelope and Stephen Levinson. 1987. *Politeness: Some Universals in Language Use*. Cambridge: Cambridge University Press.
Casson, R. W. 1997. Color Shift: Evolution of English Color Terms from Brightness to Hue. In: Hardin, C. L. and Luisa Maffi (eds.) *Color Categories in Thought and Language*. Cambridge: Cambridge University Press, 224–239.
Cheshire, Jenny and Dieter Stein. 2014. *Taming the Vernacular: From Dialect to Written Standard Language*. London and New York: Routledge.
Corbett, Greville. 1991. *Gender*. Cambridge: Cambridge University Press.
2000. *Number*. Cambridge: Cambridge University Press.
Cowie, Anthony P. (ed.). 1998. *Phraseology: Theory, Analysis, and Application*. Oxford: Oxford University Press.
Crespo-Fernández, Eliecer. 2006. The Language of Death: Euphemism and Conceptual Metaphorization in Victorian Obituaries. *SKY Journal of Linguistics* 19, 101–130.
Cresswell, Julia. 2010. *The Oxford Dictionary of Word Origins*, 2nd ed. Oxford: Oxford University Press.
Crocker, Charlie. 2007. *Lost in Translation: Misadventures in English Abroad*. London: Michael O'Mara Books.
Croimans, Ilja and Asifa Majid. 2016. Not All Flavor Expertise Is Equal: The Language of Wine and Coffee Experts. *PLOS ONE*, https://doi.org/10.1371/journal.pone.0155845.
Croom, Adam M. 2011. Slurs. *Language Sciences* 33, 343–358.
Cruse, Alan D. 1986. *Lexical Semantics*. Cambridge: Cambridge University Press.
2011. *Meaning in Language*, 2nd ed. Oxford: Oxford University Press.
Culpeper, Jonathan. 2011. *Impoliteness: Using Language to Cause Offence*. Cambridge: Cambridge University Press.
Curtis, Wayne. 2010. Who Invented the Cocktail? That Depends on How You Define Invented. And Cocktail. *The Atlantic*, www.theatlantic.com/magazine/archive/2010/06/who-invented-the-cocktail/308105/ (accessed March 16, 2020).

D'Anna, Catherine A., Eugene B. Zechmeister, and James W. Hall. 1991. Toward a Meaningful Definition of Vocabulary Size. *Journal of Reading Behavior* 23(1) (March 1991), 109–122, https://doi:10.1080/10862969109547729.

Dasen, Pierre R. and Ramesh C. Mishra. 2010. *Development of Geocentric Spatial Language and Cognition: An Eco-cultural Perception*. Cambridge: Cambridge University Press.

Dickey, Eleanor. 1997. Forms of Address and Terms of Reference. *Linguistics* 33, 255–274.

Dobrovol'skij, Dmitrij and Elisabeth Piirainen. 2005. *Figurative Language: Cross-Cultural and Cross-Linguistic Perspectives*. Leiden: Brill.

Domínguez, Pedro and Brigitte Nerlich. 2002. False Friends: Their Origin and Semantics in Some Selected Languages. *Journal of Pragmatics* 34, 1833–1849, https://doi.org/10.1016/S0378-2166(02)00024-3.

Džamić, Lazar. 2017. *Flower Shop in the House of Flowers: How We Adopted and Lived Alan Ford*. Belgrade: Deutsche Gesellschaft für Internationale Zusammenarbeit.

Falk, Julia. 1995. Words without Grammar: Linguists and the International Auxiliary Language Movement in the United States. *Language and Communication* 15(3), 241–259.

Fandrich, Ingrid. 2008a. Pagad, Chillax and Jozi: A Multi-Level Approach to Acronyms, Blends, and Clippings. *Nawa Journal of Language and Communication* 2(2), 71–88.

2008b. Submorphemic Elements in the Formation of Acronyms, Blends and Clippings: Lexis 2. *Lexical Submorphemics / La submorphémique lexicale*, 2, 105–123.

Farese, Gian Marco. 2018. *The Cultural Semantics of Address Practices: A Contrastive Study between English and Italian*. Lanham: Rowman & Littlefield.

Fischer, Roswitha. 1998. *Lexical Change in Present-Day English: A Corpus-Based Study of the Motivation, Institutionalization, and Productivity of Creative Neologisms*. Tübingen: Günter Narr Verlag.

Fletcher, Adam and Paul Hawkins. 2014. *Denglish for Better Knowers*. Berlin: Ullstein.

Foer, Jonathan Safran. 2002. *Everything Is Illuminated*. Boston: Houghton Mifflin.

Folarin Schleicher, Antonia. 1997. Using Greetings to Teach Cultural Understanding. *The Modern Language Journal* 81, 334–343. https://doi.org/10.1111/j.1540-4781.1997.tb05493.x.

Frege, Gottlob. 1948. Sense and Reference, *The Philosophical Review* 57(3), 209–230.

Friedman, Uri. 2015. How to Snore in Korean. The Mystery of Onomatopoeia around the World. *The Atlantic*. November 27, 2015, www.theatlantic.com/international/archive/2015/11/onomatopoeia-world-languages/415824/ (accessed March 15, 2020).

Fuhrman, Orly and Lera Boroditsky. 2010. Cross-Cultural Differences in Mental Representations of Time: Evidence from an Implicit Non-linguistic Task. *Cognitive Science*. https://doi.org/10.1111/j.1551-6709.2010.01105.x.

Gardner, Jeremy. 2016. *Misused English Words and Expressions in EU Publications*. Brussels: European Court of Auditors, www.eca.europa.eu/Other%20publications/EN_TERMINOLOGY_PUBLICATION/EN_TERMINOLOGY_PUBLICATION.pdf (accessed March 22, 2021).

Geeraerts, Dirk. 2010. *Theories of Lexical Semantics*. Oxford: Oxford University Press.

Gladkova, Anna. 2010. Sympathy, Compassion, and Empathy in English and Russian: A Linguistic and Cultural Analysis. *Culture and Psychology* 16(2), 267–285.

Goddard, Cliff. 2008. *Cross-Linguistic Semantics*. Amsterdam: John Benjamins.

Granger, Sylvaine and Fanny Meunier (eds.). 2008. *Phraseology: An Interdisciplinary Perspective*. Amsterdam: John Benjamins.

Grzega, Joachim and Marion Schöner. 2007. *English and General Historical Lexicology*. Eichstätt-Ingolstadt: Katolische Universität.

Hall, Edward T. 1959. *The Silent Language*. Garden City, NY: Doubleday and Co.

1966. *The Hidden Dimension*. Garden City, NY: Doubleday and Co.

Halliday, M. A. K. and Colin Yallop. 2007. *Lexicology: A Short Introduction*. London, New York: Continuum.

Hamano, Shoko. 1998. *The Sound-Symbolic System of Japanese*. Stanford, CA: CSLI.

Hardach, Sophie. 2019. How Your Language Reflects the Senses You Use, *BBC Future*, February 26, 2019, www.bbc.com/future/article/20190226-how-your-language-reflects-the-senses-you-use (accessed March 14, 2020).

Hardin, C. L. and Luisa Maffi (eds.). 1997. *Color Categories in Thought and Language*. Cambridge: Cambridge University Press, https://doi.org/10.1017/CBO978051151981.

Haspelmath, Martin and Uri Tadmor (eds.). 2009. *Loanwords in the World Languages: A Comparative Handbook*. Berlin: Walter de Gruyter.

2020. *World Loanword Database*. Leipzig: Max Planck Institute for Evolutionary Anthropology. http://wold.clld.org, (accessed March 15, 2020).

Hellinger, Marlis and Hadumod Bußmann (eds.). 2001. *Gender across Languages: The Linguistic Representation of Women and Men*, Volume 1. Amsterdam: John Benjamins.
  2002. *Gender across Languages: The Linguistic Representation of Women and Men*, Volume 2. Amsterdam: John Benjamins.
  2003. *Gender across Languages: The Linguistic Representation of Women and Men*, Volume 3. Amsterdam.
Hellinger, Marlis and Heiko Motschenbacher (eds.). 2015. *Gender across Languages*, Volume 4. Amsterdam: John Benjamins.
Herder, Johann Gottfried. 2007. *Philosophical Writings*, Desmond M. Clarke and Michael N. Forster (eds.). Cambridge: Cambridge University Press.
Hobsbawm, Eric. 1995. *The Age of Extremes: The Short Twentieth Century 1914–1991*. London: Abacus.
  1996. *The Age of Revolution 1789–1848*. New York: Vintage Books.
Hofstede, Geert. 2020. *The 6-D Model of National Culture*. https://geerthofstede.com/culture-geert-hofstede-gert-jan-hofstede/6d-model-of-national-culture/ (accessed March 15, 2020).
Hofstede, Geert and Gert Jan Hofstede 1994. *Cultures and Organizations: Software of the Mind*. London, HarperCollins.
Holm, John. 2000. *An Introduction to Pidgins and Creoles*. Cambridge: Cambridge University Press.
Hough, Carol (ed.). 2016. *The Oxford Handbook of Names and Naming*. Oxford: Oxford University Press.
Hrisztova-Gotthardt, Hrisztalina and Melita Aleksa Varga (eds.). 2015. *Introduction to Paremiology: A Comprehensive Guide to Proverb Studies*. Berlin, Boston: De Gruyter.
Hudson, Richard A. 1996. *Sociolinguistics*. Cambridge: Cambridge University Press.
IRL. 2020. *History of the IRL Scale*. Washington, DC: Interagency Language Roundtable, www.govtilr.org/Skills/IRL%20Scale%20History.htm (accessed January 14, 2020).
Jackobs, Andrew. 2010. Shanghai Is Trying to Untangle the Mangled English of Chinglish, *New York Times*, May 2, 2010, www.nytimes.com/2010/05/03/world/asia/03chinglish.html?pagewanted=1&_r=0 (accessed March 16, 2020).
Jackson, Howard. 2007. *Words, Meaning and Vocabulary: An Introduction to Modern English Lexicology*. London, New York: Bloomsbury.
Jay, Timothy. 1992. *Cursing in America*. Amsterdam: John Benjamins.
  2000. *Why We Curse: A Neuro-psycho-social Theory of Speech*. Amsterdam: John Benjamins.

Jones, Lawrence G. 1968. The Structure of the Soviet Acronyms. In: Cartier, Normand R. (ed.) *Aquila*. Berlin, Springer, 75–94.
Kachru, Braj B. 1986. *The Alchemy of English: The Spread, Function and Models of Non-native Englishes*. Oxford: Pergamon.
Kirkpatrick, Andy. 2012. *Routledge Handbooks in Applied Linguistics: The Routledge Handbook of World Englishes*. London: Routledge.
Kövecses, Zoltán. 2005. *Metaphor in Culture: Universality and Variation*. Cambridge: Cambridge University Press.
Lado, Robert. 1957. *Linguistics across Cultures*. Ann Arbor: The University of Michigan Press.
Lagerberg, Robert, Heinz Kretzenbacher and John Hajek. 2014. Forms and Patterns of Address in Russian: Recent Research and Future Directions. *Australian Slavonic and East European Studies* 28(1–2), 179–209.
Lakoff, George. 1987. *Women, Fire, and Dangerous Things*. Chicago: University of Chicago Press.
Lakoff, George and Mark Johnson. 1980. *Metaphors We Live by*. Chicago: University of Chicago Press.
　1999. *Philosophy in the Flesh: The Embodied Mind and Its Challenge to Western Thought*. New York: Basic Books.
Leaver, Betty Lou, Madeline Ehrman, and Boris Shekhtman. 2005. *Achieving Success in Second Language Acquisition*. Cambridge: Cambridge University Press.
Leech, Geoffrey N. 2014. *The Pragmatics of Politeness*. Oxford: Oxford University Press.
Levinson, Stephen C. 1983. *Pragmatics*. Cambridge: Cambridge University Press.
　2005. *Space in Language and Cognition: Explorations in Cognitive Diversity*. Cambridge: Cambridge University Press.
Liberman, Anatoly. 2009. *Word Origins and How We Know Them: Etymology for Everyone*. Oxford: Oxford University Press.
Liddicoat, Anthony J. and Angela Scarino. 2013. *Intercultural Language Teaching and Learning*. Hoboken: Wiley-Blackwell.
Lipka, Leonhard. 2002. *An Outline of English Lexicology*, 3rd ed. Tübingen: G. Narr.
Loreto, Vittorio, Animesh Mukherjee, and Francesca Tria. 2012. On the Origin of the Hierarchy of Color Names. *Proceedings of the National Academy of Sciences. May 2012* 109(18), 6819–6824, doi:10.1073/pnas.1113347109.
Lyons, John. 1977. *Semantics*. 2 vols. Cambridge: Cambridge University Press.
Macdonald, Fiona. 2015. The Greatest Mistranslations Ever. *BBC Culture*, February 2, 2015, www.bbc.com/culture/story/20150202-the-greatest-mistranslations-ever (accessed March 15, 2020).

Mackenzie, Ian. 2014. *English as a Lingua Franca.* London: Routledge.
MacQuarrie, Colleen. 2010. Othering. In: Mills, Albert J., Durepos, Gabrielle, and Wiebe, Eiden (eds.) *Encyclopedia of Case Study Research.* Thousand Oaks: Sage, 636–640.
Magga, Ole Henrik. 2006. Diversity in Saami Terminology for Reindeer, Snow, and Ice. *International Social Science Journal* 58(187), 25–34.
Malenica, Frane and Ivo Fabijanić. 2013. Abbreviations in English Military Terminology. *Brno Studies in English* 39, 58–87. https://doi.org/10.5817/BSE2013-1-4.
Malmkjaer, Kirsten. 2011. Meaning and Translation. In: Malmkjaer, Kirsten and Kevin Windle (eds.) *The Oxford Handbook of Translation Studies.* Oxford: Oxford University Press, 108–122.
Mark, David (ed.). 2011. *Landscape in Language: Transdisciplinary Perspectives.* Amsterdam: John Benjamins.
Mark, David M. and Andrew G. Turk. 2003. Landscape Categories in Yindjibarndi: Ontology, Environment, and Language. In: Kuhn, W., Worboys, M., andTimpf, S. (eds.) *Spatial Information Theory: Foundations of Geographic Information Science, LNCS,* vol. 2825. Berlin: Springer-Verlag, 28–45.
Matsuzaki, Takuya, Akira Fujita, Naoya Todo, and Noriko H. Arai. 2016. Translation Errors and Incomprehensibility: A Case Study Using Machine-Translated Second Language Proficiency Tests. *LREC 2016 Conference Proceedings,* www.lrec-conf.org/proceedings/lrec2016/pdf/921_Paper.pdf (accessed March 15, 2020).
Maxwell, Alexander. 2018. When Theory Is a Joke: The Weinreich Witticism in Linguistics. *Beiträge zur Geschichte der Sprachwissenschaft* 28(2), 263–292.
McConvell, Patrick, Ian Keen, and Rachel Hendery (eds.). 2013. *Kinship Systems: Change and Reconstruction.* Salt Lake City: University of Utah Press.
McEnery, Tony. 2006. *Swearing in English: Bad Language, Purity and Power from 1586 to the Present.* London: Routledge.
McKenna, Robert. 2005. *Bottoms Up: A Cocktail of Liquid Lore.* Mystic, CT: Flat Hammock Press.
Mencken, Henry Louis. 1919. *The American Language.* New York: Alfred A. Knopf.
Menninger, Karl. 1969. *Number Words and Number Systems: A Cultural History of Numbers.* Cambridge, MA: MIT Press.
Mills, Margaret H. (ed.). 1999. *Slavic Gender Linguistics.* Amsterdam: John Benjamins.
Mills, Sara. 2008. *Language and Sexism.* Cambridge: Cambridge University Press.

Morkovkina, Anna V. 1996. Russian Agnonyms as an Object of Lexicographic Treatment. In: Gellerstam, Martin et al. (ed.) *Euralex 96 Proceedings*. Göteborg: Göteborg University, 437–442.

Ndimele, Ozo-mekuri and S. L. Chan. 2016. *The Numeral Systems of Nigerian Languages*. Oxford: African Books Collective. http://muse.jhu.edu/book/46365.

Nishinari, Katsuyoshi, Fumio Hayakawa, Chong-Fei Xia, Long Huang, Jean-François Meullenet, and Jean-Marc Sieffermann. 2008. Comparative Study of Texture Terms: English, French, Japanese and Chinese. *Journal of Texture Studies* 39, 530–568.

Nogle, Lawrence E. 1974. *Method and Theory in the Semantic and Cognition of Kinship Terminology*. The Hague, Paris: Mouton.

Nuessel, Frank. 1992. *The Study of Names: A Guide to the Principles and Topics*. Westport, CT: Greenwood.

Núñez, Rafael E. and Eve Sweetser. 2006. With the Future behind Them: Convergent Evidence from Aymara Language and Gesture in the Crosslinguistic Comparison of Spatial Construals of Time. *Cognitive Science* 30, 401–450.

O'Mahony, Michael, Maria del Carmen, and Manzano Alba. 1980. Taste Descriptions in Spanish and English. *Chemical Senses* 5(1), March 1980, 47–62, https://doi.org/10.1093/chemse/5.1.47.

O'Neill, Maria and Montse Casanovas. 1997. False Friends: A Historical Perspective and Present Implications for Lexical Acquisition. *Bells: Barcelona English Language and Literature* 8, 103–105.

Öney Tan, Aylin. 2016. The Janissary, the Coup, and the Cauldron. *Hürriet Daily News*, July 25, 2016, www.hurriyetdailynews.com/opinion/aylin-oney-tan/the-janissary-the-coup-and-the-cauldron-102015 (accessed April 28, 2020).

Palmer, F. R. 1976. *Semantics: A New Outline*. Cambridge: Cambridge University Press.

Palmer, Garry. 1996. *Toward a Theory of Cultural Linguistics*. Austin: University of Texas Press.

Pavlenko, Aneta et al. 2017. Communicative Relevance: Color References in Bilingual and Trilingual Speakers. *Bilingualism: Language and Cognition* 20(4), 853–866.

Pereltsveig, Asya. 2012. *Languages of the World: An Introduction*. Cambridge: Cambridge University Press.

Peterson, David. 2015. *The Art of Language Invention: From Horse-Lords to Dark Elves, the Words behind Word-Building*. New York: Penguin Books.

Pinker, Steven. 2008. *The Stuff of Thought; Language as a Window into Human Nature*. London: Penguin Books.

Plag, Ingo. 2012. *Word-Formation in English*. Cambridge: Cambridge University Press.
Proshina, Zoya. 2012. Slavic Englishes. In: Kirkpatrick, Andy (ed.) *Routledge Handbooks in Applied Linguistics: The Routledge Handbook of World Englishes*. London: Routledge, 299–315.
Pym, Anthony. 2010. *Exploring Translation Theories*. London: Routledge.
Rosch, Eleanor H. 1973. Natural Categories. *Cognitive Psychology* 4, 328–350.
Rundstrom Williams, Tracy. 2006. Linguistic Politeness in Expressing Condolences: A Case Study. *RASK* 24, 45–62.
Schreier, Daniel, Marianne Hundt, and Edgar W. Schneider (eds.). 2020. *The Cambridge Handbook of World Englishes*. Cambridge: Cambridge University Press.
Schusky, Ernest L. 1983. *Manual for Kinship Analysis*. Boston: University Press of America.
Sexton, James. 1997. The Semantics of Death and Dying: Metaphor and Mortality, *A Review of General Semantics* 54(3), 333–345.
Shai, Donna. 1978. Public Cursing and Social Control in a Traditional Jewish Community. *Western Folklore* 37(1), 39–46.
Sharifian, Farzad 2011. *Cultural Conceptualisations and Language*. Philadelphia: John Benjamins.
  2017. *Cultural Linguistics*. Philadelphia: John Benjamins.
Simner, Julia and Jamie Ward. 2006. Synesthesia: The Taste of Words on the Tip of the Tongue. *Nature* 444, 438. https://doi.org/10.1038/444438a.
Simone, Rafaele (ed.). 1995. *Iconicity in Language*. Amsterdam: John Benjamins.
Šipka, Danko. 2000. *SerboCroatian – English Colloquial Dictionary*. Springfield, VA: Dunwoody Press.
  2015a. *Lexical Conflict: Theory and Practice*. Cambridge: Cambridge University Press.
  2015b. Slavic False Cognates: A Cross-linguistic Comparison. *Porta Linguarum* 14, 39–50.
Skandera, Paul (ed.). 2008. *Phraseology and Culture in English*. Berlin, Boston: De Gruyter Mouton.
Steen, Gerard. 2007. *Finding Metaphor in Grammar and Usage*. Amsterdam: John Benjamins.
Štekauer, Pavol and Rochelle Lieber (ed.). 2005. *Handbook of Word-Formation*. Berlin: Springer.
Talmy, Leonard. 1985. Lexicalization Patterns: Semantic Structure in Lexical Forms. In: Shopen, Timothy (ed.) *Language Typology and Syntactic Description, 2nd ed. vol. III: Grammatical Categories and the Lexicon*. Cambridge: Cambridge University Press, 57–149.

Taylor, John (ed.). 2015. *The Oxford Handbook of the Word*. Oxford: Oxford University Press.
W3C. 2011. *Personal Names around the World*. www.w3.org/International/questions/qa-personal-names (accessed March 16, 2020).
Wajnryb, Ruth. 2005. *Expletive Deleted: A Good Look at Bad Language*. New York: Free Press.
Weber, Elke U. and Christopher K. Hsee. 1998. What Folklore Tells Us about Risk and Risk Taking: Cross-cultural Comparisons of American, German, and Chinese Proverbs. *Organizational Behavior and Human Decision Processes* 75(2), https://ssrn.com/abstract=930085 (accessed March 15, 2020).
Weinreich, Max. 1945. *The YIVO and the Problems of Our Time*, a speech at the Annual YIVO Conference on January 5, 1945.
Wierzbicka, Anna. 1992. *Semantics, Culture, and Cognition: Universal Human Concepts in Culture-Specific Configurations*. Oxford: Oxford University Press.
  1997. *Understanding Cultures through Their Key Words: English, Russian, Polish, German, and Japanese*. Oxford: Oxford University Press.
Wilford, John Noble. 1983. Homer's Sea: Wine Dark?, *New York Times*, December 20, 1983, 55–56.
Winawer, Jonathan et al. 2007. Russian Blues Reveal Effects of Language on Color Discrimination. *Proceedings of the National Academy of Sciences of the United States of America* 104(19), 7780–7785. https://doi.org/10.1073/pnas.0701644104.
Wittgenstein, Ludwig. 1922. *Tractatus Logico-Philosophicus*. New York: Harcourt, Brace & Company, Inc.
  1953. *Philosophical Investigations*. New York: Macmillan.
WordNet. 2020. *WordNet: An Electronic Lexical Database*. Princeton: Princeton University, https://wordnet.princeton.edu/ (accessed March 15, 2020).
Yang, Xu and Terry Regier. 2014. *Numeral Systems across Languages Support Efficient Communication: From Approximate Numerosity to Recursion*. Berkeley, CA: Berkeley University, https://lclab.berkeley.edu/papers/number-2014.pdf (accessed March 13, 2020).
Young, John Wesley. 1991. *Totalitarian Language: Orwell's Newspeak and Its Nazi and Communist Antecedents*. Charlottesville: University Press of Virginia.
Zgusta, Ladislav. 1971. *Manual of Lexicography*. The Hague: Mouton.
Zhu, Pinfan. 2010. Cross-Cultural Blunders in Professional Communication from a Semantic Perspective. *Journal of Technical Writing and Communication* 40(2), 179–196. https://doi.org/10.2190/TW.40.2.e.
Zirker, Angelika, Matthias Bauer, Olga Fischer, and Christina Ljungberg (eds.). 2017. *Dimensions of Iconicity*. Amsterdam: John Benjamins.

Index of Languages

Afrikaans, a Germanic language spoken by over 7 million native speakers in southern Africa · 153, 157

Akan, a Niger-Congo language spoken by 10 million native speakers in West Africa · 65

Albanian, an independent Indo-European language spoken by 7 million native speakers in southeastern Europe · 153, 161, 176

American English, a national variety of ☞ English · 30, 36–37, 57, 59, 70, 75, 114, 120, 122, 147, 153, 169, 180, 184, 186, 198, 214, 217

Amharic, an Afroasiatic language spoken by 22 million native speakers in East Africa · 58

Anangu Pitjantjajara, a Pama-Nyungan language spoken by over 3,000 native speakers in Australia · 66

Arabic, a Semitic language spoken by 310 million native speakers in the Middle East and North Africa, with Modern Standard and various regional colloquial varieties · 33–34, 54, 58, 66, 68, 71, 94, 133–135, 139, 170, 209, 214

Argentine Spanish, a national variety of ☞ Spanish · 204

Armenian language, a separate branch of Indo-European, spoken by 6.7 million people in the Caucasus region and by a diaspora in many other countries · 215

Australian English, a national variety of ☞ English · 15, 57, 72, 187, 215

Aymara, an Aymaran language, spoken by 1.7 million native speakers in South America · 63

Bantu languages, Niger-Congo languages, encompassing Swahili, Zulu, and a large number of other languages spoken throughout Sub-Saharan Africa · 3, 40, 134

Bashkir, a Turkic language spoken by 1.2 million native speakers in central Asia · 161

Basic English, a constructed simplified variety of ☞ English · 135

Basque, an unaffiliated language spoken by 750,000 native speakers in southwestern Europe · 23, 40, 118, 161

Batak, an Austronesian language spoken by 1.2 million speakers in southeastern Asia · 118

Bavarian, a regional dialect of ☞ German · 182

Belarussian, a Slavic language spoken by over 5 million native speakers in Eastern Europe · 21, 106, 114, 135, 157, 178

Bosnian, an ethnic variety of ☞ Serbo-Croatian · 94, 212, 217

Brazilian Portuguese, a national variety of ☞ Portuguese · 87, 104

British English, a national variety of ☞ English · 15, 57, 146, 214–215, 217

Bulgarian, a Slavic language spoken by 9 million native speakers in southeastern Europe · 39, 52, 57, 113, 124, 156–157, 161, 163, 165, 176, 178, 205–206

Canadian English, a national variety of ☞ English · 30, 57

Canadian French, a national variety of ☞ French · 41

245

Catalan, an Italic language spoken by 4 million native speakers in southwestern Europe · 65, 133, 161–162, 169

Celtic languages, Indo-European languages including Irish, Gaelic, and Manx spoken on British Isles · 214

Chinglish, a developing-circle variety of ☞ English in China · 133, 170, 172

Chukchi, a Chukoto-Kamchatkan language spoken by 30,000 native speakers in northeastern Asia · 48, 114

Chuvash, a Turkic language spoken by 1 million native speakers in the Volga region of Russia · 161

Croatian, an ethnic variety of ☞ Serbo-Croatian · 21, 27, 66, 68, 159, 165, 212, 217

Czech, a Slavic language spoken by over 10 million native speakers in central Europe · 1, 15, 21, 23, 39, 57, 74, 104, 118, 124, 131, 153, 159, 161, 167–168, 176, 199, 207, 209

Danish, a Germanic language spoken by 6 million native speakers in northern Europe · 87, 106, 108, 155, 157, 162

Denglish, a developing-circle variety of ☞ English in German-speaking countries · 172

Dutch, a Germanic language spoken by 24 million native speakers in Western Europe · 30, 37, 104, 106, 108, 118, 162–163, 168, 180, 206, 209, 214

Dyirbal, a Pama-Nyungan language spoken by 29 people in Australia · 40

English, a Germanic language spoken by close to 400 million native speakers, with British, US, Canadian, Australian, and New Zealand as major varieties · 1, 3, 5, 8, 10, 13, 15, 19, 21–22, 25–26, 29, 31, 33–34, 38–40, 43–44, 46–47, 49, 51–52, 57, 60, 64–66, 68, 70–71, 74–75, 77, 81–82, 87–88, 90, 93, 102, 104–105, 108, 112–114, 117–118, 121–122, 124–125, 128–131, 133–135, 139, 143, 145, 151–152, 155–158, 161–163, 165–166, 168, 170–173, 175–176, 180, 184, 186–188, 190, 194, 196, 199–202, 204–207, 212, 214–217, 221, 230

Erzya, a Uralic language spoken by 430,000 native speakers in parts of central European Russia · 74–75

Esperanto, the most widely used constructed language · 133–135, 161, 167

Estonian, a Uralic language spoken by 1.1 million native speakers in northeastern Europe · 10, 118, 162

Eurenglish, a developing-circle variety of ☞ English in the European Union · 133, 171, 173

Fijian, an Austronesian language spoken by 333,000 native speakers in the South Pacific · 124

Filipino, a Malayo-Polinesian language spoken by 45 million native speakers in southeastern Asia · 49

Finnish, a Uralic language spoken by over 5 million native speakers in northern Europe · 3, 108–109, 112, 118, 157, 167, 214

French, an Italic language spoken by 77 million native speakers, with European, Canadian, and African as major varieties · 1, 23, 26, 39, 51, 65–66, 76, 87, 89, 103, 106, 108, 112, 117–118, 133, 135, 143–144, 155, 161–162, 167–168, 170, 172, 175, 178, 180, 196, 205–206, 212, 214

Gaelic, a Celtic language spoken by 50,000 native speakers in Great Britain and Canada · 214

Galician, an Italic language spoken by 2.4 million native speakers in southwestern Europe · 163

Georgian, a Kartvelian language spoken by 3.7 million native speakers in Eastern Europe · 23, 102, 156, 161

German, a Germanic language spoken by 95 million native speakers in central Europe, with German, Austrian, and

Index of Languages 247

Swiss as major varieties · 1, 15, 19–20, 23, 26, 29, 33, 37, 40, 47, 52, 57, 76, 89, 103, 106, 108, 112–114, 118, 122, 124, 131, 135, 139, 143, 147, 151, 154, 156, 161, 165, 167–168, 172, 175, 178, 180–181, 184, 186–187, 196–197, 201, 205–207, 209, 212, 214

Germanic languages, Indo-European languages including English, German, Dutch, Danish, Swedish, Norwegian, Icelandic, and several smaller languages spoken in central, Western, and northern Europe · 207

Germany German, a national variety of ☞ German · 147

Greek, a Hellenic language with an ancient variant, and the modern one spoken by over 13 million native speakers in southeastern Europe · 22, 79, 109, 114, 118, 123, 133, 154, 157, 161, 167–168, 214

Hawaiian language, an Austronesian language spoken by 24,000 native speakers in the South Pacific · 215

Hebrew, a Semitic language with an ancient variant, and the modern one spoken by over 5 million native speakers in the Middle East · 23, 65, 71, 123, 139, 157

Hindustani, an Indo-Aryan language spoken by 322 million native speakers in south Asia, with Hindi and Urdu as its main varieties · 135, 139

Hopi, a Uto-Aztecan language spoken by over 19,000 native speakers in Arizona · 47

Hungarian, a Uralic language spoken by 13 million native speakers in central Europe · 25, 40, 100, 105, 108, 157, 162–163, 167, 176, 206, 214

Icelandic, a Germanic language spoken by more than 300,000 native speakers in northern Europe · 34–35, 193

Ido, a constructed language, reformed Esperanto · 135

Ilocano, an Austronesian language spoken by 9 million native speakers in the Philippines · 161

Interlingua, a constructed language, based on English, French, Italian, Spanish, and Portuguese · 135

Irish, a Celtic language spoken by 750,000 native speakers in Ireland · 94, 132

Italian, an Italic language spoken by 57 million native speakers in southern Europe · 26, 52, 58–59, 87, 95, 101, 103, 108, 112, 114, 117, 135, 139, 161–163, 168, 172, 196, 206, 212, 214

Italic languages, Indo-European languages including Spanish, French, Italian, Portuguese, Romanian, and a number of smaller languages spoken in southern, Western, and Eastern Europe, and Latin America · 65

Japanese, a Japonic language spoken by 125 million native speakers in easternmost Asia · 8, 24, 29, 40, 49, 51–52, 55, 58, 64, 71, 105, 108, 116–117, 120, 139, 152, 161–162, 204, 206, 215

Kalam, a Trans-New Guinea language spoken by 15,000 native speakers in Oceania · 49

Kazakh, a Turkic language spoken by 12 million native speakers in central Asia · 74, 161

Klingon, a constructed language, created for the TV series Star Trek · 137

Korean, a Koreanic language spoken by 77 million native speakers in eastern Asia · 139, 162, 207

Kyrgyz, a Turkic language spoken by more than 4 million native speakers in central Asia · 74

Lakota, a Siouan language spoken by 2100 native speakers in north-central United States · 209

Latin American Spanish, a geographical variety of ☞ Spanish · 146

Latin, a classical Italic language, mostly extinct, in limited use in the Catholic church · 53, 65–66, 76, 124, 133, 146, 154, 160–161, 169–170, 176, 180, 196, 201, 205–206, 212

Latvian, a Baltic language spoken by over 1.75 million native speakers in eastern Europe · 118, 206

Lingwa de Planeta, a constructed language, based on most populous global languages · 135

Lithuanian, a Baltic language spoken by over 3 million native speakers in eastern Europe · 118, 162, 214

Lì'fya leNa'vi, a constructed language, created for the movie Avatar · 137

Macedonian, a Slavic language spoken by more than 2 million native speakers in southeastern Europe · 33, 39, 52, 57–58, 124, 145, 161–162, 165, 167, 176, 178, 199, 205, 207, 211–212

Malay, an Austronesian language spoken by 77 million native speakers in southeastern Asia · 29, 74, 94, 104, 118

Maltese, a Semitic language spoken by over 500,000 native speakers in Malta · 206, 212

Mandarin Chinese, a Sino-Tibetan language spoken by 920 million native speakers in eastern Asia, with Mainland and Taiwanese as major varieties · 3, 22–24, 27, 29, 33, 49, 51, 54–55, 58–59, 64, 99, 105, 133, 135, 139, 151, 157, 161, 163, 170, 172, 176, 204, 215, 229

Māori, an Austronesian language spoken by 50,000 speakers in New Zealand · 74, 124

Maung, an Iwaidjan language spoken by 371 native speakers in Australia · 49

Nahuatl, a Uto-Aztecan language spoken by over 1.8 million native speakers in central Mexico · 204

Navajo, a Na-Dené language spoken by 170,000 native speakers in the southwestern United States · 76, 151

New Zealand English, a national variety of ☞ English · 57

Newar, a Sino-Tibetan language spoken by 860,000 native speakers in central Asia · 71, 73

North American English, a regional variety of ☞ English · 15

Norwegian, a Germanic language spoken by more than 5 million native speakers in northern Europe · 117, 162, 169

Nunggubuyu, a Macro-Gunwinyguan language spoken by 273 native speakers in Australia · 70

Occitan, an Italic language spoken by 100,000 native speakers in southwestern Europe · 133, 161, 196

Old English, an early stage of ☞ English · 31

Old French, older phase of ☞ French spoken in northern France, from the eighth century to the fourteenth · 194

Oromo, an Afroasiatic language spoken by 34 million native speakers in East Africa · 58

Persian, an Iranian language spoken by 70 million native speakers in the Middle East · 22, 82, 135, 167

Pirahã, an unaffiliated language spoken by 24–38 native speakers in South America · 31

Polish, a Slavic language spoken by 45 million native speakers in east central Europe · 20–21, 26, 32, 34, 36–37, 39, 43–44, 57, 66, 74–75, 82, 100–101, 104, 106, 108, 114, 123–125, 128, 135, 139, 146, 154, 156, 159, 161, 163, 165–167, 176, 178, 196, 199, 207, 209, 214

Portuguese, an Italic language spoken by close to 223 million native speakers, with European and Brazilian as major varieties · 3, 26, 47, 68, 108, 114, 132–133, 135, 139, 156, 161, 163, 167, 170, 212, 214

Index of Languages

Romani, an Indo-Aryan language spoken by 1.5 million native speakers across Europe and the Middle East · 215

Romanian, an Italic language spoken by 26 million native speakers in southeastern Europe · 34, 65, 76, 79, 105, 124, 206, 212

Rusenglish, a developing-circle variety of ☞ English in Russian-speaking countries · 172

Russian, a Slavic language spoken by 150 million native speakers in Eastern Europe and northern Asia · 1, 3, 8, 20, 22, 25–26, 31, 34, 37, 39, 43–44, 47, 52, 55, 64–65, 67, 74, 82, 87, 107–109, 112, 114–115, 123–124, 128, 133, 135, 139, 143, 155–156, 159, 161, 163, 165, 167, 170, 172, 175, 178, 180–181, 183–184, 186, 193, 196, 199, 202, 206, 210, 212, 214, 230

Saami languages, Uralic languages spoken by 30,000 native speakers in northern Europe · 48

Samoan, an Austronesian language spoken by over 500,000 native speakers in the South Pacific · 56

Serbian, an ethnic variety of ☞ Serbo-Croatian · 28, 88, 90, 98, 171, 195, 212, 217

Serbo-Croatian, aka Bosnian/Croatian/Serbian, a Slavic language spoken by 21 million speakers in southeastern Europe, with Bosnian, Croatian, and Serbian being major ethnic varieties · 20, 26, 28, 32, 37, 46–47, 52, 54, 58, 70, 74, 76–77, 79, 81, 87, 92–94, 96, 98, 100, 103, 105–106, 108, 112–114, 117–118, 122–125, 128, 143, 146, 155, 157–158, 162–163, 165, 167, 176, 178, 180, 186, 188, 193, 196, 199, 202, 205, 207, 209, 211–212, 217

Shipibo, a Panoan language spoken by 26,000 native speakers in South America · 33

Slavic languages, Indo-European languages spoken in central and Eastern Europe including Russian, Ukrainian, Belarussian, Polish, Czech, Slovak, Slovene, Serbo-Croatian, Macedonian, Bulgarian, and a number of smaller languages · 21, 23, 26, 31, 33, 37–39, 43–44, 46, 65–66, 74, 124–125, 143, 146, 159, 165, 176, 196, 198–200, 202, 206–207, 214, 216

Slovak, a Slavic language spoken by over 5 million native speakers in central Europe · 65, 74, 124, 155, 157, 167–168, 176, 199

Slovene, a Slavic language spoken by 2.5 million native speakers in central Europe · 2, 23, 39, 44, 76, 93–94, 101, 124, 145, 156, 159, 165, 167–168, 176, 202, 205–206, 209, 211–212

Spanish, an Italic language spoken by close to 483 million native speakers, with Iberian and various Latin American as major varieties · 2, 33, 39, 47, 58, 65, 76, 102, 108–109, 114, 117–118, 120, 131, 133, 135, 139, 144, 146, 156, 161–163, 167, 170, 175–176, 205–206, 212, 214

Swahili, a Bantu language spoken by a number of estimated native speakers ranging from 2 to 150 million in eastern Africa · 21, 40, 64, 74, 134, 161, 170

Swedish, a Germanic language spoken by 10 million native speakers in northern Europe · 40, 76, 108, 112, 155, 163, 214

Swiss German, a national variety of ☞ German · 147

Tagalog, a Malayo-Polinesian language spoken by 23 million native speakers in the Philippines · 161

Tamazight, aka Berber, a group of Afro-Asiatic languages spoken by over 10 million speakers in North Africa and diaspora throughout Europe · 114

Tatar, a Turkic language spoken by 5 million native speakers in central Russia · 161

Thai, a Kra-Dai language, spoken by 30 million native speakers in southeast Asia · 19, 139

Tok Pisin, an English Creole, spoken by 120,000 native speakers in Oceania · 133

Turkish, a Turkic language spoken by over 76 million native speakers in the Middle East · 25, 28, 54, 65, 74, 89, 95, 106, 108–109, 114, 133, 156, 161, 167, 193, 196

Ukrainian, a Slavic language spoken by over 35 million native speakers in Eastern Europe · 21, 43, 74, 114, 124, 165, 167–168, 176

Uw Oykangand, a Pama-Nyungan language spoken by 2 native speakers in Australia · 33

Vietnamese, an Austroasiatic language spoken by 76 million native speakers in southeast Asia · 161, 176

Volapük, an early constructed language, mainly based on English · 135

Xhosa, a Bantu language spoken by more than 8 million native speakers in South Africa · 74

Yakut, a Turkic language spoken by 450,000 native speakers in northeast Asia · 161

Yandruwandha, an extinct Pama-Yungan language, which was spoken in Australia · 33

Yiddish, a Germanic language spoken before WWII by 13 million speakers in central and Eastern Europe · 92, 106, 135, 162, 214

Yinjibarndi, a Pama-Nyungan language spoken by 377 native speakers in Australia · 72

Zulu, a Bantu language spoken by more than 12 million native speakers in South Africa · 74

Index of Languages

Language Families Not Mentioned in the Text to Which the Languages Mentioned in the Text Belong

Afroasiatic languages (earlier known as Hamito-Semitic) – a large family of languages spoken in North Africa and the Middle East, encompassing ☞ Semitic languages, and a number of other language groups, with Somali, Tuareg, Oromo, Amharic, and other languages included.

Austroasiatic languages (also known as Mon-Khmer) – a large family of languages in mainland southeast Asia, including Vietnamese, Khmer, and Mon.

Austronesian languages – a large family of languages stretching from Madagascar to southeast Asia to Oceania, with major languages being Malay, Javanese, and Filipino.

Aymaran languages – a small family of two languages: Aymara and Jaquaru spoken in South America.

Baltic languages – a small family of two living languages, Latvian and Lithuanian, and extinct Old Prussian.

Chukoto-Kamchatkan languages – a family of languages in northeast Asia, including Kamchatkan, Chukchi, Koryak, and other languages.

Constructed languages – languages created by language planning either as means of international communication or as tools of artistic expression.

Indo-Aryan languages – a larger family of languages in northern India, south Asia, including languages such as Hindustani (Hindi-Urdu), Bengali, Punjabi, Marathi, Gujarathi, etc.

Indo-European languages – a large family stretching throughout the whole of Europe and most of Asia, including ☞ Germanic, ☞ Italic, ☞ Baltic, ☞ Slavic, ☞ Iranian, ☞ Indo-Aryan, ☞ Celtic, and other language families.

Iranian languages – a family of languages in central Asia, including Persian, Tajik, Kurdish, Pashto, and Ossetian languages.

Iwaidjan languages – a small family of languages in northern Australia, including Iwaidja, Maung and several other languages.

Japonic languages – a family of languages in Japan and Korea, including Japanese and several smaller languages.

Kartvelian languages – a small family of languages in Georgia, Eastern Europe, including Georgian, Laz, Svan, and Mingrelian.

Koreanic languages – a family of languages in Korea, including Korean and several smaller languages.

Kra-Drai languages – a family of languages in southeast Asia, including Thai, Lao, and several smaller languages.

Macro-Gunwinyguan languages – a family of languages spoken across Arnhem Land in northern Australia.

Mayalo-Polynesian languages – a large subgroup of ☞ Austronesian languages spoken in Oceania.

Na-Dené languages – a large family of indigenous languages spoken in northwestern Canada, and the American Southwest and Pacific North.

Niger-Congo languages – a large family of languages spoken in western, central, and southern Africa.

Pama-Nyungan languages – a large family encompassing most Australian Aboriginal languages.

Panoan languages – a family of indigenous languages in northwestern South America.

Semitic languages – a large subgroup of ☞Afroasiatic languages, including Arabic and Hebrew.

Sino-Tibetan languages – a large family of languages in central and eastern Asia, including Mandarin Chinese, Burmese, and Tibetic languages

Siouan languages – a family of indigenous languages in the northern midwest and central east coast in the United States and western Canada, including Lakota, Dakota, and a number of other languages.

Trans-New Guinea languages – a large family of indigenous languages in New Guinea.

Turkic languages – a large family of languages spoken in the Middle East, central Asia, and Siberia, including Turkish, Kazakh, Uzbek, and a number of other languages.

Uralic languages – a large family of languages spoken in central Europe, northern Europe, and northern Asia, including Hungarian, Finnish, and a number of other languages.

Uto-Aztecan languages – a large family of indigenous languages spoken in the western United States, western Mexico, and Central America, including Nahuatl, Hopi, and a number of other languages.

Person and Subject Index

Cases

Acitelli, Tom 228
Adams, Douglas 131
affix 13
Aitchison, Jean 226
Aleksa Varga, Melita 225
Allan, Keith 223, 226
Altshuler, Daniel 221
Annan, Kofi 65
antonyms 13
application domain 11
archaism 15
attitude 15
Augustine 62–63, 223
Austin, John L. 225
Avicenna 34

Baker, Sidney J. 215, 229
Barton, Helen xiv
Bassnett, Angela 224
Berlin, Brent 222
Berlusconi, Silvio 103
Berman, Nina xiv
Blanke, Detlev 226
Bodle, Andrew 227
Bolton, Kingsley 227
Boroditsky, Lera 224
Böttcher, Sven 131
Brixy, Nenad 87
Brown, Penelope 227
Browne, Wayles xiv
Burridge, Kate 226
Bußman, Hadumod 222

calque 15
Casanova, Montse 227
Casson, R. W. 222
Catherine, the Great 195
Chan, S. L. 222

Chesire, Jenny 229
Clinton, Hilary 87
collectivism 8
Collins, Isabel xiv
collocation 14
colloquial register 14
combinatorial potential 14
composition 13
connotation 11
context 14
Cook, James 124
Copernicus, Nicolaus 79
Corbett, Greville 222–223
core vocabulary 14
Cowie, Anthony 225
Crespo-Fernández, Eliecer 229
Cresswell, Julia 224
Croft, Lee B. xiv
Croimans, Ilja 223
Croker, Charlie 89, 224
Cruse, Alan D. 221
Curtis, Wayne 228

D'Anna, Catherine 226
Dase, Pierre R. 224
dated word 15
decimal system 23
Defoe, Daniel 65
denotation 11
derivation 13
Dickey, Eleanor 228
Dobrovol'skij, Dmitrij 224
Domínguez, Pedro 224
Doohan, James 137
Dostoevsky, Fyodor Mikhailovich 194
Dronjić, Vedran xiv
Džamić, Lazar 224

equivalence 10
etymology 14

253

Fabijanić, Ivo 228
Falk, Julia 226
family resemblance 12
Farese, Gian Marco 228
Fayndrich, Ingrid 228
Fisher, Roswitha 227
Fletcher, Adam 172, 228
Florencia Assneo María 225
Foer, Jonathan Safran 172
Folarin Schleicher, Antonia 229
formal register 14
Foster, David xiv
Francis of Assisi 111
Frege, Gottlob 12
Friedman, Uri 225
Frommer, Paul 137
Fuhrman, Orly 224

Gardner, Jeremy 171, 228
Geeraerts, Dirk 223–224, 227
Gelderen, Elly van xiv
Gladkova, Anna 229
Goddard, Cliff 223
Goethe, Johann Wolfgang 197
Granger, Sylvaine 225
Grzega, Joachim 224

Haarde, Geir 35
Hall, Edward T. 8–9, 224
Halliday, M.A.K. 221
Hamano, Shoko 226
Hardach, Sophie 223
Hardin, C.L. 222
Haspelmath, Martin 221, 227
Hawkins, Paul 172, 228
Hellinger, Marlis 222
Herder, Johann Gottfried 110, 225
high-context cultures 8
Hitler, Adolf 198
Hobsbawm, Eric 62, 223
Hofstede, Geert 8–9
Hofstede, Gert Jan 8
Holm, John 226
Hough, Carol 228
Howard, John 95
Hrisztova-Gotthardt, Hrisztalina 225
Hudson, Richard A. 228
hypernyms 13
hyponyms 13

Ikeda, Kikunae 49
individualism 8
indulgence 8

Jackobs, Andrew 228
Jackson, Howard 221
Jakobson, Roman 1, 3
Jay, Timothy 225
Jespersen, Otto 1
Jobs, Steve 57
John Paul II 122
Johnson, Mark 221, 224
Jones, Lawrence G. 228

Kachru, Braj 170, 227
Karadžić, Vuk Stefanović 125
Kay, Paul 222
Kellar, McKenna xiv
Kempis, Thomas à 201
Kennedy, John Fitzgerald 36
Khatuna, Metreveli xiv
King James II 194
Kirkpatrick, Andy 228
Kövecses, Zoltán 224, 227
Kugler, Franz 182
Kundera, Milan 131
Kuzmić, Rikard 138

Lado, Robert 229
Lagerberg, Robert 228
Lakoff, George 221, 223–224
Leaver, Betty Lou 226
Leech, Goeffrey 229
Levinson, Stephen C. 224, 228–229
lexeme 7
lexical borrowing 13, 15
lexical field 13
lexical frequency 14
lexical morphology 13
lexical network 13
lexical relations 13
lexical semantics 7
lexical stem 13
lexical transfer 15
lexical unit 7
lexicography 7
lexicology 7
lexicon 7
Liberman, Anatoly 1, 224

Person and Subject Index 255

Liddicoat, Anthony J. 226
Liebe, Rochelle 227
linear model 12
lingo 14
Lipka, Leonhard 221
Lloyd, John 131
long-term orientation 8
Loreto, Vittorio 222
low-context cultures 8

Macdonald, Fiona 224
Mackenzie, Ian 226
Maffi, Luisa 222
Magga, Ole Henrik 223
Majid, Asifa 223
Malenica, Frane 228
Malmkjaer, Kristen 224
Manzano Alba, Maria del Carmen, 223
Mark, David M. 224
Mary I, Queen of England 184
masculinity 8
Matsuzaki, Takuya 224
Maxwell, Alexander 229
May, Karl 209
McConvell, Patrick 222
McEnery, Tony 226
McKenna, Robert 228
Mencken, H.L. 214, 229
Menninger, Karl 222
meronyms 13
metaphor 11
metaphorical link 11
Meunier, Fanny 225
Mills, Margaret 223
Mishra, Ramesh C. 224
monochronic cultures 8
Morkovkin, Valery V. 128
Morkovkina, Anna V. 128, 226
Motschenbacher, Heiko 222

Ndimele, Ozo-mekuri 222
Nerlich, Brigitte 227
new word 15
Nishinari, Katsuyoshi 223
Nogle, Lawrence 222
Nomachi, Motoki xiv
Nuessel, Frank 228
Núñez, Rafael E. 224

O'Mahony, Michael 222
O'Neil, Maria 226
Ogden, Charles Kay 135
Okrand, Mark 137

paedonynic 34
Palmer, Garry 229
paradigmatic relations 14
patronymic 34
Pavlenko, Aneta 222
Perelsveig, Asya 229
peripheral vocabulary 14
Peterson, David 226
phonology 7
Pickford, Mary 184
Piirainen, Elisabeth 224
Pinker, Steven 225, 227
Plag, Ingo 227
polychronic cultures 8
Potemkin, Grigory 194
power distance 8
prefix 13
Proshina, Zoya 172, 228
prototype 12
pseudo-borrowing 15
Putin, Vladimir Vladimirovich 34, 178
Pym, Anthony 224

radial model 11
reference 12
regional differentiation 15
register 14
Rieger, Terry 222
Rorschach test 75
Rorschach, Hermann 75
Rosch, Eleanor 12, 221
Rundstrom Williams, Tracy 229

Šašić, Mladen xiv
Scarino, Angela 226
Scarpete Walters, Gina xiv
Schleyer, Johan Martin 135
Schöner, Marion 224
Schusky, Ernest L. 222
selection restrictions 14
semantic transfer 11
sense 12
Sexton, James 229
Shai, Donna 225

Sharifian, Farzad 223, 229
Shigeru Miyagawa 111
Simone, Rafaele 225
Šipka, Danko 223, 225, 227
Šipka, Ljiljana xiv
Šipka, Olja xiv
Skandera, Paul 225
slang 14
source domain 11
source language 10
Steen, Gerard 221
Stein, Dieter 229
Štekauer, Pavol 227
Stout-Smith, Kim xiv
subject matter 15
suffix 13
Sweeser, Eve 224
synonyms 13
synonymy 13
syntagmatic relations 14
syntax 7

Tadmor, Uri 221, 227
Talmy, Leonard 227
target domain 11
target language 10
Taylor, John 221
technical register 15
teknonym 34
Temkina, Elizabeth Grigorieva 195
Tolkien, J. R. R. 137

Traubert, Michael xiv
Turk, Andrew G. 224
Twain, Mark 151

uncertainty avoidance 8
usage characteristics 13

vigesimal system 23

Wajnryb, Ruth 226
Wayne, Ronald 57
Weber, Elke U. 225
Weinreich, Max 214, 228
Wierzbicka, Anna 137, 229
Wilford, John Noble 222
Winawer, Jonathan 222
Wittgenstein, Ludwig 221
word-formation network 13
Wordnet 14
Wozniak, Steve 57

Yallop, Colin 221
Yang, Xu 222
Young, John Wesley 228

Zalar, Vera xiv
Zamehnof, Ludwik L. 135
Zgusta, Ladislav 11
Zhang, Xia xiv
Zhu, Pinfan 223
Zirker, Angelika 225